Perspectives on
HARRY CREWS

Perspectives on

HARRY CREWS

Edited by

Erik Bledsoe

University Press of Mississippi
Jackson

www.upress.state.ms.us

The following articles were first published in *The Southern Quarterly* and are used by permission: "Harry Crews: Mentor and Friend" by Larry Brown; "'Is Your Novel Worth a Damn?': Meeting Harry Crews" by Tim McLaurin; "'The Use of *I*, Lovely and Terrifying Word': Autobiographical Authority and the Representations of 'Redneck' Masculinity in *A Childhood*" by James H. Watkins; "Silences, Criticisms, and Laments: The Political Implications of Harry Crews's Work" by Gary L. Long; "'Everthing Is Eating Everthing Else': The Naturalistic Impulse in Harry Crews's *A Feast of Snakes*" by Tim Edwards; "Having a Hard Time of It: Women in the Novels of Harry Crews" by Elise S. Lake; "Harry Crews's Home Place: An Excursion into Wiregrass Country and the Carnivalesque" by Jerrilyn McGregory; "Harry Crews's Away Games: Home and Sport in *A Feast of Snakes* and *Body*" by Scott Romine; "An Interview with Harry Crews" by Erik Bledsoe; "Assault of Memory" by Harry Crews; and "Keeping Up with Harry Crews: A Bibliography of Works, Interviews, and Critical Texts" by Damon Sauve; all copyright © 1998 by *The Southern Quarterly*; and "The Grit Émigré in Harry Crews's Fiction" by Matthew Guinn copyright © 1999 by *The Southern Quarterly*.

09 08 07 06 05 04 03 02 01   4 3 2 I

⊗

Library of Congress Cataloging-in-Publication Data

Perspectives on Harry Crews / edited by Erik Bledsoe.
    p. cm.
    Includes bibliographical references and index.
    ISBN 1-57806-321-3 (alk. paper)—ISBN 1-57806-322-I (pbk. : alk. paper)
    I. Crews, Harry, 1935– . —Criticism and interpretation.   2. Southern States—
In literature.   3. Rural poor in literature.   4. Whites in literature.   I. Bledsoe,
Erik, 1965–

PS3553.R46 Z84   2001
813'.54—dc2I   00-044912

British Library Cataloging-in-Publication Data available

BOOKS BY HARRY CREWS

CONTENTS

INTRODUCTION

Recently I was renewing a couple of overdue Harry Crews novels at my university library. When she saw the books, the librarian tentatively asked if I had read *A Feast of Snakes*. When I replied that I had, she smiled and began talking enthusiastically about the novel. From there we went to *A Childhood: The Biography of a Place*, and then on to other Crews novels she admired. Our discussion continued for a few minutes, it being a slow day at the library, and as I was packing up my bag and preparing to leave she said, "It's not every day that you meet a fellow Crews fan."

I tell this story because it exemplifies one of the three typical responses I received from people when I would mention that I was working on a Harry Crews project. Often, too often, I was met with blank stares. Despite having published fifteen novels, two collections of nonfiction, an autobiography that ranks among the best works to emerge from the South in the last twenty-five years, and various other limited editions and collections, Harry Crews is not very well known outside of a limited circle. As he told me, his novels typically sell fewer than ten thousand copies in hardback. Respectable, enviable even to many writers, but certainly not indicative of his power as a writer, nor of his influence upon other writers.

If the blank stares were sometimes frustrating, often enough I received responses like that of the librarian. I quickly learned that Crews has a devoted and passionate following. After putting out a call for papers I received phone calls, letters, and e-mail from people all across the United States and even a few from Europe. Some people had no intention of submitting anything—they just wanted to talk. And talk they did. They talked about Joe Lon Mackey, about the grittiness of Crews's novels and essays, about the freaks and midgets that populate his literary world. Some had been his students at the University of Florida where he taught for many years, and they talked about how he had challenged them to make their own writing honest. On a few occasions people expressed an aversion as intense as the admiration others expressed. Of those who know him or his work few seem indifferent. You either love Crews or you hate him—sometimes, as with at least one person with whom I spoke, you do both at once.

Finally, and this response usually, though not always, came from those who had met Crews, there were the stories. Stories of drunkenness, of outrageous comments made and deeds performed, of an e. e. cummings poem tattooed on his arm and a Mohawk hairdo, stories of "Harry Crews: The Legend" as I've come to call it.

"Did you hear about the time when he . . . ?"

"One time Harry and Barry Hannah . . ."

"I saw Harry give a reading when he was so . . ."

Crews has the reputation of being the baddest bad boy of American letters. It is a reputation that is both deserved and, as with all such reputations, a reputation that inevitably has taken on a life and magnitude of its own, sometimes bearing little resemblance to the truth.

Certainly, this reputation accounts for some of Crews's cult following. A certain segment of the population finds in Crews's novels and works of nonfiction a representation of the life to which they aspire—a life lived on the edge, hard and fast, no bullshit passed out and none tolerated in return. Similar to the way an earlier generation tossed worn copies paperback copies of Kerouac novels in the backseat and careened off across the country, some folks carry around well-worn copies of Crews's books. It is not surprising that Harry Crews was once asked to adapt *On the Road* for the big screen.

In recent years, however, some readers have discovered Crews by working backward as it were. With the critical and popular success of younger writers like Larry Brown and Dorothy Allison many readers and critics have returned to Crews, who was writing about what documentary filmmaker Gary Hawkings has called the Rough South for twenty years before Brown and Allison's first published fiction. The Rough South is the world of the poor white, far removed from the grandeur of Tara and *Gone with the Wind* (as least as Hollywood created it, even if Margaret Mitchell did not write it quite the same way). The Rough South is often a world of acute desperation matched only by its profound faith. A harsh and violent world. It is a world that Harry Crews, Larry Brown, Dorothy Allison, and Tim McLaurin know well, for it is their home place. They were born there, lived there, have kinfolk there, and they return there in their works and in their lives. When the younger authors write understandingly of the Rough South they are working ground plowed earlier by Crews.

I must confess that I, too, came to Crews via the works of Brown, Allison, and McLaurin. Or at least really came to them. I had read a couple of his novels, had enjoyed them, and made a note to return for more, but other interests delayed that pursuit. I was working on a paper about writers of the Rough South, and I knew that I needed to at least acknowledge Crews's work. I picked up *A Childhood* and the power of his language, his ability to invoke a world that is essentially alien to me and to make poetry out of its roughness amazed me. Quickly I read everything else I could find and then turned to the criticism to help me sort out what I was feeling. I was amazed at the paucity of the scholarly attention. There were a few very fine articles and a nice collection, but there seemed much more that could be said, that needed to be said. I wrote to Stephen Flinn Young, editor of *The Southern Quarterly*, and suggested the journal should devote a special issue to Crews. Stephen agreed, and asked me to assemble it.

Most of the essays in this collection were originally published in that special issue. When the University Press of Mississippi invited me to turn the issue into a book, I added three new essays to round out the collection. The essays collected here offer new perspectives on the work of Harry Crews and suggest new fields waiting to be plowed. Particularly in the public press, those who write about Crews have tended to focus on a limited range of topics: the freaks, the violence, the machismo, etc. Certainly, these are important elements of Crews's writing, and they fit well with "Harry Crews: The Legend"; however, we should be careful of pigeon-holing his work. The critical essays herein attempt to offer new insights about his work, while drawing upon the best of what has been previously written. It is my hope that while offering new paths to explore this book also has the secondary effect of focusing our attention more upon the work and less upon the legend.

Larry Brown and Tim McLaurin offer pieces of appreciation to Crews. Both writers tell of a man who encouraged them when they were struggling, of a man who gave his time to help younger writers. Once in conversation, Crews expressed to me his admiration for Andrew Lytle, who had been his mentor when he began writing. Lytle, Crews said, had given him the only gift that really mattered because it is the most valuable gift one can give—his time. It is obviously a lesson Crews learned well. Brown and McLaurin tell just how important Crews has been to them both as an unofficial mentor and as a friend.

James H. Watkins places Crews's *A Childhood: The Biography of a Place* in a long tradition of southern autobiography and then shows how the book gives voice and a sense of humanity to a class, the poor white, that has often been excluded from that tradition. Gary L. Long combs nearly the entirety of Crews's literary output for insights into his world view. Ultimately, Long argues that Crews is a traditionalist, that in his critique of modern society he posits an idealized, agrarian past. Given Crews's comments over the years about how he differs from Andrew Lytle, an original contributor to the Agrarian manifesto *I'll Take My Stand*, it is an interesting position in which to find him (see, for example, my interview with Crews reprinted here).

Richard Rankin Russell's essay is the first of the three new pieces. Crews has often expressed his admiration for Graham Greene and stated that he studied the British writer's works carefully. Russell's essay probes the questions of why Greene and what Crews may have learned from his studies. While Russell looks to provide connections between Crews and one particular writer, Tim Edwards examines Crews's relationship to a particular style of writing. Edwards seeks to relocate our discussion of Crews away from the traditional paradigm of the southern gothic and instead examines Crews in terms of American naturalism, with a postmodern twist. Edwards's comments about the implications of such an approach for how we view Crews's female characters leads nicely into Elise S. Lake's more extended discussion of Crews's women. Lake takes as her starting point previous critical assessments that have labeled as sexist both Crews and his work. Rather than a simple misogyny Lake finds a series of complex mixed messages that perhaps reveals more about Crews's view of humanity as a whole than about his views of women.

Jerrilyn McGregory takes the commonplace notion that southern writers have a distinctive sense of place and shows how rather than a monolithic South there are actually many Souths, various subsections with their own codes and customs. Viewing Crews's work through the lens of Bahktin, she shows how the Wiregrass region of Georgia has impacted his work and how this specialized sense of place allows him to overturn and lampoon traditional hierarchies in his work. Matthew Guinn's essay on the grit émigré is the second new piece in the collection. He points out that while Crews characters often have their origins in sharecropper country, what often captures Crews's imagination is how those characters fare when they leave the home place and attempt to make a new life for themselves elsewhere. Scott Romine is also interested in the notion of place and home. By looking at the obsessive game playing that occurs in many of Crews's novels, Romine finds characters who seek in the games the structure that is denied them as exiles from a home place.

Nicholas Spencer's essay focusing on *Karate Is a Thing of the Spirit* is the final new addition to this collection. Spencer takes as his starting point the question of why Crews's works have not attracted greater interest from cultural theorists. He illustrates that Crews and theorists such as Judith Butler share many of the same concerns, especially in regard to issues of language and the body.

As I edited hours of taped conversation with Crews into a printed interview brief enough for this issue, I realized the difficulty of capturing a personality on paper. I hope that the interview provides a taste of Harry Crews the person while offering insights into Harry Crews the writer. Damon Sauve operates an excellent web site devoted to Crews. He has graciously allowed me to publish here a portion of the bibliography he maintains there. The web site provides an invaluable service for those working on Crews (the url is given at the beginning of his piece). The bibliography printed here lists the critical work done on Crews and the short pieces Crews has published in magazines and newspapers.

Finally, when I timidly asked Harry Crews if he would give me something (anything) of his to print, I was thrilled when he agreed. A few weeks later when a large manila envelop arrived I was surprised to find within it the first two chapters of *Assault of Memory*, a work-in-progress and the follow-up to his highly acclaimed *A Childhood*. Many readers consider his autobiography to be his best work and have eagerly awaited Crews once again turning to his life in narrative form. The excerpt printed here only heightens our anticipation.

I would like to end this introduction by sharing one of the tamer stories I heard about Crews while putting together this issue. Evidently, at some departmental meeting back when Crews was teaching at the University of Florida someone made a disparaging comment about how "creative" works should weigh in relation to "scholarly" work in tenure decisions. Crews stood up and announced his willingness to pile his books on the goddamn scale, match them up pound for pound against the production of any scholar in the room. No one took him up on it. The reason I like this story better than most is that while it is about Harry Crews—the man, the legend, the rebel, whatever—and while it captures perfectly a bit of his personality, ultimately the story comes down to the work. Long after Harry Crews the man is dead we will have the work; long after the death of everyone who ever saw him drunk, or claimed to have seen him drunk, the works will still be around. Harry Crews is a character, all right, but more importantly he has given us books filled with characters that are hard to forget. The books, by the way, weigh in at over twenty-four pounds according to my bathroom scale.

I would like to thank Stephen Flinn Young for allowing me to organize the special issue of the *Southern Quarterly* that became this book. That issue would have never appeared, however, without the diligent work of Lola Norris, editorial assistant for the *Southern Quarterly*. I would also like to thank Seetha Srinivasan, director of the University Press of Mississippi, for believing in this project. Also, Anne Stascavage was a careful editor who kept me on task when other activities sought to lure me away. Many others at the press also labored anonymously to ensure that this project would come to fruition. Chip Arnold provided valuable comments that made the collection tighter and better. The people at Simon & Schuster and at John Hawkins and Associates provided me with information and needed materials. The contributors to this volume all worked diligently making changes and meeting deadlines. Finally, I owe a great debt to Harry Crews, without whose work this collection would not exist, of course. Over the past few years he has given me the most valuable commodity a writer has—his time. Thank you, my friend.

Perspectives on
HARRY CREWS

HARRY CREWS

Mentor and Friend

Larry Brown

I've been reading Harry Crews for so long that I can't really remember when I first discovered his work. It was probably way back in some dim year close to the time when I started writing, and that was in 1980. I remember that my friend and cousin, Paul Hipp, came over one afternoon when my wife and my children and I were living in the house with my mother-in-law. He had in his hand a paperback copy of a book called *A Feast of Snakes*, and he loaned it to me. I can remember sitting on the front porch in the swing, reading it. My children were small then, Billy Ray only three or four, Shane just a baby, LeAnne not even born yet. I remember how that book moved me, shook me, riveted me.

I'd never read anything like it and didn't know that such things could be done in a book. I didn't know that a man could invent characters like Joe Lon Mackey, or his warped sister, Beeder, or Buddy Matlow, the sadistic yet lovestruck peg-legged sheriff. It was an unearthly combination of hilarity and stark reality and beauty and sadness, and I could only shake my head over the power of the imagination that created it.

Since then I've read it many times, and like all great books, it only gets better with each successive reading.

I'd already seen some of his essays in places like *Playboy* and *Esquire*, and somewhere along in there I went to Richard Howorth's fledgling bookstore in Oxford and bought a book of essays called *Florida Frenzy*. From the library in town I checked out a book called *Blood and Grits*, and another one called *A Childhood: The Biography of a Place*. I was awed by the writing in these books, by the stories of his life, his childhood, his struggles to become a writer, the places he had been and the things he had done, but mostly, the things that he *felt*.

His novels were harder to find. The public library had a couple of them, *The Gypsy's Curse* and *The Hawk Is Dying*. I read both of them and loved them tremendously, but I couldn't find any more of his fiction. I knew it was out there somewhere, but nobody seemed to know where.

I don't know how long a period of time this reading covered, but I must have been trying to write by then. I was in the process of trying to find mentors, writers whose work I could look up to and gain inspiration from. I wanted to read the rest of those books, novels that were listed in the front pages of his other books, novels with names like *Karate Is a Thing of the Spirit*, *Car*, *Naked in Garden Hills*, *This Thing Don't Lead to Heaven*, *The Gospel Singer*. I went in search of a larger library, and found it out at Ole Miss. I learned all over again how to use the card catalog, and then, armed with a piece of paper I had scribbled numbers and letters on, I began to prowl the semi-dark aisles of the stacks. And I began to find the books. Most of them were there, minus their dust jackets, and I checked them out and took them home and read them.

Car was reissued in paperback and I bought it, and when *The Gospel Singer* was finally released again in 1988, I bought it. As the newer books have come out, things like *The Knockout Artist* and *All We Need of Hell* and *Body* and *Scar Lover* and *The Mulching of America*, I've bought them. I've read or bought everything by him that I've been able to get my hands on, and I'm grateful that a writer like him walks this earth.

By 1985 I had written five unpublished novels and almost one hundred short stories that had, for the most part, gone begging also. There was a reason for that: most of it was no good. I'd sold one story to *Easyriders*, one to *Fiction International*, and one to a now-defunct magazine in New York called *Twilight Zone*. I had learned by then that the price of success for a writer came high, that there were years of a thing called the apprenticeship period, and that nobody could tell you when you'd come to the end of it.

You just had to keep writing with blind faith, and hope, and trust in yourself that you would eventually find your way, that the world would one day accept your work. Whenever I fell into a black period of depression, which was fairly often, I could get one of Harry's books of essays and read again about what he had gone through, how he had worked for years with no success. It was comforting somehow to know that a man of his great talent had not been born to it, but had learned it, and had possessed the perseverance or the stubbornness or the internal character or whatever it was that he possessed that allowed him to keep on writing in the face of rejection. I read about how much he had lost: his wife, and one of his little boys. He never once complained about how tough it had been. He never said how hard it was to put the right words down. What he said was that you had to keep your ass in the chair. Even if he couldn't write anything one day, if the words wouldn't come at that particular sitting, he would make himself sit in the chair for three hours anyway.

I knew that back in those early days when he was unpublished, he must have wanted success as badly as I did then. And I was tremendously heartened to read these things. It meant that I was not the only writer who had ever gone through what I was enduring, that it was probably a universal experience, this apprenticeship period, this time of years when you wrote things that were not good only to throw them away or have them rejected in order to write enough to eventually learn how.

I learned to use the trash can. I burned one of my novels in the backyard. I collected my rejection slips and kept them in a worn manila envelope. I kept writing, and hoping, and trying to do better. I pulled a twenty-four hour shift at the fire department in Oxford ten days a month, and on the other days I drove nails or sacked groceries or cleaned carpets, whatever it took to make a few extra dollars to feed my growing family, heat the house, pay the endless bills that everybody has. On the weekends or for a few hours at night I would go into the kitchen and try to write something that made some sense. I was still writing stories, and I had started another novel.

That year I wrote a story about a man and a woman sitting in their bedroom and watching an old movie, *The Lost Weekend* starring Ray Milland. It was a turning point for me, that story. All the things I had written and thrown away over the years had been leading up to the writing of that story, one that was called "Facing The Music." By then I had found some additional mentors, a few other role models. They were William Faulkner, Flannery O'Connor, Raymond Carver, Cormac

McCarthy, and Charles Bukowski. Along with Harry Crews they were the writers I admired most, and still do.

Two years later I finally sold the story, and I was offered a book contract for ten stories, and I sent them, and they were accepted and my apprenticeship period was over after seven years. Harry's had been ten, and it wasn't lost on me. When my publisher asked me to suggest some writers they might send galleys to for blurbs, I named my Mississippi friends Barry Hannah, Ellen Douglas, Jack Butler, and Willie Morris. And I asked them to send a galley to Harry Crews.

Some time passed, the galleys went out, and the blurbs began to come in. My editor sent them to me as they came, and we were glad to have them. All my friends said nice things about the book, and I walked around for a long time with my head in the clouds. And then one day my editor mailed a postcard to me, a postcard that had come to her from Harry Crews, and he had responded kindly and favorably as well. I was grateful to my friends, and grateful to him. But I never thought of trying to write to him and thank him. I figured he was a busy man, and I didn't want to bother him. I held him in such high esteem, and respected him and his work so much, that I thought it would be best to just be grateful from a distance, and try not to intrude on his life.

Harry kept writing and so did I. I kept buying his books as they came out, and I published my first novel, and kept writing stories, and in 1990 Algonquin published another collection. It was in October of that year when I read a review of the book that Harry Crews had written in the *Los Angeles Times*. The review was very good, even better than I could have hoped for, but what surprised me the most was what he said about the first book, that in twenty-five years of writing it was the first time he'd picked up the phone and tried to call the author.

He hadn't been able to get ahold of me, but I decided then that I would write him, and thank him for the things he'd done for me, and try to tell him how much I'd admired his work through the years and how much it had meant to me in my struggles to become a writer. I got his address from my editor and wrote the letter and sent it, along with my phone number, and then sometime later on a Saturday afternoon when I was sitting out in my room working, the phone rang, and it was him. I was so glad to hear from him. I think we talked for about an hour and a half, and then we began to write back and forth. We talked about writing, about our lives, about dogs, about drinking, about women, about everything. Once in a while I would call him up and he would do the same. Eventually he arranged a reading for me at the University of Florida, and offered to let me stay with him for a couple of days, and I quickly accepted.

When I walked off the plane at Gainesville, he was leaning up against a wall, wearing a pair of jeans and running shoes and a black Oakland Raiders sweatshirt with the sleeves hacked off. The sides of his head were shaved. There was a silver skull with ruby eyes in one ear, and on one shoulder he wore the tattoo of a death's head, and underneath it the legend:

How do you like your
blue-eyed
boy now, Mr. Death?

We got into his black pickup and we started talking and didn't stop for several days. He drove me over to his house and I unloaded my suitcase and he put me into the spare bedroom he had. He'd called earlier to ask me what kind of beer and whiskey I liked, and he had laid in a supply of both for me. We sat and talked in the living room for a while, and out in the backyard where his deck overlooked a wild piece of land, a creek, tall trees. His living room was sunken from the rest of his house and I met his old dog Heidi, and then he took me to a good seafood place for something to eat. I gave the reading that night and don't even remember what I read, but the place was packed and he introduced me. It was one of the high points of my life. Later that night we sat in the living room and read to each other pieces from the books we were working on. The next day I went to his class with him, and that night he gave a party at his house. He treated me like a favorite uncle would, and told me that if there was anything I needed and didn't see it, to just ask for it. The time with him passed by too soon, but just to get to hang out with him for a while was a great gift that I've never forgotten, never will forget.

We've continued to stay in touch over the years, and I know that he's still working, that he hasn't finished his writing, since that is the thing that makes him most alive. I understand that because it's the same way for me.

It's important to have people to look up to at the beginning of your career. You have to find people who have found their own way of saying the things that you yourself want to say. It never comes easy, and I believe now, while I'm engaged in writing my tenth novel, that it may even get harder the older you get and the more you write. The apprentice approaches the pinnacle slowly, with much stumbling and cursing, constantly going down one-way streets and taking off on tangents that go nowhere. The incredible amount of things that have to be written and then thrown away is probably what discourages a lot of young writers. I don't think Harry ever thought of quitting. I know I certainly did, but something kept me going. To a large degree it was Harry Crews and his work. Knowing about those hard early years made me see that it was possible to succeed at what I was trying to do, and it pulled the blinders off my eyes about what was required. In the beginning I was very naive. In the beginning I thought I'd write a novel and mail it off to New York City, and they'd mail me a check back for a million dollars, and it took a couple of years for me to find out that it doesn't work that way. A fluke does happen once in a while, but the person who sets out to write literature has already fixed himself up with a hard row to hoe. By its very nature, literature is the hardest thing to write, because the standards are so high, and there's sometimes little market for it, and the majority of the world does not read it. It's probably nearly impossible to make a living solely from it, unless you get lucky. Most of the literary writers I know teach somewhere, and write their books in between classes and working on students' stories. Harry did that for a long time, and I've done a good bit of it myself, even though I'm uneducated in the formal sense and barely got out of high school.

I heard a while back that he had finally retired, but I haven't talked with him in a spell. The last time I saw him was a few years ago, when he came over to Oxford to read at Square Books from his latest work. My friend Mark and I watched him get off the plane at Memphis, and were waiting on him when he got to the top of the stairs. He grabbed me in a bear hug and gave me a smile, and shook hands with Mark and told him how much he'd enjoyed his book, and then we drove him down to Oxford in Mark's old Caddy. I got pretty drunk on him that night, and felt bad about it afterwards and apologized to him for it, but he told me later in a letter to forget about it, that it went with the turf. I knew he meant it, and I stopped worrying about it. But I was glad to get to spend some more time with him again.

Once when I was in Washington, DC, rehearsing a stage adaptation from one of my novels, we had a bad day. Actually a terrible day. Nothing went right and the lines I'd written with my director were wrong and everybody kept missing their cues and forgetting their lines and it got so bad that the director, Rick Corley, finally threw up his hands and sent everybody home. Opening night was not far away, only a few days, and I went down a dark snowy street to a liquor store and got a fifth of Wild Turkey and went back to my hotel room and tried to crawl inside it. Sometime later, after I'd gotten good and drunk, I dug Harry's number out of my briefcase and tried to call him, but his answering machine was on and all I could do was leave a message. I wanted to tell him how badly things were going, and ask him what it was that I needed to do. He didn't call back that night, but he did call the next morning, full of good humor and reassurance. He told me of rehearsing his own play in Louisville, and of how terribly things sometimes went, but how it all came together before opening night, and he let me know that the same thing would happen for us. And he was right. Rick and I fixed the lines, and the actors pulled things up out of themselves that we had never seen coming, and on opening night the play fit together like the corners of a finely mitered box. He knew what he was talking about.

If not for having written a few books I would not know Harry Crews, or be able to count him as a friend. In a business that involves staying by yourself most of the time, and working uncertainly and usually fearfully toward an uncertain goal, the rewards can be few and far between and the very nature of the thing you are doing can cause a man to question, and often, the sanity of it. But other writers understand what you do and what is required of you to do it. And nothing matters but the finished book. It doesn't matter how much pain it costs you. You can't bitch or whine about it, you just have to do it. I think that's probably the most valuable lesson I've learned from Harry: do the best work you can, whatever it takes to do it, whatever the price is that you have to pay.

And when it goes right, when you *know* that what you've done is good, then you know what your existence on earth is all about, and why you keep doing what you do.

I wish that everybody in America would read some of his work. I wish everybody in America would find out what a great writer we have living down in Gainesville, Florida. Even if Paul hadn't brought that first book over that day, I still would have discovered him.

I would have heard his name mentioned somewhere, because I hear it mentioned everywhere I go. It doesn't matter if it's Seattle or St. Paul, people know about Harry Crews and his work. I think that's a pretty fine tribute, for his name to be scattered so far and so wide. It is only just and fitting. He is one of the greatest treasures that we have.

Thanks, Harry, for all you've given us.

"Is Your Novel Worth a Damn?"

Meeting Harry Crews

Tim McLaurin

My first novel was in galley form, and I was on my way back from a canoe trip in the Everglades when I decided to veer through Gainesville, Florida. I hoped there was a slim chance that I might contact my favorite writer, Harry Crews.

I had been turned on to Harry by the poet James Seay a couple of years before. After reading *A Feast of Snakes*, I repeatedly returned to the library and bookstore until I had read everything he had in print. Here was a man who wrote about people with scars— folks who cheated and shit and prayed and puked as they searched for their own sense of salvation. He wrote about midgets and obese people, men who ate cars chunk by chunk and fought pit bulls and preached a sold-out gospel. But, by the end of the books, I did not see the characters as freaks or outcasts, but as people with hopes and fears and triumphs and failures like my own. Crews was not afraid to write about the ugly parts of life because he knew that by having a man or woman face adversity a window opened into their true heart and soul.

Despite never having met him, I felt a certain camaraderie with Crews. Both of us had grown up rural and poor. We both joined the Marines at eighteen. With my novel approaching the publication date, we both would have our first books printed in our mid-thirties. We wrote about basically the same people—the underclass, folks who worked with their hands and grasped and snatched life from day to day.

I rolled into Gainesville in the late afternoon and got a cheap motel room. After downing a few beers for courage, I opened the phone book to the *C* section. To my surprise, a "Harry Crews" was listed. All of the writers I knew back in my home state of North Carolina had unlisted numbers. I funneled another beer, then took a deep breath and dialed. The phone rang a couple of times, then I heard a click and a thundering voice rang out—"HARRY CREWS!" I nearly dropped the phone. Stammering at first, I introduced myself, told Harry that I was a big fan of his work, a first-time novelist, and wondered if I might buy him a beer or a cup of coffee. He told me to meet him at his office the following morning at the university. I was elated when I hung up.

At nine a.m. I stood outside his office. Shortly, he turned a corner in the hallway, a large man, limping, craggy-faced, with intense, piercing eyes. He looked about as much like the public-imagined "John Updike" image of a writer as Peter Pan did to Godzilla. We shook hands, then went to McDonald's for coffee.

I admit I was in awe. I knew probably a couple hundred other young writers and fans had sought his time. But despite his gravelly voice and fierce stare, he seemed truly interested in my recall of the one hundred-mile canoe trip I had just taken and the novel I had forthcoming. Under the table, I picked at my nails and tried to work up the courage to address one of the reasons I had called him. I guess he sensed that.

"Well, send me a galley, and if I like it I'll give you a blurb for the dust jacket."

Harry was good for his word. When I received an advance copy of my book, of several notable writers who had endorsed it, I was proudest of seeing his words and name. A few years later, I wrote my third book, a memoir of growing up in the South that had been inspired by the raw honesty of Harry's own memories of his youth in *A Childhood: The Biography of a Place*. Again, he gifted me with a quote that I have often said is the best piece of writing in the book.

Harry Crews taught me that I should write what I know about, and that the characters and their words and actions should be true to the reality of their lives. I learned that by taking this route, I will probably never make the bestseller list, but the people who do read my books will look forward to the next and will remember the previous ones. He also taught me that if a man writes of the affected, of those who live hard and hope mightily, he is usually himself of that caste and should not live too insulated from his past. Today, after six books, I still have a listed phone number. Some callers are kooks that I endure; others leave tears in my eyes from kind words I know they pulled from their guts. Nearly a decade has passed since that first conversation with Harry, but I cannot and will not forget the young writer who dialed the number of a man he admired, and that man who answered and spoke his name.

"THE USE OF *I,* LOVELY AND TERRIFYING WORD"

Autobiographical Authority and the Representation of "Redneck" Masculinity in A Childhood

James H. Watkins

N ear the beginning of his memoir, *A Childhood: The Biography of a Place* (1978), Harry Crews describes an incident in which he first feels the impulse to engage in the autobiographical act. In this scene, twenty-one-year-old Crews, who has returned home for a visit after finishing a stint in the Marines, has been taken by his mother's brother to a section of his home county in South Georgia where his father, Ray Crews, lived as a young man. There he listens to his father's old friends and acquaintances as they recount one story after another about the elder Crews, who died when the author was an infant. One particularly colorful account involves a practical joke his father and an unnamed "taleteller" played on Tweek Fletchum, a local moonshiner, who revealed his lack of appreciation by peppering the two fleeing pranksters with a shotgun blast. When Crews expresses incredulity the man then bends forward, pulls up his shirt, and exposes the "sign of the bird shot" as evidence of his truthfulness, to which the author observes to the reader, "Wounds or scars give an awesome credibility to a story" (21). Unsettled (though apparently not unpersuaded) by the corporeal nature of the evidence, Crews shifts his attention from his father's past to his own future and beyond, wondering "what would give credibility to my own story if, when my young son grows to manhood, he has to go looking for me in the mouths and memories of other people. Who would tell the stories?" Realizing that his son is never likely to have an opportunity to hear stories about him in such a communal setting, he arrives at a conclusion that signals the germinal moment of the text: "It was in that moment and in that knowledge that I first had the notion that I would someday have to write about it all, but not in the convenient and comfortable metaphors of fiction, which I had been doing for years. It would have to be done naked, without the disguising distance of the third person pronoun. Only the use of *I*, lovely and terrifying word, would get me to the place I needed to go" (21).

Here Crews demonstrates his awareness that the transmission and reception of autobiography and memoir involve a different set of conditions and consequences than does fiction.[1] The logic of his implicit comparison suggests that autobiographical writing is to fiction what physical scars are to mere words; it is concrete rather than abstract, immediate and self-evident instead of distanced and cloaked in the disguise of art(ifice). While some readers may be inclined to regard with suspicion any autobiographer's explicit claims to narrative truth—in much the same way that we become suddenly wary when someone we have just met at a party prefaces an account with, "I swear this really happened"—the fact remains that we do respond differently to autobiography than we do to other genres. That response is characterized, as Crews clearly understands, in large part by a desire for the "truth" of a life, a longing that does not disappear completely simply because we may lack faith in the credibility of a narrator or even in the representational capacity of language itself. As theoreticians Elizabeth Bruss and Philippe Lejeune have shown independently, autobiography is accorded a special status among the other literary genres which allows it to speak with a degree and specific form of authority that are not granted to fiction or poetry.[2] By means of this particular form of discursive authority, the apparent immediacy and "nakedness" of the autobiographical "I," Crews makes an especially convincing claim of attachment to the "place" of Bacon County and its people, and by extension to the larger geographical and figurative South surrounding it. More specifically, by investing his representations of poor whites with this autobiographical authority, Crews makes a bid to flesh out and humanize the southern "redneck" and thus reverse a centuries-old trend in which this class of southerners is maligned and demonized, on the one hand, or treated as comic figures, on the other.

As the subtitle of *A Childhood* suggests, Crews takes pains to locate his autobiographical persona within a particular ethnographic context, describing throughout the narrative the relationship between the essential qualities of the land and the character of the people who live there. The setting of the country store where the men are gathered, the communal nature of their memories of their long-dead friend, and the mannerisms they display during the gathering serve to conflate the identity of Ray Crews with a traditional culture still tied to that specific locale. Thus, the scene is presented as a rite of passage in which the narrator inherits not only a sense of geographical and cultural belonging but also a more secure position within a patriarchal order anchored in that geography and culture. (Though the narrative features two strong maternal figures—his mother, Myrtice, and an elderly African American woman called Auntie—Crews gives considerably more attention to men in *A Childhood* than to women, none of which seem to be at the store in this scene.) But we are asked to accept the narrator's claim that without the intervening agency of the autobiographical "I" the figurative patrimony the men have bequeathed to him is as momentary and impermanent as his physical presence in that place. The timing of and rationale behind Crews's impulse to engage in self-representation link his autobiographical project to an ambivalence about paternity, which in turn points to an underlying concern with defining poor white southern masculinity that runs throughout *A Childhood*. Indeed, this attention to the problem of masculinity is a feature common to the most prominent new branch of life writing in the South, the "redneck" autobiography.[3]

In a nation where culturally dominant definitions of manhood have long been tied closely to an individual's ability to provide material prosperity for himself and his family, men from poor white backgrounds have, like others locked in poverty, found themselves unable to measure up to national norms, frequently resulting in low self-esteem that is reinforced by other pervasive negative stereotypes of the "redneck." Furthermore, the excessive drinking and physical violence exhibited by and reinforced among poor and working-class southern white men, while providing some opportunity to vent frustrations and anxieties, surely inhibit emotional growth and have wreaked havoc on domestic life. Crews shies away from none of this in *A Childhood*. Yet, for all the attention he brings to the kinds of shortcomings that have provided fodder for stereotyping poor white men over the centuries, he also uses the medium of autobiography to address their strengths and virtues. In this sense, he participates in a trend Patrick Huber has described, in which so-called "rednecks" have "rehabilitated the derogatory stereotypes ascribed to them by using language to fashion an identity as honest, hard-working folks" ("Short History of *Redneck*" 146). Crews's ability to convincingly render poor white masculinity can be attributed partly to his craftsmanship as a writer and his unflinching willingness to expose both its positive *and* negative characteristics, but the degree of authority he brings to that project is made possible largely by the special status accorded to autobiography. Just as members of other marginalized groups in the U.S. and elsewhere have engaged in self-representation to resist sexist and racist stereotypes, southern whites from lower-class backgrounds are now using the autobiographical "I" to claim a degree of dignity historically denied them in literature and film.[4]

Whether as indolent reprobates, members of lynch mobs, victims of social forces beyond their comprehension, or hillbilly comics, poor whites from the South have historically been painted in broad strokes rarely approaching fully human terms. Not surprisingly, it would take an insider's perspective to bring a degree of complexity to the portrait. While many upper- and middle-class white southerners used the autobiographical occasion during the civil rights period to criticize or defend segregation, poor whites continued to refrain from engaging in self-representation.[5] By the end of the sixties, popular perceptions of poor southern whites had reached their nadir, largely as a result of the nation's revulsion over southern whites' violent attacks on civil rights activists. However, by the mid-seventies, negative perceptions of this group became ameliorated if not eclipsed by less pejorative associations, a trend culminating in the enshrinement of Billy Carter as everyone's favorite good old boy. Because this trend was largely a corrective reaction to the demonized image of the bigot "redneck," the good old boy image was nearly as much of a caricature as the image it sought to replace. The self-declared "redneck" men who engaged in self-representation at this time brought a much-needed complexity to the subject by exploring both the successes and the failures of this class of southerners, while investing their portraits with the discursive authority specific to autobiographical writing.

Perhaps the most notable feature of this new branch of autobiographical writing from the South is the shift away from southern liberals' near-obsession with racial guilt to a preoccupation with failed masculinity. For instance, Paul Hemphill's *The Good Old Boys* (1974) begins with a section entitled "Growing Up Redneck" in which the author focuses on his ambivalence towards his father, an independent ("wildcat") semi-truck operator whose marriage suffers as a result of his alcoholism and womanizing. As a young boy he enjoys the prestige among his peers derived from his father's "snarling four-ton Dodge pulling a sleek aluminum trailer, which was, unlike the portfolio of the insurance salesman or the samples of the salesman, something a kid could sink his teeth into" (20). Yet as a teen his father's racism and alcoholism cause Hemphill to lose respect for the man, which is regained only after the author gains in his maturity "a new frame of reference" that allows him to recognize and appreciate in his elder "an involvement with and a passion for life, a willingness to take on the world if necessary, the courage to endure" (34). Another redneck autobiography of the mid-seventies, William Humphrey's *Farther Off from Heaven* (1976), is structured around the death of the author's father, whose love of whiskey and fast cars catches up with him on a two-lane road outside of Clarksville, Texas, in 1937. The portrait Humphrey paints of his father is characteristically ambivalent, detailing the monumental and ultimately successful struggle the man makes to pull himself up from his sharecropper origins and establish himself as the owner of the town's first auto garage while also revealing in grim clarity his propensity to violence, drinking, and adultery. One of the most remarkable memoirs by a self-described redneck, Mississippi native Will D. Campbell's *Brother to a Dragonfly* (1977), details the author's relationship with his brother, Joe, an alcoholic drug abuser who commit-ted suicide. Though he ultimately has more to say about the intersections of race and class exploitation in the South (Campbell, a "renegade" Baptist preacher, was one of the few white southern members of the clergy to work in the front ranks of the civil rights movement, yet also went on to minister to Klan members toward the end of the movement), he sheds considerable light on the ways in which behaviors common to the popular image of the "redneck" can inhibit emotional growth and contribute to self-destruction. Despite their shared interest in revising negative ste-reotypes of the "redneck," none of them does so with the nuanced complexity that characterizes Crews's approach in *A Childhood*.

To the delight of his long-time admirers, Harry Crews is currently enjoying a much-deserved resurgence in critical attention and popular acclaim. However, be-cause his literary reputation has been built primarily on the considerable body of fiction he has produced over the past thirty years (more than a dozen published novels and counting), scholars are clearly more interested in exploring his novels than his autobiographical writing. This is not to say that *A Childhood* has been ignored altogether. Following excellent reviews upon publication, it languished out of print for a number of years, but is available now in two reprint editions, ensuring that it will continue to captivate new readers and admirers.[6] Nevertheless, the little scholar-ship that has been directed towards *A Childhood* has tended to focus—productively, I would add—on its significance in relation to Crews's fiction or, more generally, to his development as an artist while generally disregarding any textual issues especially relevant to the process of self-representation.[7] Crews manages to humanize the poor white without mitigating the violence and grotesquery typically associated with representations of this class of southerners by means of a sophisticated self-representational strategy in which he calls attention to the apparent ugliness of his childhood environment only to reveal, from the perspective of the self-imposed exile, its harsh beauty. This syncretic strategy, in which the reader is continually reminded of the chronological and intellectual distance between the events being described and the radically improved circumstances under which Crews writes of them, emphasizes the creative process of remembrance, as do so many writers' memoirs. But where this method of autobiographical self-disclosure runs the risk of elevating the act of remembrance, and by extension the author's ego, at the expense of the individuals who actually populate those memories, Crews avoids this pitfall by creating an autobiographical self that exists primarily in relation to others. Thus, the narrator's own identity emerges to the extent that he successfully reveals with some degree of complexity and sensitivity the humanity of the people who populated and constituted the place of his childhood.

For some theorists, the tendency to define oneself primarily in relation to others is a defining characteristic of marginalized subjectivity, something that distinguishes women's and minorities' experiences of selfhood from the autonomous individualism commonly associated with those who enjoy racial, gender, or class privilege. For instance, Mary G. Mason writes that the "recognition of another consciousness . . . [the] grounding of identity through relation to the chosen other, seems . . . to enable women to write openly about themselves" when they would otherwise feel uneasy about calling undue attention to themselves ("Voice of the Other" 210). Similarly, Susan Stanford Friedman argues, drawing from the work of psychoanalytic theorists Sheila Rowbotham and Nancy Chodorow, that the canonical emphasis on "individualistic paradigms" of selfhood in autobiographies is a critical bias that has devalued *identification, interdependence,* and *community,*" traits she names as "key elements in the development of a woman's identity" ("Women's Autobiographical Selves" 38). Yet, the tendency to represent one's own sense of self through one's relationships with others is a feature common to southern autobiography in general—including those by white men of all classes—though for different reasons than those given by scholars to explain this pattern in women's and African Americans' life writing. The most likely explanation for the emphasis on relationality in southern autobiography may lie in what Fred Hobson has identified as a "compulsion to tell about the South" which is so widespread among southern writers "that explaining the South is almost a regional characteristic" (*Tell About the South* 8–9). The primary method of self-disclosure used by southern autobiographers—white and black, male and female, upper- middle- and lower-class—has been to write of their communities, their family members, and their own sense of place within those communal and familial contexts. Since "place" for southerners typically connotes social and racial hierarchies as well as a specific locale, this method of self-representation is ideally suited to the task of "explaining" the South to non-southerners.[8] Though much has been made of the ways in which southern novelists and short story writers have conveyed a "sense of place" in their writings, southern writers have also invoked the special authority given to autobiography to legitimize or question regionally-specific class, race, and gender hierarchies. As the example of the slave narrative and its post-emancipation counterparts clearly indicate, marginalized groups within the South, as elsewhere, have found self-representation to be an especially useful way to counter "official" histories written by those who wish to minimize social or racial conflict and maintain the status quo. One of the most recent examples of this phenomenon, the "redneck" autobiography, seeks to accomplish at least one objective that concerned writers like Frederick Douglass and Harriet Jacobs: to resist through the use of the autobiographical "I" negative and demeaning stereotypes resulting from others' representations of their group.

For the majority of redneck autobiographers, though, this process of discursive resistance has involved a cold, unsparing look at the human costs of trying to live up to the excesses associated with lower-class southern white masculinity. In particular, the image of the father broken by poverty and alcoholism figures prominently in all but a few autobiographical works by southern writers from working-class backgrounds.[9] In redneck autobiographies and memoirs from Humphrey's *Farther Off from Heaven* and Hemphill's *The Good Old Boys* to more recent examples such as Tim McLaurin's *Keeper of the Moon: A Southern Boyhood* (1991), Dorothy Allison's *One or Two Things I Know for Sure* (1995), and Rick Bragg's *All Over But the Shoutin'* (1997), we witness the same near-obsession with the embodiment of contested masculinity and with the psychological effects of hard drinking, hard work, and hard fighting on the father.

Much of the eloquence and acuity that Crews brings to the subject of poor white masculinity in *A Childhood* can be attributed to his considerable literary skills and narrative expertise (he had already published eight novels by the time he wrote his autobiography). But at the heart of his discursive method lies a willingness to expose the vulnerabilities of his loved ones so that he can then make his readers aware of the core of humanity that is revealed in their failures. More than the poverty he and his family endured (which most people in the depression-era rural South experienced to some degree), the particular circumstances of his paternity likely gave him the perspective and motivation to explore the spectrum of popular images of the poor white. Crews has two fathers to write about in *A Childhood*: his biological father, Ray, who died when the author was an infant, and his stepfather/paternal uncle, Pascal, who, in a plot turn reminiscent of *Hamlet*, divorced his first wife and married his brother's widow eight months after Ray Crews's funeral. Crews divides his autobiography into two separate sections, the first drawing heavily on passed down memories and encompassing Ray Crews's adulthood and untimely death, the second relying on his own personal memories and generally tracing the break-up of his mother's marriage to Pascal Crews. As can be expected, the picture of the father that emerges in Part One is less distinct but more positive in comparison to that of the stepfather in Part Two. The two figures combine to form a composite portrait of poor white masculinity, with Ray Crews embodying the best qualities, and his brother Pascal representing the darker side, of the social type. For all their differences, though, both figures are intrinsically linked to the notion of failure—attributed in Ray's case to economic forces that trap the individual in a cycle of class exploitation, and in Pascal's to self-destructive behaviors strongly associated with poor white southern masculinity—that ultimately rend the fabric of the Crews's domestic life.

The autobiographical identity that Crews presents in *A Childhood* is constructed in relation to his family and neighbors, but within a context of loss and deprivation that affords him a unique perspective he otherwise would not have. This discursive strategy is used to particular advantage in his representations of masculinity, but we see it in practice when he discusses his identification with the "place" of Bacon County, as well. He writes, "I come from people who believe that the *home place* is as vital and necessary as the beating of your own heart. . . . that if you do not have a home place, very little will ever be yours, really *belong* to you in the world" (13–14). Yet, because the family farm was lost after Ray Crews's death, and because his stepfather's drinking problems caused them to be "driven from pillar to post" as his family moved from one tenant farm to another, he has been left with no single place he can point to as "home." As a result, he observes, "Bacon County is my home place, and I've had to make do with it. If I think of where I come from, I think of the entire county. I think of all its people and its customs and all its loveliness and all its ugliness" (14). Here Crews employs a confessional motif to authorize his description of Bacon County, implying that more privileged citizens of the county lack the kind of inclusive identification with the downtrodden that comes from hardship and dislocation.

Frequently, the idea of lack is manifested in explicitly physical terms. For instance, he writes, "Nearly everybody I knew had something missing, a finger cut off, a toe split, an ear half-chewed away, an eye clouded with blindness from a glancing fence staple. And if they didn't have something missing, they were carrying scars from barbed wire, or knives, or fishhooks" (54). These bodily deformations function as signs of "difference" for the young Crews, who becomes aware of his marginality by comparing his people to the "perfect" faces and "unscarred bodies" he finds in the Sears, Roebuck catalog. Yet, he also finds in those scars a text that speaks to him of virile masculinity. For instance, "under the left eye" of his stepfather (called "Daddy" during most of Part Two) is "the scarred print of a perfect set of teeth." Rather than frightening young Harry, the teeth marks signify to the boy his daddy's manhood: "I knew he had taken the scar in a fight," he observes, but it "only made him seem more powerful and stronger and special to me" (49). By far the most remarkable example of how contested masculinity is inscribed on the body can be found in the opening scene of the book. There Crews describes a series of events culminating in the amputation of one of Ray Crews's testicles, which had become painfully swollen after he contracted a case of syphilis while working on a road construction crew deep in the Everglades. The operation leaves Ray under the impression that he is incapable of fathering children, an assumption that, according to the author, impels him to excessive fighting, drinking, and womanizing when he returns to Bacon County upon the completion of the road construction project. The prospect of remaining childless would have caused his father pain, he observes, not simply because children were needed to assist in the farm and house chores, but because in rural Bacon County ". . . a large family was the only thing a man could be sure of having. Nothing else was certain. . . . The timber in the county was of no consequence, and there was very little rich bottomland. Most of the soil was poor and leached out, and commercial fertilizer was as dear as blood. But a man didn't need good lands or stands of hardwood trees to have babies. All he needed was balls and inclination" (13). Although Ray Crews was lacking in one of those components, apparently he made up in inclination what he lacked in the other department. As one of the men at the country store tells the author, " 'It'll take a lot of doing, son, to fill your daddy's shoes. He was much of a man' " (18).

Crews suggests that his father's untimely death may have resulted directly from his mistaken belief that "balls and inclination" are enough to see a man out of poverty. When Ray settles down, marries, and—much to his amazement and delight—begins a family, he turns his attentions to farming with the same vigor he had given to his youthful pursuits. However, we are made to understand that sheer determination was simply not enough, for "[t]he world that circumscribes the people I come from had so little margin for error, for bad luck, that when something went wrong, it always brought something else down with it" (40). The force of will his father exerted in the fields was "born out of desperation and sustained by a lack of alternatives," and ultimately insufficient. Just as he pulls the family out of debt and pays off the mortgage on a 200-acre farm, ". . . it all caught up with him, and he went down." Though Crews goes into vivid detail in recounting the discovery of the corpse and his mother's subsequent hysteria, those ten words capture more of the pathos of his father's demise than all that follows. The "it" that finally gains the advantage on Ray Crews is the chaos that always lurks beyond the narrow "margin for error" in the lives of the poor, while the actual "going down" connotes the defeat of the contender who has just received the knockout blow.

Part One of *A Childhood* concludes with another loss of flesh, though of a very different type than the one that begins the narrative. Two nights after Ray Crews's funeral, a neighbor steals the entire store of meat from the family smokehouse, "everything but one little piece of meat about as big as a man's hand hanging in the back" (42). Because the meat was tangible evidence of a man's efforts to sustain his family, its absence represents the ultimate futility of those efforts. But once again Crews uses the "ugliness" of this incident to illustrate through the privileged perspective of the insider the motivations that prompted the action. We are told that the culprit, who remained unpunished for the crime against his neighbors, lies buried not far from his father's grave. But, Crews confesses, "I see no reason to name him." Not many people would be able to "sympathize" with a man who would steal food from the family of a friend who had just died, "but I think I do," he writes, invoking autobiographical authority. Because of the hardships they faced in that time and place, "a lot of men did things for which they were ashamed and suffered for the rest of their lives. But they did them because of hunger and sickness and because they could not stand the sorry spectacle of their children dying from lack of a doctor and their wives growing old before they were thirty" (43). Rather than avoid the issue of moral weakness and dishonesty, one prominent feature in traditional representations of poor whites, Crews forces his readers to consider the conditions that reduce a man to theft. Then, by using the position of the aggrieved party to offer understanding and forgiveness to the perpetrator, he challenges readers to suspend their judgement on all those who have been locked out of middle-class prosperity.

While Crews renders with sensitivity the conditions that force men to steal from their neighbors, he is even more effective in his treatment of violence, another major component in popular stereotypes of the "redneck." Rather than downplay this "ugly" side of poor white masculinity, Crews uses his authority to distinguish between necessary and unnecessary forms of physical brutality. In some respects, Ray Crews, the "good" father, is no less violent than his brother, Pascal, but the author takes pains to contextualize the behavior of his biological father so that his actions appear perfectly legitimate, given his circumstances. "These were not violent men," he writes in Part One, "but their lives were full of violence" (7). He goes on to remark that the sheriff was not to be sent for if you had a dispute with a neighbor, because ". . . if you had any real trouble. . . . [y]ou made it right yourself or else became known in the county as a man who was defenseless without the sheriff at his back. If that ever happened, you would be brutalized and savaged endlessly because of it. Men killed other men oftentimes not because there had been some offense that merited death, but simply because there had been an offense, any offense. As many men have been killed over bird dogs and fence lines in South Georgia as anything else" (8).

For Crews, utility and self-restraint are key to distinguishing between desirable and undesirable forms of violence, as evidenced in the way he describes his natural father's relationship with his mare, Daisy. Administered in exacting proportions, he suggests, physical brutality can bring about understanding, even intimacy. "They knew what to expect from one another," he writes. "He knew dead solid certain that she would kick his head off if she got the chance. And she knew just as surely that he would beat her to her knees with a singletree—the iron bar on a plow or wagon to which the trace chains are hooked—if she did not cooperate" (31). Anticipating his reader's revulsion, Crews acknowledges, "It sounds like a terrible thing to talk about, hitting a mare between the ears with a piece of iron," only to explain, "but it was done not only out of necessity but also out of love. . . ." After describing the manner in which his father and Daisy would work the field, Crews creates a syncretic moment in which the reader is pulled back into the "present" time of narration, where the author retrieves from an old shoe box an aging photograph of his four-year-old brother sitting atop Daisy without a saddle. "Nobody is holding her rein," he observes, "and she is standing easy as the lady she became under my daddy's *firm, gentle,* and *dangerous* hand" (italics mine).

In contrast to the measured application of violence exhibited by Ray Crews, the author's stepfather is prone to explosive bouts of shouting, gun-waving, and wife-battering. Yet Crews initially juxtaposes the man's propensity to drinking and violence against his capacity for tenderness and affection. Although the author associates the smell of whiskey with the "ugly sound of breaking things in the night," he notes that "[t]he stronger the smell of whiskey on him . . . the kinder and gentler he was with me and my brother" (49). One night, after hearing the "dull, unmistakable thump of flesh on flesh," Crews and his brother are jolted out of bed by a shotgun blast from within the house (124–25). Despite the fact that the narrator "knew for certain it was not unusual for a man to shoot at his wife" (125), his mother takes the two boys and moves to the Springfield section of Jacksonville, Florida, where she finds employment in the cigar industry.

It is in that setting, among the dislocated rural people of South Georgia who have come to the city in search of a better life, that we are made to understand that Pascal's weaknesses are not special. Once he discovers where his wife and stepsons are living, he begins showing up in the middle of the night, drunk and singing on the sidewalk outside. "But I never thought too much about it all, one way or the other," Crews writes. "Certainly it did not cause me any shame. How could it when half the fathers and husbands at any given moment were swooning and crooning along the sidewalks and at the bedroom windows of the Springfield section . . . ? Daddy was neither better nor worse than the rest. He was simply one of them" (144–45). Finally, after having a restraining order placed on him, he ceases stalking his ex-wife and disappears from the author's life. In a scene that begs comparison with the scene at the country store in which he first feels the urge to translate his life into writing, Crews describes going back to Jacksonville, while he was a student attending the University of Florida, to look for his stepfather. He finds him "not far from where I lost him. . . . sitting in the back of a tiny store, huddled beside a stove in a huge overcoat. He was very nervous. He did not want to talk. I left minutes after I got there. We never touched each other, not even to shake hands" (147). Crews does not explore the psychology of his stepfather, though no doubt he must have wondered what demons drove the man to behave so. Instead, Pascal becomes less distinct as an individual as Part Two of the narrative progresses, finally fading into anonymity with the other broken, dislocated men from South Georgia who populate the Springfield section.

In the end it is Crews's maternal uncle, Alton, who serves as the father figure in his later youth after Myrtice Crews and her two sons have moved back to Bacon County. He takes the boy hunting, teaches him to fish, shows him how to perform the tasks necessary to survive in the country. "But perhaps the best thing he ever showed me—made me *feel*—" he writes, "was that a man does not back down from doing what is necessary, no matter how unpleasant" (164). Crews emphasizes the tactile here because that is precisely what Alton does one afternoon when the family's rooster becomes sick. Enlisting the author's aid, Alton performs surgery on the bird to remove an object from his craw. But first, he places the boy's hand gently on the rooster's neck so that Harry can fully appreciate the necessity of the act. Then, after the "horrible and beautiful moment" when the incision is made and the object is retrieved from the craw, Alton asks his nephew to take over the job of suturing the craw. Crews writes, "Uncle Alton's hand moved to take the rooster's feet and my own fingers were suddenly deep in the wound, the living flesh slipping and throbbing" (165). The operation is successful and every time he sees the rooster after that, he recalls, he would "remember that his blood had been on my fingers, and more, that I had touched his blood because Uncle Alton had treated me like a son he trusted" (165–66). In this scene a coming-of-age ritual is enacted in which the author is anointed with the symbolic mark of manhood. But for all the emphasis Crews gives here to the idea that masculinity is defined by "doing what a man's gotta do"—to borrow a cliche not of Crews's choosing—he also makes it clear that the emotional significance of the moment lies in his uncle's trust in him and the feeling of confidence that gives him. The scene also suggests that it is men like Alton, whose humility and quiet dignity bear little resemblance to the rowdiness of the young Ray Crews or his brother, Pascal, that truly represent the best attributes of the lower-class rural southern male.

Despite the South's economic revitalization and the alleviation of most of the social and racial inequities that caused the region to be seen by non-southerners (as well as non-whites within the South) as a national "problem," southerners and non-southerners alike continue to perceive the region as culturally distinct from the rest of the U.S.[10] Judging by the recent spate of self-demeaning "redneck" humor, it also appears that negative stereotypes of lower- and working-class whites continue to loom large in popular images of the South. As long as the figure of the "redneck" remains a part of the landscape of the imagined South, then, writers who identify with this class of southerners will have some motivation to engage in self-representation. For nearly three centuries, the figure of the poor white figured prominently in representations of the South. Now it appears that lower- and working-class southern whites have achieved a voice of their own with which they can resist and redefine those earlier representations and, thus, contribute to a more complex understanding of the South and the southerner. Although the critical reputation of Harry Crews rests primarily on his achievement as a novelist, he should also be credited with writing the quintessential redneck autobiography. For all the attention his novels have deservedly received, it may be that *A Childhood* leaves a more lasting influence on the literature of the South than all of his fiction combined.

TRAVELS IN GREENELAND

Graham Greene's Influence on Harry Crews

Richard Rankin Russell

Despite a relative lack of critical attention, Harry Crews has had a
magnificent career as a novelist, essayist and general commentator
on American life. The criticism that does exist on Crews tends to focus
on individual readings of his novels, discussions of his freakish characters, his image as literary outlaw, or his influence on other authors such
as Larry Brown. However, to truly appreciate and delineate Crews's role
as author and social critic, a recognition of literary influences upon him
must be fostered. Of these, no writer has been more important for him
than the British author Graham Greene. I argue here that Crews has
been profoundly shaped by Greene, who to this day remains an abiding
influence. Crews has often pointed to Greene as his literary mentor. He
has explicitly noted that:

if any novelist has ever influenced me, it's been Graham Greene. I've read
Graham Greene very closely with the conscious idea of seeing how in the hell
he did things. . . . Graham Greene's seemed closer to my story-telling sense than
other people's did. So I took one of his novels [*The End of the Affair*] and reduced

it to numbers: how many characters, how many days did the novel take; how many cities were involved; how far into the novel did I understand the climax to take place; where did the action turn; how many men, women, children, rooms. Then I sat down and tried to write a novel using that skeleton. . . . Needless to say, the novel that resulted from this was an abominable piece of work—arbitrary, mechanical, and uninteresting. At the same time, I think I learned a great deal from that exercise . . . matters of physical transition . . . psychological kinds of transitions. (Watson 64)

Crews also told David K. Jeffrey and Donald R. Noble in an interview which took place in the early 1980s that "I think I've learned more from Graham Greene than I've learned from any other writer. To the best of my knowledge, I've read everything that he's ever written" (142). While Crews's "apprenticeship" to Greene may not have given him an immediate grasp of the subtleties necessary in crafting a successful novel, I believe several attributes of Greene have become hallmarks of Crews's writing and helped form his conception of the role of the artist: a commitment to traditional fictional elements, driven by a spare prose style; perseverance in the face of near-constant despair; and a conception of himself as a moral writer, augmented by a problematic belief in orthodox Christianity.

Crews clearly sees himself as a storyteller in the tradition of Greene. He has vigorously maintained that his own writing is storytelling, plain and simple. To wit, he emphatically told Sterling Watson in a 1974 interview, "I think of myself as a very traditional storyteller. . . . the writers I've read who undertake to do these things—Robbe-Grillet, or whatever his name is, the Frenchman—simply seem to me not to render the human condition in a human way. It all becomes too intellectual, too complicated for complication's sake" (65–6). Nearly twenty years later he maintained the same position on his narrative style: "I always admired writers that told you a story, and I think of myself as a storyteller. . . ." (Lytal and Russell 538). Interestingly, Crews's earlier remarks closely parallel Greene's about his own penchant for storytelling, down to the elder writer's clear realization that experimental writing simply does not convey a story in the manner in which realistic fiction does. For instance, Greene told Marie-Francoise Allain in the early 1980s that "I've always enjoyed telling stories, and my impression is that readers prefer this to the *nouveau roman*, for instance. . . . I like Robbe-Grillet very much, but I think that certain experiments in writing can't be extended beyond a rather limited number of years" (147). It should go without saying here that Crews's lack of interest in Robbe-Grillet specifically and writers of his ilk generally was undoubtedly influenced by Greene's refusal to be influenced by them in his own traditionally constructed novels.

Crews then, scorns the omission of such standard elements as plot, characterization, and normal settings in time and space in the *nouveau roman*, preferring to use these standard fictional devices to render the condition of his characters clearly and perspicaciously.[1]

In developing his minimalist prose style Crews needed to look no further than Greene. Greene's writing resonates with the tautness of a bowstring; modifiers are stripped away and action is paramount. He honed his distinctive prose style as sub-editor on *The Times* in London as he learned to pare a story down to its essence. In his autobiography, he gratefully recounts the formative influence of his newspaper editing on his own style: "And while the young writer is spending these amusing and unexacting hours, he is learning lessons valuable to his own craft. He is . . . compressing a story to the minimum length possible without ruining its effect" (*A Sort of Life* 181). Later on in this account of his early life, Greene remembers his epiphany about the type of writing he was supposed to carry out: "the sort of novel I was trying to write, unlike a poem, was not made with words but with movement, action, character. Discrimination in one's words is certainly required, but not love of one's words—that is a form of self-love, a fatal love. . . ." (203). Crews is one of the foremost literary inheritors of Greene's terse, pointed prose style, which enables Crews's writing to carry such formidable force.

It is no accident that Crews started his career, not by writing newspaper columns, but by writing in another genre usually governed by relative brevity—short stories. His own ongoing interest in compression in the three early short stories, "The Unattached Smile," "A Long Wail," and "The Player Piano"—all of which were published before his first novel, *The Gospel Singer*, in 1968—has undoubtedly colored his minimalist fictional prose. But Crews is really not a short story writer: he is at his best in a handful of novels—*A Feast of Snakes* and *Scar Lover* both come immediately to mind—his autobiography, *A Childhood: The Biography of a Place*, his forthcoming memoir, *Assault of Memory*, and his essays. He excels in distilling his meditations upon a given subject in the more limited space of an essay; however, this is not to dismiss the undeniable achievement of his several fine novels. The novels I have mentioned and indeed, all of his novels, are longer meditations upon a variety of subjects that can all be grouped under the heading of man's place in the world. What characterizes the typical Crews novel is its concision, its distillation of the essences of life into the essences of fiction: plot, character, dialogue, and storytelling, the last of which is driven by a love of concrete prose. As he has noted recently and explicitly, "Writing is good to the degree that it is concrete and specific. And bad to the degree that it is abstract and vague" (Bledsoe 99). In all of these, but especially in his sparse prose style, his model has been Greene. Finally, what Cedric Watts has noted about Greene's prose could also be easily applied to Crews's forceful writing: "At its frequent best, Greene's prose is never inert; ruthlessly, it shuns the easy platitude, the convenient cliche, the waffling digression" (166).

While Greene's conception of the novelist as storyteller, coupled with his powerfully precise prose, have strongly influenced Crews's notions of the novel, one of his most enduring characters has been a powerful and long-running influence on Crews's personal persistence and staying power as an author. If Greene is the dominant literary influence on Crews, his most powerful work for Crews is surely *The Power and the Glory*. Time and again, both Crews and his fictional characters muse over the protagonist of that novel—the nomadic whiskey priest on the run from the authorities in 1930s Mexico, where Catholicism and its practice has been banned. The priest himself is a bundle of contradictions: he has had a child out of wedlock, but refuses to conform to the new laws for priests and marry; he abuses wine but still believes it becomes the blood of Christ during communion; he is literally fleeing for his life but uncontrollably giggles in the most dangerous situations. Scorned by even his own parishioners, he stolidly carries on his offices, administering Mass and performing baptisms. Even though he is betrayed and executed, the novel ends hopefully, as another priest appears and is joyfully received by Juan, a boy of fourteen who has formerly scorned the Church.

Crews greatly admires this character and even identifies his role as a writer with him. The nameless priest embodies Crews's own struggles with writing and living and the desire to press on towards the mark, along with a sense of ambiguity. Evidence of his empathy with Greene's protagonist abounds. When I helped interview Crews in 1992 during his time at The University of Memphis for the River City Writers Series, our concluding question to him was, "Do you have any other advice for those who wish to write?" He had already given us advice on how to write when "mentally constipated," but his answer to this final question reveals his purpose as a writer, indelibly shaped by Greene:

> If you're gonna write, for God in heaven's sake, try to get naked. Try to write the truth . . . Graham Greene has a book called *The Power and the Glory*. It's got a priest in it, in a state down in Mexico. . . . *And he was totally flawed. He had a child out of wedlock, and he was a drunk.* Everything was wrong with him, except he could intercede between man and God. With all the other stuff that he had done and was, *that man was God's man in that place.* He was God's representative. And God's representative was *failed and flawed*, as are all of God's representatives

that it has been my good fortune to meet. . . . And I'll tell you something else: when I write, when you read my stuff, I want to hurt'cha. I wanna hurt'cha by turning you back upon your own heart. I want to make you look into yourself. . . . See, if I do my job right when I'm writing, I will really get you turned back on yourself, and on your own code of ethics or morality or vision of the world or sense of self or whatever. If I get you turned back on yourself, then I done my job. (Lytal and Russell 552–53, my emphases)

Crews's writerly intent, to "get you turned back on yourself," owes something to Faulkner's famous statement in his 1949 Nobel Prize acceptance speech that "good writing" is essentially concerned with the "human heart in conflict with itself," but what is more striking is the inclusion of a discussion of Greene's masterpiece in his reply. He clearly identifies his own failings with those of the priest's, but goes on to imply that both he and the priest still have the power to place their characters and parishioners, respectively, in moral dilemmas, out of which hopefully will come tenable, realistic solutions—though these will never be cheap or easy, purchased as they are with gritty experience.

And just as Crews the author has often taken Greene's famous priest as a personal and artistic model, so have Crews's characters. A fictional protagonist who also likes *The Power and the Glory* is Marvin Molar in Crews's seventh novel, *The Gypsy's Curse*. At one point, tired and frustrated, he relates, "I even took down my favorite book in all the world, one I've read more times than I know, Graham Greene's *The Power and the Glory*, and tried to read in it" (270). Molar, whose crippled legs remain bound behind him while he walks on his hands, cannot find solace in the novel. But Crews, whose own legs were also mysteriously drawn up behind him for a time in early childhood does, returning to it again and again, through his fictional protagonists and in personal interviews.

Crews's ongoing concern with Greene's masterpiece shows through his empathetic portrayal of Duffy Deeter in his 1987 novel *All We Need of Hell*. With his divorce pending, Deeter searches for stability among the bookshelves of his Winnebago. What he finds for his evening reading is telling:

He opened the grate and took out one of his favorite books, Graham Greene's *The Power and the Glory*. He knew it was the book he needed because the moment he saw it, he remembered the whole thing as vividly as he remembered his own father, dead now these many years. He remembered the man at the center of the book, a wonderful, *totally fucked-up priest, a Catholic priest who is a drunk, who has a child out of wedlock, and who is at the same time God's man in the world*. The priest does not just believe he is God's man, or just know he is God's man, but he acts on the knowledge and belief to administer last rites even though in his time and place Catholicism has been outlawed. And the penalty for administering last rites is death. *Totally flawed and fucked up, the priest remains the perfect instrument of God.* Wonderful. Everything works together. Everything is of a piece. (50, my emphases)

The wording of this passage at times is very similar to Crews's own remarks cited earlier about the novel in my interview with him. Certainly it is reductive to consistently identify Crews with his fictional characters, but the repeated appearance of Greene's priest throughout Crews's writings makes him both an artistic symbol and source of refuge for Crews. Since this passage is featured so prominently in Crews's return to writing long fiction, he probably also drew upon Greene's character for inspiration during his hiatus.

In short, Crews has not only perfected Greene's prose style, but he has adopted Greene as his artistic inspiration. He sees Graham Greene as a kindred soul, someone who suffered just as he has, but nevertheless doggedly plodded on, committed to posing moral questions in fictional forms. Greene's first volume of autobiography, *A Sort of Life*, reveals his lifelong boredom, which he occasionally alleviated by playing Russian roulette to charge and refire his senses. More important, he speaks again and again in those pages about his failures as a writer. Certainly writing itself is composed of various false starts and the starving artist is an overused cliche. But Greene really felt like a failure throughout his life. When reminiscing about publishing his first piece of fiction in his school magazine, he grimly observes, "never again did the idea hold such excitement, pride and confidence; always later, even with the publication of my first novel, the excitement was overshadowed by the knowledge of failure, by awareness of the flawed intention" (*A Sort of Life* 110–11). Nevertheless, he determinedly pursued a career as a writer. Later, while recounting his two-week stint with the British-American Tobacco Company after graduating from Oxford, he writes of his second attempt at a novel and being torn between a "respectable career" and becoming a writer: "How could I abandon the chance of being a businessman, when it seemed my only escape from the hated obsession of trying to make imaginary characters live?" (154–55). But abandon it he did, eventually signing a three-year contract with the London firm of Heinemann.

Crews, too, has struggled with writing and speaks of it in similar terms of loathing and need: "I'm compulsive about going to the typewriter. There again it has nothing to do with liking to do it. I don't think that compulsive horse players like to go to the track particularly. I think they enjoy themselves sometimes, but they do it because it's in them to do it" (Watson 70–71). Never one to go about something halfway, he remains deeply committed to his craft. After attempting to write a novel again after his decade-long abstinence, he admitted his compulsion about writing to interviewer Michelle Green in 1987: "If I'm away [from a manuscript] for even a day, it's like I left all those people stuck in a frozen tableau, lifting the forks to their mouths. Once you've come this far with them, you feel you're not just doing them a disservice, you're being gravely inconsiderate leaving them, so you've got to go back and free them" (75). And in freeing his characters, Crews seems able, however temporarily, to slip free of his own demons.

Crews further adheres to Greene's belief that "For a writer . . . success is always temporary, success is only a delayed failure" (*A Sort of Life* 219). Both men seem to cling to their work as a lifeline in a sea of failure which threatens to subsume them. But for Crews, it is precisely his failure that reassures him and enables him to continue writing. In his finest essay, "Climbing the Tower," he again points toward Greene as an example for the artist generally and himself specifically: "Graham Greene said: 'The artist is doomed to live in an atmosphere of perpetual failure.' I am very nervous about the word artist. . . . But I know what it means to live in an atmosphere of perpetual failure. . . . All of us whose senses are not entirely dead realize the imperfection of what we do, and to the extent that we are hard on ourselves, that imperfection translates itself into failure. Inevitably, it is out of a base of failure that we try to rise again to do another thing" (212). Crews has admittedly made a mess of his personal life, and the literary value of his work has consistently been questioned. But through it all, he has remained committed to what he sees as his God-given office, rising repeatedly from the ashes of his life in his determined pursuit of writing.

For instance, in his "Introduction" to *Classic Crews*, after reviewing his year and a half spent roaming and working across America and Mexico, he recalls:

> That learning to write was taking so long did not surprise or discourage me. At least I tried not to let it. No one knew better than I how hit-and-miss my learning had been. But I remained convinced in my belief that all anybody needed to develop as a writer was access to a good library and the willingness to play fast and loose with his life. . . . And I knew there was not a mother's son or daughter in the world who could tell any apprentice artist, no matter how much potential and willingness to work the apprentice had, whether he would in fact catch the brass ring or spend the end of his days just as he spent them in his youth: floundering and flopping about and still failing. (14–15)

The traveling, the writing, the hard living—with Crews as with Greene, it is all of a piece and completely necessary to complete an apprenticeship with life's realities which inspire and become the material of their writing.

Furthermore, Crews's life experiences have helped him attune himself to suffering and essential questions of morality. Earlier in our interview with him, he suggested something akin to Flannery O'Connor's concept of the mystery at the heart of the novel when asked, "How much time do you spend editing?" His reply was that he rewrites a great deal in order to "find out what I'm writing about, what the subject is. . . . I mean is it about despair, or the healing nature of forgiveness and compassion, or somebody as *flawed and failed* as I am? At the center of all books or poems or plays, there is a mystery, a mystery that cannot be solved or resolved or explained, but only kind of meditated upon and wondered at. And meditating upon that, and wondering about it, you inevitably have to wonder about yourself, and meditate upon yourself" (551, my emphasis). This description of himself, coupled as it is with his description of the "failed and flawed" whiskey priest shortly afterward and his wish to turn his readers back on themselves, implies that he himself, though scarred and imperfect, is essentially a moral writer, more concerned with creating and posing ethical questions than he will directly admit.

His remarks about *The Power and the Glory* further suggest his belief that Greene was a moral writer. Greene's position as a writer is complex but recently critical opinion has come to agree that he was not merely a Catholic writer (a title which he disliked as much as Crews dislikes being called a Southern writer) but one whose work carries an undeniable weight of morality. For instance, in his *A Reader's Guide to Graham Greene*, Paul O'Prey points out that "Greene writes as a moralist as well as a realist, concerned with the moral complexity and ambiguity at the centre of life as well as with the actual experience of life, and his greatest achievement is in those books, such as *The Power and the Glory* and *The Honorary Consul*, in which he achieves a careful balance of the two . . . with a sensitive and profound treatment of important moral issues" (12). O'Prey's observation is especially important in that it recognizes the means by which Greene effected his fictional questions of morality—through ambiguous characters like the whiskey priest who, through his perseverance, forces the reader to reflect upon his own life and question his values and beliefs.

Another Greene critic has also noticed how uncertainty and morality interact in his fiction. For instance, R. H. Miller points out in his *Understanding Graham Greene* that "he writes from a highly developed moral perspective and invests his narratives with a deep moral concern, most so when in the novel or story there seems no basis for any kind of moral meaning in life" (1). Greene then, is that most troubled of moralists, not pontificating from his literary pulpit, but asking soul-searching questions about the nebulous areas of our lives.

The uncertainty inherent in Greene's *oeuvre* stems at least in part from his own deracination. For instance, Philip Stratford points out that Greene had "a carefully nurtured ambiguity. From his earliest days, when he used to play a game in the family garden called 'England and France,' Greene was irresistibly drawn to frontiers. . . . One must be able to write, he says . . . 'from the point of view of the black square as well as of the white' " (ix–xi). Greene's most memorable characters seem developed from his own lifelong quarrel with himself; thus we have the priest who believes but is hopelessly sunken in depression in *The Power and the Glory* or Scobie in *The Heart of the Matter*, torn between two women, and agonizing over his relationship with God and the possibility of eternal damnation.

Similarly, Crews's interest in creating ambiguity in his fiction has almost certainly arisen from his uncertainty about himself. For example, in the opening pages of *A Childhood*, he notes that "it was just for this reason that I started this book, because I have never been certain of who *I* am. I have always slipped in and out of identities as easily as other people slip into and out of their clothes. Even my voice, its inflections and rhythms, does not seem entirely my own" (4).[2] After leaving Bacon County, Georgia, at seventeen, Crews has traveled extensively, but also ensconced himself in the northern Florida town of Gainesville. While he does seem comfortable there, the location is admittedly a necessary distance from his famous upbringing in south Georgia, as he notes in his essay, "Why I Live Where I Live": "I've tried to work—that is, to write—in Georgia, but I could not. Even under the best of circumstances, at my mama's farm, for instance, it was all too much for me. I was too deep in it, too close to it to use it, to make anything out of it. . . . Living here in Gainesville seems to give me the kind of geographic and emotional distance that I need to write" (47). Crews's displaced identity and geographic distance from his early home, far from disorienting him, have instead proved to be a source of strength for him, as he has been able to adapt to constantly changing conditions around him, just as Greene did. He seems to revel in the contradictions which have always swirled around him: he is alternately seen as either a misogynist or a feminist, fighter or pacifist, believer or nonbeliever. It is the last of these paradoxes which most links him to Greene, in that both authors share a conflicted faith in God.

Besides their shared deracination—this is of course, an affinity between the two rather than a straightforward case of influence from Greene upon Crews—both writers are problematic Christians, espousing, at times, a belief in central tenets of the faith, but whose lives and characters radically depart from any sort of normative Christianity. Greene converted to Catholicism in 1926 after deciding to marry Vivienne Dayrell-Browning, an ardent Catholic. He described his experience in characteristically terse prose: "I can only remember that in January 1926 I became convinced of the probable existence of something we call God. . . . I remember very clearly the nature of my emotion as I walked away from the Cathedral: there was no joy in it at all, only a somber apprehension" (*A Sort of Life* 168–69). Later, he divorced Vivienne, and was involved with numerous affairs the rest of his life. By the end of his life, he admitted to his biographer Norman Sherry that he doubted his belief in God, but he remained committed to a nominal faith.

He further yoked his tenuous faith in Catholicism to an abiding interest in political issues and social justice throughout his career. Towards the end of his life, he told Marie-Francoise Allain, "My interest in politics goes back a long way. Don't go thinking, as many others have done, that I've undergone some evolution from religion toward politics. . . . There's a certain coherence, a certain continuity between *It's a Battlefield, Brighton Rock* and *The Honorary Consul*: it's my concern with the possibility of social change" (87–88). He later told this same interviewer that he recognized the "first inroads" of his faith "during my visit to Mexico [the inspiration for *The Power and the Glory*] in 1938. It's all bound up with my loyalty to the underdog—and so it has been ever since" (154). Greene long championed the rights of the oppressed, variously supporting persecuted Mexican Catholics in the 1930s, Fidel Castro in the 1950s, and the Sandinistas of Nicarauga in the early 1980s.

In much the same way, Harry Crews, both personally and in his fiction, has had difficulty in adopting or believing orthodox Christianity. As an internal émigré in the Bible Belt, he has come to decry organized religion but still often discusses his thoughts on his faith (or lack thereof) and consistently features characters who struggle with God or their faith in Him. He has recently claimed that, "all of my books, everything I've written, as a matter of fact, including the journalism, in one way or another is either about people searching for something to believe in, something that has to do with faith, or the nature of faith" (Bledsoe 105). While his conversion experience was dramatically different from that of Greene—based on emotion, not argument—it rings similarly hollow. In an hilarious passage from his autobiography, Crews recounts his baptism under pressure at the hands of an itinerant Baptist preacher around the age of six: "When a man like that told you God, by God, was coming soon, was probably on His way this very night to touch you with His Love if you didn't come on home to Jesus right now! you didn't argue about it, resist it, or even think about it. You just shit in your pants, stood up and staggered down the aisle toward the altar, blinded by tears and terror. But I had always known

I would someday have to do God. I had been watching people do Him all my life: fainting, screaming, crying, and thrashing about over the floor. My turn had come and I'd survived him" (*A Childhood* 168). This experience seems more an encounter with God's representative than God Himself. But admittedly, it is representative of a fundamentalist Protestant salvation experience in the American South.

During our interview with him, when asked his position on salvation, he evasively and defensively replied: "Well now, you've got to ask somebody with a better mind and a better heart, and who knows things in a way that I don't know them, to get an answer to that. As a matter of fact, I am not interested in talking to you about what I believe or do not believe about God or the absence of God or heaven or hell or any of that. That's just a little too big for me. And I stand—if I stand any way before it—in fear and trembling" (Lytal and Russell 545). However, when pressed upon the same issue eleven years earlier, Crews unequivocally stated, "I have no book that does not in some way concern itself with man's relationship to God. . . . I am a believer. I am not a spark of electricity. I am not an accident. I was made" (Jeffrey and Noble 147). Surely, then, if not Christian, Crews's position is at least strongly agnostic or even deistic.

More recently, Crews has indicated a grudging awareness of God. For example, in a short essay entitled, "A Lesson in Desperation and Stupidity," he recounts being caught in Hurricane Elena on the island of Cedar Key with the young woman he is seeing. He opens the piece by recollecting his refusal to believe the hurricane could hit the island, expressing a characteristically agnostic view of God: "Only God knows and He never speaks" (47). She replies that he shouldn't joke about hurricanes—that they are serious—and he agrees. Late that night, they are awakened to find their room awash in water. After they have fled across the rickety wooden bridge that connects the island with the mainland—a move that defies all common sense—Crews turns to the girl and asks, "Do you remember early today when I said God never speaks?" After she nods, he observes flatly, "I think he just spoke" (48). This skeptical belief in God often emerges only in crisis situations for Crews or his characters.

However, many of his novels, while having a number of Christian elements and characters, end in horrific or ambiguous ways, further demonstrating how his penchant for ambiguity colors his "faith." For example, the righteous snake-handling preacher of *A Feast of Snakes*, Victor, is gunned down by the novel's protagonist, Joe Lon Mackey, in the final pages of that novel. And just as ambiguity abounds in Greene's works, it flourishes in the pages of Crews's writing. As Frank W. Shelton has noted in an article appraising Crews's fiction written after his autobiography, "If there is one constant in Crews's best fiction, it is uncertainty . . ." (9). Greene's critics have coined the term "Greeneland" for his literary landscape, which was characterized by seediness, ambiguity, and questionable characters. Similarly, the background against which Crews's well-known freaks and other disturbing characters move is the gritty territory of the down and out, the oppressed, and the lonely. At times, his characters are offered hope and redemption, at others, there is nothing waiting but the slash of the hatchet and the razor blade (in the ending of *The Gypsy's Curse* and *Body*, respectively), or the repeated boom of the shotgun (in *A Feast of Snakes*).

Crews's interest in religious matters has been noted by a number of his critics. For example, in an essay dealing with Crews's work through 1979, William J. Schafer cites as one of his major themes "the tension between faith and doubt— modes of belief. Beginning with the obvious themes of *The Gospel Singer*, a consistent spiritual enquiry runs through Crews's novels. His characters quest after spiritual certainty and meaning, seek paths to salvation. . . . The vision permeating Harry Crews's novels is a satiric, mordant picture of secularized, isolated and spiritually undernourished people seeking beyond themselves for redemption" (85, 87). Schafer curiously omits one of Crews's finest novels, *A Feast of Snakes*, from his discussion. However, Ruth L. Brittin notes that this novel is another example of how "Crews again deals with Southern religion; again his protagonist resists its claims; and again that protagonist cannot escape its powers" (98). In his early fiction, between 1968 and 1979, Crews is definitely concerned with spiritual matters, which enabled him to pose moral questions while often satirically (and almost nihilistically) sneering at us.

But what role does Crews's faith play in his later work, which has appeared starting in 1987 after his much-publicized hiatus from writing novels? *Scar Lover*, published in 1992, is the most redemptive of these later novels, not in an orthodox Christian sense, but in a profoundly human one. Despite his surname, the protagonist of the novel, Pete Butcher, is the healer of the various people afflicted with scars. He takes up with a neighbor named Sarah and her family. After her father dies, he assumes the role of man of the family, helping to pacify her mother, who is slowly growing mad. In the process, he forgives himself for the maiming of his younger brother Jonathan with the claws of a hammer. I agree with Robert C. Covel, who sees *Scar Lover* as "significant in the Crews canon because it demonstrates how one might take at least one step beyond violence, namely, by developing compassion for the physically and emotionally scarred people who inhabit the developing megalopolis of the New South" (86). Whereas in an earlier novel like *A Feast of Snakes* no redemption is offered, here Crews features characters who break through their stultifying environment and psychological hang-ups to build a bridge of connection to others.

It is Graham Greene, however, not his fictional priest, who has functioned as the model for Crews's compassion. A typical example of the priest's attitude towards the poor occurs after he is captured by the lieutenant, when he asks the officer, "Oh, I know we are told to give to the poor, to see they are not hungry—hunger can make a man do evil just as much as money can. But why should we give the poor power? It's better to let him die in dirt and wake in heaven—so long as we don't push his face in the dirt" (*The Power and the Glory* 199). Greene, with his lifelong compassion for the oppressed of the world, not the priest, with his opposition to a redistribution of wealth, is the exemplar for Crews's ongoing concern for his displaced and often poor characters. In fact, the problematic faith of both writers is thoroughly imbued with aspects of socialism.

While Graham Greene emphatically denied he emphasized politics over religion later in his career, Crews seems to be drifting toward social commentary with only faint overtones of his faith. He has always been concerned with the clash between southerners and nonsoutherners, rural and urban, but one of his overriding concerns—and one which is intertwined with his personal and fictional search for faith—has been with the damaging effects of consumerism on America. He charts his disdain for the effects of mail order shopping in an early essay entitled "L. L. Bean Has Your Number, America!" In this piece, a bemused Crews finds himself outside the headquarters of the mail-order giant L. L. Bean in Freeport, Maine, sniffing "the green smell of money [which] was everywhere in the air" (24). After touring the outfit and observing rabid customers engaged in a feeding frenzy of shopping, Crews points out that the contemporary company has drifted far from its origins as an outfitter for real hunters, but that all their products are marketed so that "suburban America [is given] the slightest whiff of a blood spoor" (*Blood and Grits* 28). Often Crews, as he does here, plays the intermediary between the world of the suburbs and the grittier rural world which is being relentlessly invaded by the mass media and mass marketing. He has not hopped on the bandwagon of rampant capitalism, but realizes he cannot live in the agrarian past either.

In one of his most recent novels, *The Mulching of America*, Crews skillfully exposes the deleterious effects of marketing on our society in his typically wry manner. His protagonist is a door-to-door soap salesman, Hickum Looney, who has been bound to his job at Soaps for Life for the past twenty-five years. Traditional religion has been replaced by salesmanship in the novel. Looney and his cohorts literally worship the head of the company, who is variously called The Boss, Elmo Jeroveh (surely a play on Jehovah), and the Big Man:

> People all over the country working in the Soaps For Life Company were waiting for what they had been promised, waited with all the fervor of their being, with hope, with a certain anxiety and fear, and, yes, with prayer. . . .
>
> As will sometimes happen in matters of such kind, the three names became mixed and meshed and confused, one with the other, without the supplicants ever knowing it. Apparently it never seemed blasphemous to them when it all became tightly knotted together, and inseparable, into Elmo/the Big Man/ the Boss—and without any of those on their knees realizing it—God. (203–04)

The Boss has constructed a Trinitarian religion based on buying and selling. His salesmen have what amounts to their Bible in the Company Manual, which is full of the Boss's exhortations on how to sell more soap: "The bedrock on which the Boss's Theory of Salesmanship was built was that the consumer in America was the world's most terrified individual. . . . Anybody could make an excellent product and sell it. But it took a genius to make a piece of shit and sell it" (103). And that is precisely what his legions of salesman are pushing—a product that they have never even seen but which nets Jeroveh a great deal of money. They are selling an image, an idea, foisted upon the public through the vacuous medium of television. Just as L. L. Bean sells "a whiff of blood spoor," they dupe their consumers with colored wax samples of soap.

The cost of this consumer mentality runs throughout the novel. After Looney has sex with Gaye Nell Odell, a prostitute who has been living with her dog Bubba in an abandoned Volkswagen van, he muses on her plight from the comfort of his air-conditioned Lincoln Town Car: "How does anybody, especially here in the U. S. of A., land of the free, home of the brave, and breadbasket to the rest of the world—in such a country, how does anybody manage to end up living in a ruined vehicle?" (88). After this passing shot at our consumer-oriented culture, Crews's story hurtles on with typical verve to its ending, where the "mulching" of the title is finally explained. Hickum is summoned before Ida Mae, who has assumed control of the company. Both he and the Boss have outlived their usefulness and are to be mulched, their bodies ground up and used in flowerbeds. As the novel closes, Looney protests to Ida Mae, "But what about Gaye Nell and her dog. . . ." Her reply is succinct and horrifying: "Don't trouble yourself, dear boy. It will all work out. The world grinds on." And then, right before he dies, Hickum realizes the fraud to which he has committed the better part of his life: "the fire in the hearth was, in fact, a fake, not fire at all, only colored light" (268).

Matthew Teague has argued persuasively that "The new novel is . . . Crews's attack on capitalism and the American ideal of 'progress,' both of which he views as having bastardized any semblance of spirituality. . . . In Crews's fiction, a spirituality muted by a secular world cripples his characters, who worship that which does not satisfy human need" (71). Because its theme is characteristic of his body of work, this novel clearly is consistent with Crews's artistic and moral vision. Crews's warning to us all here is clear—if we let our consumer culture control our lives, we will soon become soulless, devoured in the maws of mass production. Thus his concern with issues of faith remains in this novelistic admonition about the danger of letting money become our religion.[3]

In many ways, the question of belief in Crews's life and work is characteristic of an ongoing phenomenon in American writing that Alfred Kazin chronicles brilliantly in his final book, *God and the American Writer*. As Kazin notes in his "Afterword,"

> If the American writer is usually alone in his imagination and in his devotions a secret to the rest of us, one reason is that religion is so publicly vehement, politicized, and censorious. . . . Still, so much radical individualism is bracing as opposition and innovation, never as belief in itself. There is no radiance in our modern writers, just stalwart independence, defiance of the established, and a good deal of mockery . . .
>
> *Faith is nothing but itself, is what remains within the anguish of seeing so many things destroyed in life*—not least the belief in immortality, which has been submerged in American writing since the passing of Puritan theology. Though it pitifully rises again from the mass devastation and grief of war, *it is soon lost again in our insistence on unlimited progress and prosperity as the goals of life.* (my emphases, 257–58)

For Kazin, the real religious life for American writers has gone on in their studies, not in the churches of our land. Though Crews is far from the Dickinsonian model of the lonely writer in her garret, he nonetheless conveys the same sense of privacy about faith which Kazin charts in Melville, Dickinson, Eliot, Frost, and other American writers, while also raging against its annihilation or effacement by unchecked consumerism and progress.

But he has had for example no living American novelist who has engaged with tough questions of faith and man's place in the world. Walker Percy comes to mind, but Crews has never mentioned him as a literary influence and would probably term him too philosophical. Perhaps this is one reason why he turned to Graham Greene. In Greene he found another author with a reckless temperament, another writer removed from his home, someone who had already stared death in the eyes and won. This initial attraction has been ongoing and pervasive for Crews. From Greene he learned what the writer's strong points should be—the strong narrative line and dialogue. Additionally, his prose style is heavily indebted to Greene's sparse style. Through his reading and re-reading of Greene's work he absorbed and has come to stake a claim on a minimalist style which is the most effective medium for conveying his taut stories. He has come to see himself as a storyteller in much the same fashion that Greene saw himself; each author is simply not interested in postmodernism and its self-referential fiction, preferring instead to let his characters and words speak simply and for themselves.

Besides adopting Greene's minimalist style and reportorial eye in his fiction, non-fiction, and autobiographical writing, Crews has repeatedly looked toward Greene as an example of a literary artist who has persevered in the face of constant failure. His determination to pursue a career as a writer (his goal for years when writing has been 500 words a day, a dictum which Greene followed for much of his career) and rise through the bizarre tragedies of his life is epitomized by the nameless whiskey priest of Greene's masterpiece, who pops up repeatedly in Crews's fiction and interviews. Both men are admittedly imperfect but continue carrying out the office to which they believe they have been born. And closely linked to Crews's qualified adoption of Greene's whiskey priest as his authorial persona is his conception of himself as a moral artist.

Finally, what has become a hallmark of Crews's fiction, uncertainty, stems from his own outlook toward his faith, and undergirds his artistic position as a moral writer, committed to challenging his audience on timely ethical issues. Just as the priest in Greene's novel is failed and flawed but still able to challenge his scattered parishioners to examine their own lives, Crews readily admits that while he may not be the most moral person or writer, his purpose in writing—in fact, the purpose in writing generally—is moral. As he has noted recently, "writing is a moral occupation practiced by not necessarily moral men and women" (Bledsoe III). In short, Crews's absorption in Greene's life and work has given him the courage to plumb the depths of his own somewhat shaky faith—to doubt his doubt, as it were—through his fictional characters. And like Greene, who steadfastly maintained that all of his works stem from a faith-based concern for the oppressed peoples of the world, Crews remains committed to a role as satiric purveyor of an ultimately religious worldview increasingly carried out as a social commentator concerned with the dehumanizing effects of our consumer culture on American society. This rampant greed was one reason Greene abhorred the United States; in discussing his revulsion toward America at the end of his life, he said, "The terrifying weight of this consumer society oppresses me" (Allain 94). Perhaps Harry Crews, in his attempts to throw off the albatross of our moneyed culture from our necks, is once again echoing his literary mentor. But his echo is achieved with his own distinctive flair, through his desire to "cut things and leave an imprint, a design" (Lytal and Russell 546).

SILENCES, CRITICISMS, AND LAMENTS

The Political Implications of Harry Crews's Work

Gary L. Long

The most awful thing . . . I can imagine is a kind of moral vacuum . . . to be cut loose from the universe . . . [with] no sense that it is all working somehow. . . . I suspect that . . . [is] what . . . my work comes out of. . . . I am aware of the black kind of vacuum . . . [of] no belief. . . . If I could anchor myself irrevocably in belief and order, and put God in His Heaven . . . I would do that irrevocably. Some days I can, and some days I can't. It is . . . not knowing what and where I am . . . that I struggle with.

—Harry Crews (Foata 217)

Harry Crews is a man of traditional society. Son of a sharecropper, Crews climbed from humble beginnings to become writer-in-residence at University of Florida, Gainesville.[1] Crews left the red clay of South Georgia to become a writer, but he did not escape it. His works are filled with the culture and the experiences of rural poverty. In his writing, he marshals both his rural background and his upward climb to produce stories about destructive aspirations. For Crews, a culture of individual achievement can be hostile to life.

In this paper, I focus on political implications in Crews's work. Using his novels, essays, journalistic pieces, and interviews, I attempt to distill indications of his ideological leanings. Crews asserts that his writing does not contain messages. Taking cues from silences, paradoxes, and contradictions in his work, I argue otherwise.

For example, the individual seems to be the only legitimate agent of action in Crews's novels; yet, individual actions are usually ineffective, and collective action is anathema. A critic of American society, Crews is angry about pain in contemporary life. Pain and thwarted ambitions foster meanness and an inclination to reckless violence in his characters. But, Crews is ambivalent, unwilling to forego pain completely; pain is central to the realist perspective from which he writes.

Crews's fiction suggests a tragic view of life, his characters' efforts to alter their lives are futile. Crews's critiques of modernity seem to be founded on conservative assumptions. Instead of prescriptions for change, he instructs by implication, counseling accommodation. Anger is dissipated in despair. Some aspects of his work—e.g., fatalism and an admiration for traditional morality—may be connected to his southern roots.

In what follows, I develop these assertions about Crews and his work. Subsequently, I endeavor to document them with examples from his writing.

AMBIVALENCE

Crews seems to be a man of ambivalence, a study in paradox. In his own words, he is an angry moralist; yet, he disavows ideology. Crews's writings contain savage judgments of American life, but he denies writing theses, disclaims polemics: "If you want social reform, . . . stand for public office . . . if you want to preach, . . . take a pulpit . . . if you want to send messages, use Western Union" (Foata 216).

An example of the American parable of success, Crews's escape from rural poverty testifies to his personal determination and to his belief in culturally prescribed virtues. In his quest to become a writer, Crews taught English during the day to support his family, and wrote instead of sleeping at night. Over several years of failed manuscripts, he trained himself in his craft. Along the way, he wrote inspirational stories about individual achievement for Nelson Boswell, a Florida radio personality in the mold of Paul Harvey.

Upward mobility is a continuing theme in Crews's work. His characters believe in success and persevere in the face of adversity (e.g., *Naked in Garden Hills*, *The Gypsy's Curse*, *Body*, *The Knockout Artist*, *This Thing Don't Lead to Heaven*). However, Crews writes not about success, but of false hopes and failure. He seems to debunk bootstrap individualism as a harmful illusion, and implies the existence of obstacles that cannot be surmounted by effort and will. By experience a mobile man, Crews exposes the emptiness of America's obsession with individualized destiny. Nevertheless, he celebrates the determination of characters engaged in hopeless attempts to take control of their lives.

In fiction, Crews challenges the efficacy of individual action; goals elude his characters. He also warns against collective action. Challenge and warning suggest that Crews is not sanguine about human agency. For his characters, the possibilities seem to be inaction or dramatic gestures of protest with unfortunate consequences. On the other hand, collective action—spontaneous, concerted, typically irrational—is dangerous. In Crews's books, people in the aggregate are out of control. Freed by anonymity from responsibility for their deeds, people become crazed mobs or crowds run amok (*The Gospel Singer, Karate Is a Thing of the Spirit, A Feast of Snakes*).

Crews questions American beliefs about success, but does not relinquish belief. He populates his books with believers. Some of his characters seek belief for its own sake; some pursue the promises of worldly faiths. He seems to be fascinated with belief: "I take all my books to be about the nature of faith. How does a man come to believe what he believes? How do you . . . hold on to . . . [belief], God, wife, job whatever" (Burt 119).

Apparently not a religious man, Crews does not build magic, redemption, or inevitable justice into his plots. There is no unseen designer behind the march of events in his novels. In the face of trouble, his fictional people are thrown back on their own resources. Crews describes himself as different from Flannery O'Connor, yet wishes he could believe: "Sometimes I think I am a believer with nothing to believe. . . . On any given day I am a believer or not . . . but always there is a thing in me that desperately would like to be" (Foata 209).[2] Exposing his characters' beliefs as illusions, Crews seems to applaud their audacity and to deplore their fates.

In Crews's writings, modern society is inhospitable to human beings. Liberated from absolutes, cut loose from obligations to others, people are free to join communities of limited commitment made possible by urban living—communities of interest, or specialized purpose, or of common predicament (e.g., a karate commune, professional bodybuilders, a senior home, Fireman's Gym). These secular enclaves offer no equivalents for the moral certainties of the past. Their absolutes are narrowly circumscribed; standards are group specific. Surrogates for traditional communities, they are unable to warrant enduring meanings.

Crews seems to admire the functions of traditional morality. In books and journalistic pieces, he poses success against survival—belief in individual achievement, and the resulting anomie, against the morality, duty, and solidarity of communities in the rural South. Measuring modern society by the organizing principles of the agrarian past, the present against a way of life which produced hardship for his own people, Crews opts for the latter. A manipulator of symbols who is alienated from the immediacy of experience within traditional society,[3] he laments the displacement of regional culture by a homogeneous national culture of abstract symbols which his vocation presupposes.

IMPOSSIBLE QUESTS: TRAGEDY AND HUBRIS

Within Crews's novels are recurring patterns. "[M]adness and absurdity are everywhere . . ." (Crowder 105). People commit themselves to impossible tasks. Hubris begets tragedy. Usually from rural origins, Crews's central characters are misfits in a contemporary landscape. Whether "freaks" (midgets, handicapped, grossly overweight) or "normals," they are almost always "grits" speaking the dialect of his people, and they believe in the religion of individual success.

Accepting diligence and discipline as redemptive, Crews's characters attempt to remake themselves. Through effort and will, they expect to overcome deformities of body, escape disadvantages of low birth, or to surmount cultural irrationality. Believers in grand nouns (normality, self-determination, love, morality, justice), in the connection between hard work and rewards, and in emblems of success marketed by Madison Avenue, Crews's characters are deluded. In a culture of empty symbols, they seek substantive outcomes. Misunderstanding life in twentieth century America, they are destined to fail.

Typically the characters in Crews's novels are obsessed with controlling their lives. Single-mindedly they pursue impossible goals. In *Naked in Garden Hills*, a fat man (Mayhugh Aaron, Jr.) consumes Metrecal by the case and "Eat-&-Grow-Slim Wafers" by the handfuls, gaining weight while eating to grow thin. Mistaking the consequence of his wealth for its cause, Fat Man tries to keep his privileged position in Garden Hills by consuming prodigiously. In the same book, a failed black jockey who will not ride because he fears pain maintains his self-conception as a competitor by dressing in silks and riding the backs of chairs while watching televised horse races.

In *Car*, the son of a wrecking yard owner has an unnatural attraction to cars. In order to escape domination by the automobile, Herman Mack attempts to destroy the fetish by consuming a Ford in half-ounce chunks on stage in a Jacksonville, Florida, hotel. His eatings and passings before audiences will be broadcast worldwide on *Wide, Wide World of Sports.*

An enthusiast of physical training, the central character of *All We Need of Hell* tries to impose order on his disorderly life through muscular control. Duffy Deeter disciplines his body on a Universal machine and refines his technique on a lightweight racing bike, in long-distance running, on the handball court, at karate, and during sex. A stopwatch is his indisputable standard for perfection.

Old people in a nursing home seek to avoid physical degeneration and death by subjecting themselves to painful massages in *This Thing Don't Lead to Heaven.* The midget masseur, Jefferson Davis Munroe, is pursued by a spinsterish mail-sorter who believes him to be the six-foot-plus man of her dreams. Wanting to be normal, Munroe, seeks a magic to make himself grow tall.

Eugene Talmadge Biggs, a boxer with a glass jaw, punishes himself for failure in *The Knockout Artist.* He makes a living and maintains a string of wins in miniature rings at sadomasochistic theme parties in decadent New Orleans, by knocking himself out with a punch to his chin. Eugene resists acknowledging that he is just another pornographic exhibit in a city of perverted displays. In letters to his dirt-farm parents in Georgia, he encloses money and writes of pugilistic successes.

In the same book, Charity, a demented daughter of a wealthy oil man—who will subsidize her only if she remains in graduate school—vainly attempts to maintain her illusions by manipulating others. Dismissed from a doctoral program in psychology because of her own illness, she conducts research for a dissertation and the definitive book on madness by tape-recording case histories while engaged in sex with her subjects. Risking their rage, Charity punctures the defenses of both males and females in order to bring them to realizations about their abject lives.

Crews's characters generally fail to achieve their goals. Control eludes them. Quests end in ambiguity or defeat. Outcomes are inconclusive or tragic.

In *The Hawk Is Dying,* a successful small businessman turns to the past to escape the emptiness of his urban existence. Abandoning his auto upholstery shop and rejecting the platitudes of his family, George Gattling immerses himself in the ancient lore of the austringer and straps a raptor to his arm. Instead of people, he will dominate a hawk. Despite interference from relatives who consider him insane, Gattling prevents the bird from starving itself, successfully "mans" the animal, and trains it to attack a lure. The novel ends with the hawk driving its talons into a rabbit on the first field trial. Unresolved is whether the hawk returns to George's gloved hand.

Eating and passing half-ounce pieces of a Ford cause Herman Mack unimaginable pain in *Car*. Unable to destroy the thing he loves, he leaves the stage of Homer Edge's hotel ballroom in defeat and returns to the heap of junk cars that defined his childhood.

In *The Gypsy's Curse*, Marvin Molar, a deaf midget with flippers for legs—adept at walking inverted, reading lips, and talking with his hands—longs to be "normal," to possess a female with a "fantastic lap." Marvin realizes his dream with the beautiful, neurotic Hester. A malign influence in Fireman's Gym, Hester wrecks the all-male refuge that shelters four "losers"—Marvin, an aging stunt-man crippled by feats of strength, and two punch-drunk ex-fighters—by rekindling the men's hopes for competitive success. Hester adds excitement to her life and makes Marvin prove his love by betraying him. On the way to prison after killing Hester and her lover with an axe, Marvin thinks of himself as a real man, a "swinging-dick" male.

At best, control in the lives of Crews's characters is limited. Sometimes they destroy themselves, controlling only the moments that seal their fates.[4] In *Body*, Dorothy tries to overcome her lower-class origins, and to take charge of her life, as a world-class female bodybuilder. She reshapes her physique, changes her identity, and vies for the title of Ms. Cosmos.

Dorothy's independence as "Shereel" is temporary—experienced during her few minutes competing on stage and in the final preparations preceding them. Win or lose, her past as Dorothy Turnipseed from Waycross, Georgia, awaits her in the wings in the person of Nailhead, her brutal, psychotic boyfriend. After losing the competition to the black, male-defined body of marvelous Marvella, Dorothy commits suicide, a final assertion of autonomy.

Even when Crews's characters succeed, they fail. Goals sour or turn out to be hollow. Fat Man's dreams of food come true in *Naked*. Suspended from the ceiling in a golden cage in a tourist trap in Garden Hills, he must eat to maintain his status as the star attraction in Dolly's sideshow of freaks. Unable to keep his position at the top of Garden Hills by consuming, Fat Man falls into poverty, humiliation, and mandatory gluttony. Jester's success is also his failure. Dressed in the silks of a jockey, he rides his adoring, faithful, ex-whore Lucy on stage for the entertainment of strangers. Prisoners of their delusions, both men are sad spectacles.

In *Knockout*, Mr. Blasingame, a wealthy, manipulative New Orleans businessman, destroys people with opportunities. Washed-up fighters Eugene and Pete dream of owning and managing a boxer. Blasingame helps them to realize their dream and then chains them to it. Acquainting them with the facts of exploitation, Blasingame confronts Eugene and Pete with their own weaknesses and ruins their friendship. Managing an eager young boxer means using him. Pete is amenable; Eugene can exploit himself but not others. Instead, he escapes opportunity and the evil city into a life of uncertainty, on the road with no destination.

Frequently, Crews's fictional characters are engaged in self-destructive quests.[5] In *The Gospel Singer*, an amoral god-singer exploits religion to satisfy an insatiable desire for sexual variety. His rapacious appetite turns his childhood sweetheart, MaryBell, into a scheming whore, and his childhood friend, Willalee Bookatee Hull, into her murderer. Trying to save his friend, the Gospel Singer confesses his sins and his inability to heal at a tent revival. Unwanted revelations to worshipful believers turn backwoods fundamentalists into an angry mob. They hang both the Gospel Singer and Willalee from the same tree.

The central character in *A Feast of Snakes*, Joe Lon Mackey, recent high school graduate, a football star who failed to qualify for a college scholarship because he never learned to read, sells moonshine whiskey to blacks, supervises the placement of chemical toilets at a tourist campground, abuses his child-faded wife, and yearns for the glory of his playing days. Pampered in the past by females, his coach, and fans because of his prowess on the gridiron, Joe Lon regains public attention and takes "control" of his life with a shotgun. He kills his former girlfriend, a deputy sheriff, a snake hunter, and a snake-handling preacher during the annual rattlesnake roundup. When his gun is empty, a crazed mob of tourists throws him into a pit of rattlers.

In Crews's fiction, traditional morality is a disadvantage in an amoral marketplace. Physical impairments do prevent normal lives. Adaptations that protect handicapped characters by limiting expectations are undermined by dreams of competitive success. Words are empty and people are not what they seem. Medieval pastimes offer no escape from market exploitation. Standards for measuring achievements at the fringes of society have only limited applications to life. People are prisoners of the automobile. Self-discipline does not guarantee transcendence. And, there are no enduring meanings in pain.

Crews's characters are defeated. Hopes prove to be irrational; beliefs are false. Characters cannot overcome their rural origins, limitations of body and birth, or the insanities of modern culture. Ultimately, they do not control their own fates. Crews seems to imply human efficacy is an illusion, a dangerous hubris.

Theodicy of Suffering

In interviews, Harry Crews talks about pain—damaged knees, rejected manuscripts, hangovers, and broken relationships. For him, pain is expected and familiar, to be endured: ". . . if you can't play with pain, you can't play" (Nuwer 46). In *A Childhood: The Biography of a Place*, Crews's autobiographical account of hardships on a Georgia tenant farm, pain is a fact of life.[6] The quests of his fictional characters typically entail pain.[7] Crews seems to suggest that pain is a constant in life. What makes it bearable is belief. What distinguishes traditional from modern society is the kind of pain to be tolerated, and the beliefs which legitimate it.

Rooted in absolutes of God, kinship, community, and soil, agrarian life was harsh and demanding—incessant work but uncertain subsistence. People's fates were determined by birth, accidents, and disease. Survival depended upon luck, markets, insects, and weather.[8] In the past, *necessary* pain was part of a divine plan. Religion made stoic acceptance into a measure of character.[9] Labor was dignified by a morality of workmanship (e.g., plowing straight rows in *A Childhood*). Promising justice in a final accounting of human affairs, religion offered moral clarity and made action consequential. Acts were binary, right or wrong. People could control their spiritual fates through work, self-restraint, and by submission to the Word. Religion shielded them from the terrors of death.

By contrast, Crews suggests that the modern theology of individual achievement makes *voluntary* pain a virtue. Belief in self-determination, and success as a universal goal, entails pain as both means and ends. Pain is a condition for pursuing illusory ends (e.g., everlasting life in *Heaven*, domination of the machine in *Car*). Pain also measures goal attainment.

Celebrating *unnecessary* pain as character-building, contemporary society encourages sadomasochism. Competition pits people against each other and sets them against themselves. Absent is a transcendent justification for suffering anchored within stable communities that protect people from overweening ambitions. Disconnected from the past (except in media fantasies),[10] from kin, and from shared meanings, people are rootless wanderers seeking and giving pain.[11]

Lamenting the passing of traditional society—an order sustained by religion—Crews seems to search for substitutes.[12] Through non-religious characters, he examines justifications for suffering within circumscribed sub-worlds at the peripheries of modern America. Here, there are promises of meaning and control, moralities of self-discipline, standards for achievement, and beliefs justifying *avoidable* pain—self-inflicted or voluntarily accepted from others. Within the bounded, rule-governed activities of sports (football, boxing, karate, handball, bodybuilding, training a hawk) are pockets of certitude and mensurable outcomes. Vestiges of traditional community exist within self-contained collections of "unusual" people—in Fireman's Gym (*Gypsy*), the karate commune (*Karate Is a Thing of the Spirit*), and a retirement home (*Heaven*), among side-show "freaks" (*Gospel*), cockfighters ("Cockfighting: An Unfashionable View"), and carnival people ("Carny").

But Crews's sub-universes of self-justifying meaning and pain-centered absolutes can be sustained only outside the mainstream, on the margins within carefully restricted forms of existence, or in an obsolete past. Collectivities organized around individual sports (e.g., boxing, bodybuilding) tend to be pseudo-communities, fragile assemblages of uneasily interdependent, competitive individuals. Sub-communities united by disciplines of the body (Fireman's Gym, the karate commune) are vulnerable to disruption by competition and cultural illusions.

In the social mainstream, standards are flexible, meanings uncertain. Pain is "purified," dissociated from specific purposes. Isolated people live "naked" in the moment, without ties or obligations.[13]

Crews's characters—typically marginal people imbued with contemporary aspirations—seek a *modus vivendi* with society at its edges. Their failures to reconcile traditional and modern seem to echo his own. Apparently, rapprochement is impossible, another chimera.

AN ABSENCE OF ORGANIZATIONS AND STRUCTURED INEQUALITY

Crews writes about underdogs. Typically from backgrounds dominated by morality and duty—wherein appearances and essences coincide, and words are binding—his characters usually lack the advantages of money or connections. With a few exceptions (Charity in *Knockout* and Berenice Sweet in *Feast* have wealthy fathers), their assets are of the flesh—e.g., a golden voice (Gospel Singer in *Gospel*); beauty (Dolly in *Naked*); athletic prowess (Joe Lon in *Feast*); a glass jaw (K.O. in *Knockout*); and deformities of size, limb, or stature (Fat Man, Jester, and Jefferson Davis Munroe in *Naked* and *Heaven*, Foot's enlarged foot in *Gospel*, Marvin Molar's flippers for legs in *Gypsy*). " . . . [D]oing the best they can with what . . . [they've] got" (Burt 118), Crews's characters generally attempt to parlay their physical singularities into financial security, autonomy, or other dividends. They tend to be blind to forces that shape their goals and chances for realizing them.

In Crews's novels, ironies and delusions abound; but connections between culture and economy, and between structured inequality and individual life-chances, are not made. Power, economic forces that change mores, and vested interests in illusions are missing. Crews's critiques of America tend to be ahistorical and indifferent to persistent features of society.

Large organizations appear in Crews's novels, but their internal workings are missing. Details about corporate entities or government bureaucracies are confined to his essays. For example, in "Going Down in Valdeez," modernity in the guise of big oil invades a fishing village on the coast of Alaska. Building the trans-Alaskan pipe line to exploit North Slope deposits, a consortium of oil companies (Alyeska) is despoiling the land and destroying the traditional subsistence community of Valdez.

In "Poaching Gators for Fun and Profit," Crews explains the alligator's decline in the Okefenokee as the work of the federal government. Subsistence hunting did not jeopardize the animal's existence; the Corps of Engineers drained the swamps for big farmers and cattle ranchers. In "L. L. Bean Has Your Number, America!," Crews looks behind the facade of the famous Maine country store to describe computerized, mail-order marketing of high-quality outdoor gear and frontier survival myths to suburban "woodsmen."[14]

Large organizations may transform the landscape and people's lives, but how they do so is not made clear in Crews's fiction. For example, in *Car*, America is in thrall to the automobile; American culture is permeated by auto-culture. The countryside is overlaid with concrete freeways crowded with traffic, and littered with junk cars.

Life is indelibly marked by the automobile. The ultimate consumer fetish, people worship it. How it became dominant is a mystery; the idol has no history. Connections between auto manufacturers, oil companies, the poverty of public transportation, federal highway subsidies, and real estate interests are unmade. Agents that transformed Americans into transients on wheels are unmentioned.

In some of Crews's books, there are indications of industrial blight. Water-filled, scummy tailings of a played-out phosphate mine—the creation of a god-like absentee industrialist who ravages the Florida landscape for profit—are central to the plot of *Naked*. An engineer of fate, Jack O'Boylan is a faceless exploiter of resources and people. Michelangelo's *Creation* is his corporate logo; his business is destruction. In the novel, the inner workings of O'Boylan's organization are inscrutable.

In other novels, Crews makes passing references to environs befouled by people and commerce. In *Car* and *Scar Lover*, there are stinking rivers contaminated with chemicals and human waste, legacies of modernity. Unmentioned are the politics of pollution, or vested interests profiting from poisoning water and air. Instead, Crews seems to imply that modern people are tainted. Urban, remote from the land, they necessarily destroy what they do not understand. Fault is nonspecific because it is universal.

Stratification and power also are obscured in Crews's fiction. Class hierarchies are virtually unnoticed. The usually poor, displaced Southerners on whom Crews concentrates have folkways and mannerisms in common, but not common interests. Inequality is personal and idiosyncratic. Discreet individuals of wealth and power—Doctor Sweet in *Feast*, Mr. Blasingame in *Knockout*, Jack O'Boylan in *Naked*, and Homer Edge in *Car*—are prominent. Compared to those below them, their lives are merely different and easier.

When they make appearances in Crews's writing, the wealthy and powerful are not fully-drawn. (Iron-willed Dolly who acquires position at the expense of Fat Man in *Naked* is an exception.) The exercise of power is seldom depicted in detail. Instead, power is mystified; machineries of exploitation are hidden. Illustrated are the consequences for the powerless.

An example is Mr. Blasingame in *Knockout*. Rich, head of a large organization in New Orleans, Blasingame controls the lives and fates of other characters from behind the scenes. Other than wealth, the source of his power is a puzzle. Crews hints at unusual proclivities, Blasingame's perversions as Oyster Boy, but does not detail the mechanisms by which he dominates people. Heavily made-up because of a skin disease, the powerful Mr. Blasingame's face is, literally, masked.

When it happens in Crews's novels, rational action is individual action; he seems not to trust people in groups. Usually, characters resolve crises individually by dramatically defying fate, through violent protest, or by withdrawing from the field. (Herman and Margo the whore retire to the bottom of the Autotown junk heap in *Car*; K.O. leaves immoral New Orleans for a life on the road in *Knockout*; Beeder recoils into "insanity" and television in *Feast*; Duffy in *Hell* and John Kaimon in *Karate* escape into love; others escape into death.) In Crews's novels, human action is limited. Individual acts tend to be expressive and ineffectual. Usually, outcomes are violent, self-destructive, and tragic.

In a society of large organizations, class divisions, and enduring elites, Crews's characters strive and fail as individuals. Debunking bootstrap individualism, his books seem to discount success as merely a dream. On the other hand, Crews offers no alternatives to individuals pursuing illusive goals. Collective action is impulsive and vicious. Collectivities legitimately exist only as extended families or as romanticized traditional communities of the past. In the present, there are only marginal communities, pseudo-communities, and masses—anonymous individuals in crowds.[15]

Crews's fiction seems to entail both fatalism and nihilism. Characters' dreams are foolish; belief in transcendence is an illusion. Action is presumptuous. Contemporary culture is malign; retreat into the past is impossible. There is no escape at the margins of society. What remains are individual accommodations to the inevitable —submission to life as it is—or dramatic, futile acts of protest. Crews's critiques of modernity create an impasse. They resonate resignation and an angry, reckless despair.

REALITY AND TRUTH: BODY, PAIN, DUTY, AND BLOOD

Crews's frequent use of the phrase "wish in one hand and shit in the other—see which one fills up first" suggests he distrusts abstractions. For him, meaning seems to be body-centered, grounded in the tactile and the tangible.[16] The body and the social obligations in which people are enmeshed are anchoring points for truth. Blood, blood-kin, blood sports, self-discipline, pain, and mastery of a body of knowledge rooted in experience are baselines for measuring human experience.[17] Control is imperative. With blood, pain, and mastery, Crews invokes a kind of "naked" realism for comprehending life.[18]

Several of Crews's characters are enthusiasts of the body. Flagellants of different kinds living in ascetic worlds, they seek perfection by mortifying their flesh, by embracing pain.[19] Crews is an enthusiast. He admits to weight-lifting and to jogging despite the pain of knees damaged in motorcycle accidents.

When Crews comments on his writing and his life, discipline and control are recurring themes. Asked in interviews about writing habits, he avows self-repression. Crews trained himself to write by painstakingly disassembling a Graham Greene novel seeking to discover how to accomplish literary effects (Watson 64). Talk about his work is full of failed manuscripts, and persistence.[20] Crews describes writing as a spartan activity. For several hours each day, he sits at the typewriter. Permitting himself no distractions, he must do the time whether or not he produces. His goal is two pages; the alternative is boredom.

In Crews's own words, the activity of writing affords him a measure of order in a disorderly life. Characters follow his designs: "I can control that . . . [manuscript] by the typewriter. . . . Them suckers . . . [characters] go where I tell them. . . . Sometimes they're rebellious, but I got a rein on them. . . . Controlling my own life, so I could be called a civilized human being—I've often been unable to accomplish that" (Green 80).

Discipline is apparent in the factual details of Crews's work. Some of the activities about which he writes are grounded in first-hand experience. Crews kept and trained hawks ("The Hawk Is Flying"), took karate lessons, lived with and trained a female bodybuilder, and spent time in a gymnasium as a youth.

In some of his journalistic pieces ("Reminiscences of a Blind Muleman," "Cock-fighting," "Poaching"), Crews celebrates the knowledge of people who train cocks, poach gators, and trade mules. As he describes them, these are people accomplished in lore, informed by practice, and constrained by experience; their knowledge is empirically grounded.

In "Muleman," Crews describes a retired, blind mule trader. Mr. Shingler knows how to judge an animal's age by its teeth or walk, how to alter its age by re-cupping and staining teeth worn from years of grinding feed, and how to recognize this deceit. Raised on tenant farms, Crews knows something about mules. He is not a modern man with only secondhand knowledge, but he is inferior to the real thing. Compared to the old muleman with a lifetime of experience, Crews thinks of himself as a "cheap imitation."

Crews parodies modern people's lack of experiential knowledge, their ignorance of nature and of danger. Modern woodsmen "camp out" in self-propelled trailers with televisions and indoor "shitters" in "L. L. Bean." Japanese tourists in the Shenandoah Valley National Park are without the good sense to fear a trapped bear in "The Wonderful World of Winnebagos." Unknowing about the ways of animals, tourists in the Okefenokee Swamp stumble into confrontations with alligators in "Poaching."

A man who makes a living with words, Crews seems to argue that words are hollow unless grounded in needs of the body or anchored in duty. Within his books, words like "love" usually are meaningless. Central figures are misled by abstractions, disoriented by a language of empty promises.[21]

In "The Wisdom of the Groin" Crews writes: "Since we came out of the caves . . . the . . . needs of the groin have been tempered . . . by . . . abstract nouns . . . : responsibility, concern, compassion, mercy and the really big one . . . love. . . . [B]elief in only the language of the head and heart . . . leads to genuine evil. . . .

[M]ajor religions of the world have taught that the head and the heart must rule whatever is below. . . . I . . . have always despaired of that" (158).

The abstractions of contemporary life may be misleading, but for Crews, absolutes of the flesh seem to function as touchstones for what is real. Violence is one such absolute. (Physical violence is a form of human communication that is difficult to misunderstand. Several of Crews's characters—Joe Lon, Duffy Deeter, Marvin Molar resort to the palpable language of violence.) Pain and blood are others. Nothing seems to be as fundamental and as real as blood. In his words:

> Are you plagued with a sourceless anxiety? Do you worry about . . . the existence of God and whether . . . there *is* order in the universe? . . . If the answer . . . is yes, *then go out and get your ass kicked* . . . the ultimate refreshment. You will be purified and holy. . . . Nothing gets you back in touch with yourself like a little of your own blood. A broken nose or . . . rib centers a man . . . mentally like nothing else can. . . . Nose-to-nose combat is better than a psychiatrist, . . . never as humiliating and . . . [less] expensive ("The Violence That Finds Us" 186).[22]

In his work, Crews celebrates immediate experience and elemental facts of life. Human beings are carnivores; they need blood rituals; they are fascinated by blood sports. To be human, they require stabilizing obligations to blood kin. Duty, discipline, violence, pain, and death are essential aspects of human existence. For Crews, authenticity requires acknowledging the skull behind the smile, and the flies waiting for our eyes.

A Mythic Resolution

A man who escaped from the bottom of an agrarian order wherein religion and tradition justified inequality, Harry Crews uses traditional society to measure modernity. A moralist angry about a culture of unnecessary pain (". . . to write out of my kind of outrage, you've got to be a . . . hard-core moralist" [Oney 34]), he also glorifies pain. Hostile to inflexible conceptions of normality, nevertheless he implies that absolute standards—preferably rooted in experience—are necessary for measuring character and accomplishments.[23] Creator of characters who seek to take control of their lives, he argues that people need limits. Southerner, American, cultural critic writing from an individualistic perspective, Crews finds wisdom in the past.

In the past, traditional communities imposed order on human life. Absolutes clarified morality. The threat of sanctioned violence ensured connections between words and deeds. Obligations to kin and community stabilized identities.[24] Duty set out guidelines for conduct. Embedded within groups, tied to place, constrained by duty, people behaved predictably.[25] Incorporating ritual, an understanding of blood, a realistic appraisal of human nature, and familiarity with the land, traditional communities acknowledged survival imperatives and restrained people's aspirations.

Crews's writings suggest that the enforced realism of the past has been lost in modern society. Out of touch with knowledge on which life depends, contemporary culture denies limits and ignores human needs. Falsifying experience by packaging history as frontier fantasies, fostering myths of unlimited opportunities and personal success—while organizing human existence as unnecessary pain—contemporary culture promotes pernicious illusions. Wishes and hyperbole have displaced reliable standards for measuring accomplishments. With no distinctions among efforts and no ways of judging outcomes, people become foolish. Everyone is a hero.

By persuading people to believe they are solely responsible for their fates, modern society destroys community. Freed from constraints, rootless, anonymous individuals are not accountable for their actions. Anonymous people in crowds "revert to the . . . grinders." They are dangerous and scary.[26]

In Crews's writings, there seems to be no escape from the madness of modern life except into love or death. He does not prescribe reforms.[27] In the small towns of his novels—Enigma, Garden Hills, Mystic—and in essays about Valdez, dog fights, the Appalachian Trail, and the Everglades, change seems to be a problem. Change has turned Southerners into wandering tourists in Winnebagos, vacationers in the woods, believers in Disney versions of history, solipsistic achievers, and Americans lacking geographically distinct dialects.

Angry at the inhumanity of modernity, Crews ignores inequalities and the powerful. He attacks cultural illusions. Suggesting that belief can destroy, he implies that everyone is at risk. How an ideology of individualistic success might serve some people's interests is not addressed. Crews's books depict suffering at the bottom of society. "Topdogs"—those who encourage illusions and who benefit from pain—are unseen.

Crews's critiques of modernity are romantic, and *idealistic*. Invoking a past, better way of life, he emphasizes beliefs. In his work, solutions to contemporary madness seem atomistic.[28] The organization of life is given. Poverty, inequality, cultural irrationalities, and physical deformities limit human options. Apparently, the proper response is an *individual response*—strip away illusions and somehow live with what is. People need to examine their hearts, to disbelieve, to adapt.[29] The alternatives seem to be acts of madness, individual self-destruction, or collective hysteria. The message—ultimately a conservative plea for limits—is also one of estrangement, resignation, and defeat.

Thus, to the fatalism associated with traditional, southern society, Crews weds a pessimistic individualism. An article of faith in the culture he critiques, individualism encourages private acts instead of social actions. Both Crews and his characters seem to be prisoners of cultural assumptions.[30]

Built into Crews's work is a prescription for inaction and a recipe for despair. His anger translates into biting irony, parody, black comedy, a bleak hopelessness, and a wail of pain. Nevertheless, Crews does suggest a solution to modernity—an imaginary one existing in a mythical past as another cultural ideal. Against the pernicious character of modern society, he poses an image more authentic and humane. As he recalls it, life in the agrarian South, although brutal, was closer to nature and to human nature. Crews counters contemporary illusions with historical fantasy. Against the present he marshals the organic wholeness of community in the old South, and the benefits humans derive from moral absolutes.[31]

"EVERTHING IS EATING EVERTHING ELSE"

The Naturalistic Impulse in Harry Crews's
A Feast of Snakes

Tim Edwards

In a 1978 article, Allen Shepherd warned readers about Crews's disturbing brand of Southern gothic: "Reading Crews is not something one wants to do too much of at a single sitting: the intensity of his fiction is unsettling" (61). Although Shepherd's study examines several of Crews's novels, he concludes with a reading of *A Feast of Snakes*, a "very nearly thesis-bound" text[1] that attacks the "American ethic [of] setting men, women, children, dogs, and snakes against each other" in brutal competition (60). In thus labeling the text, Shepherd pointed the direction for future readings of *A Feast of Snakes*, readings that focus almost inevitably on the violence and grotesqueries of Crews's "powerful and idiosyncratic" vision of the contemporary South (Shepherd 61).

A Feast of Snakes tells the story of Joe Lon Mackey, the illiterate former football star for the Mystic, Georgia, High School Rattlers and his psychological deterioration over a four day period leading up to Mystic's annual November Rattlesnake Roundup. Mackey's illiteracy destroyed his hopes of playing football for Bear Bryant, and, as the narrative opens,

Joe Lon faces a stunningly unheroic existence as a liquor store proprietor, occasional wife-beater, and manager of the chemical toilet maintenance at the snake rodeo. In an apocalyptic conclusion echoing Nathanael West's *The Day of the Locust*, the novel explodes in violence as Mackey unleashes his frustrations in a murderous rampage at the rattlesnake rodeo, killing four people before being hurled by the vengeful crowd into the collection pit full of rattlers. This final sequence in the narrative, shocking as it is, unfolds with an ominous inevitability: Joe Lon himself seems to arrive at a kind of dark epiphany: "All morning he had felt as though he was going to do it today. But he had not known what *it* was" (176). As Joe Lon methodically slaughters his victims, "[he] felt better than he had ever felt in his life. Christ, it was good to be in control again" (176). Indeed, until this point in the narrative, Joe Lon clearly has not been in control of his destiny—nor have many of the other inhabitants of Mystic we encounter in the novel: as Allen Shepherd observes, the characters in Crews's novels enjoy "slim hopes of escape from life's entrapment" (53), and in *A Feast of Snakes* in particular Crews's universe is shaped by a "fatal determination" (61). And it is this sense of entrapment that pushes Crews's fiction beyond the narrower regionalist parameters of Southern gothic and locates his work in a larger tradition of American fiction. It is impossible to deny the inherent Southernness of his work, but to best appreciate Harry Crews's achievement, we need to see his fiction as essentially emerging from the naturalist stream of American literature.[2] Indeed, doing so allows us to address more fully issues that have concerned critics since the novel's publication—issues regarding how we should see the character of Joe Lon Mackey—(is he a victim or a monster?)—and how we should read Crews's depiction of women characters. These matters become clearer when we recognize that, in *A Feast of Snakes*, Crews taps into the rich vein of naturalism that has shaped social criticism in American fiction since the 1890s.

Donald Pizer describes literary naturalism as "one of the most persistent and vital strains in American fiction," asserting moreover that "[few] of our major twentieth-century novelists have escaped its 'taint'" (*Theory and Practice* 13). Harry Crews may not yet be considered a major novelist—indeed, he may never be, but certainly the tradition of American literary naturalism endures in his work. As we examine the controlling themes and tropes at work in *A Feast of Snakes*—the pervasive animal imagery, the Darwinian sense of competition and struggle, the bewildering hopelessness of the individual consciousness confronting inexorable outside forces—we see the text clearly emerging as a naturalistic statement, though the novel certainly bears the stamp of Crews's own uniquely disturbing *Weltanschauung*.

In *Twentieth-Century American Literary Naturalism: An Interpretation*, Pizer describes naturalism as an amorphous and flexible narrative technique—more a sort of tradition, he contends, than a disciplined school of fiction. It is this very malleability, Pizer believes, that has allowed the naturalistic impulse in American fiction to endure well into the twentieth century, as American novelists have redefined the naturalistic tradition, contouring and reshaping the tradition to fit the changing literary terrains of each new decade. Despite the Protean nature of literary naturalism itself, Pizer insists that we can agree upon "a variable and changing . . . set of assumptions about man and fiction which can be called the naturalist tradition" (xi). Certain basic tenets of literary naturalism remain fairly constant: "the tragic incompleteness of life" (8); "the demonstration that man is more circumscribed than ordinarily assumed" (xi); the confluence of "the more sensationalistic aspects of experience with heavily ideological (often allegorical) themes" (xi).

And we can identify even more specific themes and devices as definitively naturalistic. Charles Child Walcutt's *American Literary Naturalism, A Divided Stream* establishes the general criteria of the tradition: "*determinism, survival, violence,* and *taboo*" (20). As Walcutt points out, an essentially Darwinian world view lies at the core of naturalistic fiction, a literature that examines " '[the] lower nature of man' " (20). Determinism, Walcutt asserts, "carries the idea that natural law and socioeconomic influences are more powerful than human will" (20). Moreover, such a perspective also suggests the notion of biological competition in that "[animal] survival"—and man is an animal in the naturalist tradition—"is a matter of violence" (Walcutt 20). The intrusion of taboo subject matter into the naturalistic novel has encouraged naturalism's dismissal as "sordid and sensational" (Pizer, *Theory and Practice* 13). But as Walcutt observes, these taboo subjects—"sex, disease, bodily functions, obscenity, depravity" (21)—expose the animal nature of humankind. In short, the naturalistic novel depicts man locked in a Darwinian cosmos, competing, often violently, with those around him and at the mercy of forces greater than himself—a kind of "pessimistic determinism," to employ an enduring label Oscar Cargill coined in 1941.

Clearly, then, the literary devices that emerge from this school work hard to undermine any transcendent conceptions of man. Animal imagery, for instance, is pervasive in the naturalistic novel (Howard 81), with human beings consistently figured as beasts. And larger fictional techniques serve to underscore the brutal in man. The plot of decline, too, is a common narrative strategy in naturalist fiction, a downward spiral of a character into an increasingly brutal existence (Howard 98–99). And, again, external forces are at work to brutalize these characters—economic depravity, abuse at the hands of other brutal characters, diseases and manias of various sorts, and, very commonly, alcoholism (Pizer, *Twentieth-Century* 188).

The animal imagery, the plot of decline, the violence, the sense of competition inherent in the American system—all of these primary naturalistic tropes isolated by Walcutt, Pizer, and others hold pivotal positions in *A Feast of Snakes*. True to the naturalistic form, for instance, the novel posits a world of pessimistic determinism. And, in fact, a number of critics have already engaged with the issue of responsibility and blame in Crews's text. Most recently, Michael Spikes has taken to task what he considers the most common reading of the novel's main character, Joe Lon Mackey: "Most critics have interpreted Joe Lon's situation and his responses to it as unavoidable, almost fated. . . . None of these critics, in sum, feels that Joe Lon has a choice, or any control over his own condition" (83). For Spikes, Joe Lon possesses free will but lacks the energy or desire to change his circumstances. A close reading of *A Feast of Snakes* demonstrates, however, that Joe Lon is in fact "trapped in a bizarre and fallen world," as David K. Jeffrey has asserted (53). But to say that Crews's text is simply one more reworking of the naturalist theme of determinism is too shallow. Recent reconsiderations of naturalism and how it has transformed itself in the postmodern era go far in explaining how—and where, exactly—Crews's novel locates itself in the naturalistic tradition.

Pizer identifies three well-defined phases of American literary naturalism—one in the 1890s, of course, one in the 1930s, and the most recent naturalistic wave, beginning in the post war period and continuing at least into the 1970s. Each phase, as Pizer sees it, is a response to the peculiar social, political, and economic pressures of its cultural milieu—and naturalism is in fact a literature of failure, a literature of "hard times" in America (Pizer, *Theory and Practice* 168). Thus the 1890s strain of naturalism responded to "the rapid shift from a predominately rural, agrarian civilization to an urban, industrial society, and the transition from traditional religious faith and moral belief to skepticism and uncertainty" (17). And the naturalism of the '30s stemmed from the economic strains of the Depression and the Marxist intellectual currents of the period. The latest incarnation of naturalism is driven by the same sense of chaos and despair that has shaped the projects of postmodern writers such as Thomas Pynchon and Kurt Vonnegut—"[the] extermination camps, the atom bomb, the cold war in Europe and the hot war in Korea, the McCarthy witch hunts" (29). In an examination of Norman Mailer and William Styron, Pizer brings his discussion of the resurgence of naturalism into the late '70s, arguing that Vietnam, Watergate, the continuing threat of nuclear devastation, economic recession, and the violence and poverty of the cities have created a new sense of " 'hard times' in America" (170).

Crews's novel conforms to Pizer's rubric on a number of levels. Several critics have noted how *A Feast of Snakes* depicts a new industrial and urban South, yet one still in transition, still echoing its agrarian past. DeBord and Long see *A Feast of Snakes*, along with *Car*, *Naked in Garden Hills*, and *This Thing Don't Lead to Heaven* as novels of "social history" and "culture in transition" (41): "Central to these novels," they assert, "is the change from agricultural to industrial values and from subsistence to individual achievement" (41–2). So DeBord and Long actually discover in Crews's canon thematic concerns that link his work directly with that of the first wave of late nineteenth-century naturalistic novelists. Similarly, Robert C. Covel sees the tragic conflicts in Crews's work emanating from "value systems . . . based on outmoded lifestyles that conflict with postmodern urban values" (75).

In fact, we find Crews's novel laced with many of the cultural markers Pizer identifies in contemporary literary naturalism—references to Vietnam, the Holocaust, the alternating violence and vapidity of the pop culture waste land of television. And although these references are often brief, they are far from marginal. Buddy Matlow, in typical naturalistic fashion, is powerfully shaped by his Vietnam experience. The perverse and sadistic Matlow even provides a crude but vivid image of the kind of pessimistic determinism characteristic of the naturalistic novel: " '. . . I was born in trouble. It's been trouble ever since.' He slapped his right thigh. 'That fucking stick leg is trouble . . . Everybody's got their load of shit to haul' " (*Feast* 36). It is difficult to imagine that Buddy Matlow was anything but cruel in his former life, but clearly his experiences in Vietnam—"[stepping] on a pungy stick that had been dipped in Veet Nam Ease shit" (15)—have intensified his anger and brutality. But Buddy is not the only character in Mystic who was "born in trouble"—the other figures we encounter have their own "[loads] of shit to haul." In one of the most unsettling sequences of a deeply unsettling narrative, Duffy Deeter prolongs his sexual stamina by diverting himself with visions of the Holocaust: "Duffy Deeter with an effort of will was thinking of Treblinka. He had already finished with Dachau and Auschwitz. Images of death pumped in his head" (79). And we see where those images originated, because Duffy himself tells us: " 'Before television. We used to get the news at the neighborhood movie,' he said. 'They told us everything. I loved it. One disaster after another. Burning blimps. Collapsing buildings. Ships blowing up' " (81). And the two most clearly insane citizens of Mystic—Beeder and Lottie Mae—are similarly inundated with the pageant of postmodern terrors parading through the media. Beeder, of course, is addicted to television—anything on television, from game shows to Johnny Carson. But Lottie Mae, like Deeter, responds to more specific—and more troubling—cultural cues: "Lottie Mae recognized the man who talked when the guns and the planes and the bombs stopped. It was the NBC Nightly News. It was Lottie Mae's favorite program . . . NBC Nightly News went straight to the robbing and killing, the crying and the blood, burning buildings and mashed cars. Them NBC Nightly News sumbitches was mean. Soon kill you as look at you. Killed somebody ever night" (130–31).

The free indirect speech Crews so often uses in *A Feast of Snakes*—as in the above quoted passage—is a narrative device Pizer links to contemporary naturalist writers such as Norman Mailer (*Theory and Practice* 177–78), an author for whom Crews has expressed considerable admiration (Bonetti 163). As Pizer sees it, this narrative device is primarily useful for fashioning a "sense of intimacy of knowing" (*Theory and Practice* 179). In the case of Mailer's *The Executioner's Song*, through free indirect speech "we come to understand the desperation that underlies [Gary Gilmore's] frustrated and failed life and the tormented self-destructiveness behind his actions" (179). Similarly, Crews employs this strategy to help us enter the consciousness of his characters and thus unravel the mystery of their violent, brutal, or insane behavior. We learn, for instance, that Joe Lon, abusive as he is to his wife, nonetheless regards Elfie as "as good a woman as a man ever laid dick to" (*Feast* 12). But his confining life with Elfie and two wailing babies "ruined his nerves completely. Hell, he guessed that was to be expected. But it didn't mean he ought to treat her like a dog. Christ, he treated her just like a goddam dog. He just couldn't seem to help it" (12). We see here, in language appropriate to Joe Lon's character, the first hints of Mackey's decline into the murderous brute he becomes in the closing scene of Crews's novel, and we see, too, that Joe Lon, like Buddy Matlow, instinctively recognizes how forces seemingly beyond his control are shaping his destiny. Joe Lon knows, too, that "[everybody's] got their load of shit to haul." But these broader links to literary naturalism become clearer when we consider the more specific naturalistic tropes at work in Crews's text.

The animal imagery employed by Crews is the most self-evident naturalistic element in *A Feast of Snakes*. Edward C. Lynskey suggests, in fact, that "[man] and beast are made to reverse roles in the novel" (197). But Crews's novel does not really deconstruct the traditional binary opposition of man/beast; instead, it shows us that ultimately there is no difference between the human and the brute, between man and beast. Even relatively minor characters are figured as brutes: Hard Candy, for instance, is described in serpentine language—she felt "slick as oil, in all the joints of her body, her bones, in the firm sliding muscles, tensed and locked now, ready to spring—to *strike*" (*Feast* 3). Her boyfriend, the new Boss Snake Willard Miller, is rendered in equally appropriate terms; indeed, he, quite literally, looks like a snake: "He had a direct lidless stare and tiny ears. His hair was cut short and his round blunt head did not so much sit on his huge neck as it seemed buried in it" (19). And the pattern extends throughout the novel: in Lottie Mae's twisted consciousness, Brother Boy transforms into a snake; Buddy Matlow, after donning a snake-headed condom, is butchered like a hog (160); and Joe Lon responds to meeting Berenice's new boyfriend by thinking, "Shep was a fucking dog's name, wasn't it?" (61).

More importantly, the characters' actions are equally bestial. Critics are fond of noting how frequently Joe Lon howls. But Joe Lon is not the only brute prowling the Darwinian jungle of Crews's novel. Willard's sexual trysts with Hard Candy are described as "brutal," an adjective that appears with significant frequency in the text—sex is brutal (5); Susan Gender, despite her graduate education, is considered brutally ignorant by Deeter (81); and of course the fighting dogs themselves are described as brutal (52), underscoring again how distinctions between man and animal are radically blurred in the text. Characters are forever grunting with pleasure (70) or with challenge (89), or "growling and slobbering" (140). And in the chaotic dog fight scene that foreshadows the narrative's explosively violent conclusion, we see that Joe Lon is not the only character given to fits of howling: as Big Joe kicks the defeated Tuffy to death, "he and the crowd howled with a single voice" (167).

But it is the theme of competition in Crews's novel that brings this animal imagery into focus. We need to recognize, too, that the obsession with competition that saturates the text is Crews's extension of the classic naturalistic patterns derived from Herbert Spencer's form of social Darwinism, framed in the infamous catch phrase, "survival of the fittest." Joe Lon's insane sister, Beeder, conveys this idea with more terrifying clarity: " 'That hurts. God, it hurts, that everthing is eating everthing else' " (47). And, indeed, we find that not only are the characters of Crews's universe feasting on snakes; they are feasting on each other: as Edward C. Lynskey sees it, Crews's novel becomes "a dark mirror held up to the national arena" (195), showing how in the era of late capitalism in America "personal lives are thrown into the meatgrinder of competition and, through a combination of luck, chance, and attrition, the winners emerge" (197).

The sports and gaming metaphors that recur throughout *A Feast of Snakes* are of particular interest. Donald Pizer tells us that naturalistic narratives are often heavily ideological or allegorical. While political commentary, per se, is absent from Crews's text, we do see the kind of social criticism at which the naturalistic novelist aims. The central events of the novel invariably focus on competition—football, pit bull fighting, the snake hunt itself. And Edward C Lynskey clearly sees this competitive theme as an allegorical stroke against the American system: "Published during the bicentennial year, the title and theme of Crews's . . . novel suggest what the author's vision, growing progressively darker with each novel, has finally come to—a nation gorging itself on the traditional symbol of evil, the snake" (195). Characters seldom lose an opportunity to face off with each other in animalistic bouts of competition. Duffy Deeter can not resist engaging in a brutal weightlifting duel with Joe Lon and Willard; Susan Gender and Hard Candy compete fiercely in an impromptu baton twirl off; and we are reminded constantly of the competitive nature of the American system even in the minor details of the text—the boisterous game shows on Beeder's constantly blaring television, the litany of competitions surrounding the snake rodeo: "prizes for the heaviest snake, the longest snake, the most snakes, the first one caught, the last one caught. Plus there would be a beauty contest" (*Feast* 17). Joe Lon and Willard, moreover, come close to blows on several occasions, a competitive electricity sparking between them at the slightest provocation. Upon betting on when one of Mackey's snakes will strike a rat, for instance, what should be a friendly wager turns startlingly belligerent: "You ain't bettin with me,' said Joe Lon. 'I'll make you bet with me,' said Willard. They were both off their stools now, kind of leaning toward each other across the counter. They were both smiling, but there was an obvious tension in the attitude of their bodies" (21).

In fact, in Darwinian terms, tension between Joe Lon and Willard should not surprise us: we can see Joe Lon as having been displaced from his leadership position in the herd. Although he occasionally consoles himself by reflecting on his past triumphs—"*That's all right. By God, I had mine*" (7)—he finds himself presently trapped in "a constant state of suffocating anger" (8). As Boss Snake, Joe Lon "was stronger and faster and meaner than other boys his age and for that he had been rewarded" (49). Part of the "load of shit" Joe Lon has to haul is that his former dominance "had been terribly satisfying while it had been going on, but now it lived in his memory like a dream. It had no significance and sometimes inexplicably he wished it had never happened" (50). Those unable to compete in the system—the grunions on the football field, the pathetic Poncy whom Joe Lon and Willard mercilessly torture, or, as Lynskey argues, the deranged girls, Beeder and Lottie Mae (199)—

simply have no chance in the "meatgrinder of competition" (Lynskey 197). Just as disturbing, perhaps, is the suggestion that a similar fate awaits even those seemingly best suited for surviving the meatgrinder—like Joe Lon, like Berenice. In Crews's world, even the fittest don't survive.

At issue in any naturalist text is the problematic question of determinism. As Donald Pizer concedes, "naturalists [critics charge] have been hopelessly confused because they introduce elements of free will and moral responsibility into accounts of a supposedly necessitarian world" (*Twentieth-Century* x). As we have already seen, this sort of debate has erupted around *A Feast of Snakes* in Spikes's response to those critics who see Joe Lon as a doomed character. By way of engaging this question, we need to examine how deterministic elements are deployed across the landscape of Crews's text. *A Feast of Snakes* clearly follows a typical naturalistic narrative pattern, the plot of decline—accelerated into a four day descent into madness; and Crews's tale of Mackey's decline is urged along by another privileged naturalistic device, alcoholism. When we first encounter Joe Lon, "[he] had been drinking most of the day" (8). Over the four day period the narrative recounts, a bottle is never far from Joe Lon's reach. Indeed, he remains, it seems, "lost in the sour mist of bourbon whiskey" (55) throughout most of the novel, drinking to collapse at night, and chasing coffee with whiskey at breakfast. Clearly, Joe Lon is in an alcoholic tailspin. But alcoholism is not the only force forging Joe Lon's dark destiny.

The presence of Willard, the return of Berenice, the oppressive sameness of his "*goddam life listening to nigger talk and . . . totin whiskey to them*" (57)—all serve to conjure up troubling reminders of his former life as Boss Snake, images of past glories and present and future failures. Pizer finds in later naturalistic writers "a refinement of the naturalistic stress on the conditioning or determining force of the world": "the burden of the past, a past, . . . inseparable from place and family [operates as] a powerful constraining agency," and characters are incessantly "haunted by errors, failures, and deficiencies of their former lives" (*Theory and Practice* 190). In *A Feast of Snakes*, of course, the errors and deficiencies of Joe Lon's life are largely of the present. In his past life, "the world was still a place where such things"—his relationship with Berenice, his reign as Boss Snake—"were not only possible but also a great singing joy in his heart" (56). But when his football career ended, "it took everything with it . . . If it had meant anything then, he had forgotten what; and merciful God, it meant nothing now. His life had become a not very interesting movie that he seemed condemned to watch over and over again" (102). But, of course, what Joe Lon had before, his past, does mean something now, shaping as it does his violent nature, and underscoring for him what a failure his life has become in contrast to his halcyon days when "on any given day in his senior year of high school, [he] could have run through the best college defensive line in the country" (6). His immersion in the savage culture of football allowed him to hone his naturally violent nature to a keen edge, giving him "great opportunities to run over people and step on them, mash their heads and their hands, kick their ribs good" (7).

Joe Lon's family heritage plays a particularly important role. We clearly see that not only has Big Joe passed the family business on to his son, but also some especially troubling personality traits, such as his taste for whiskey. But alcoholism isn't the only trait shared by the Mackey men. Although his father "would have killed [Joe Lon] if he ever found out he punched Elfie" (40), Big Joe shares Joe Lon's savage impulse: we learn that he "once castrated a Macon pulpwood Negro," "scalped a white man," and produced the best fighting dogs in Georgia "because he treated them with a savage and unrelenting cruelty that even other pit bull owners could not bear to witness or emulate" (40). And though Big Joe ostensibly "didn't hold with hurting women" (40), he sets a precedent for Joe Lon's abuse of Elfie by triggering his wife's suicide, which, of course, wreaks its own tragic consequences on Beeder. Indeed, Big Joe, though something of a background character in the narrative, serves as a kind of metaphorical figure embodying the determining forces in the text. He sets in motion the forces that, in part, drive Joe Lon toward his homicidal rampage at the close of the novel; his wife's suicide leads to Beeder's madness; and Beeder, in turn, inadvertently encourages Lottie Mae's horrific murder of Buddy Matlow. And the treadmill Big Joe uses to train Tuffy comes to signify the brutal forces at work driving all of these characters toward the abyss: "*Before he's through,*" Lottie Mae tells us, "*he gone tie everone on it*" (133).

Clearly, an intricate web of forces is entrapping Crews's characters. And this is perhaps no better illustrated than in the female characters in *A Feast of Snakes*. In her article, "Crews's Women," Patricia V. Beatty argues that Crews's sexist depictions of women are limited to two categories—"devouring monsters or pathetic victims" (112). In *A Feast of Snakes*, Beatty's analysis is, at least on one level, viable—the women in the novel are indeed either monsters or victims. However, virtually every character in the novel—male or female, human or animal—is, as we have seen, either a monster or a victim, or in most cases, I would argue, both. Beatty, moreover, calls Crews's women in *A Feast of Snakes* "Barbie dolls run wild" (119), and it is true that the novel's narrative voice is careful to describe the sexual charms of the "honey-legged" Berenice (*Feast* 55), her prancing sister Hard Candy, and the "long-legged, black-haired cream-colored" Susan Gender (84). But a naturalistic reading of the novel provides some perspective on Crews's women.

First, women are commodified in the text—objects for male consumption. In a footnote to her essay, "What More Can Carrie Want? Naturalistic Ways of Consuming Women," Blanche H. Gelphant connects "studies of women as objects, rather than subjects, of desire" (201) with representations of the feminine, and, specifically, the female body, in naturalistic texts. Women characters in Crews's novel are clearly objects of desire, objects to be possessed and devoured, and, as such, they are determined, in a sense, by the male spectators who fix these women in their gazes. The narrative voice opens with the male gaze lingering over the body of Hard Candy as she works out on the practice field. As this opening description pans back for a broader perspective, we see that the male gaze of the watching Joe Lon still fixes Hard Candy. Thus is foreshadowed the tricky interplay between the familiar third-person narrative voice and the episodes in the novel in which women characters are possessed by the male gaze. Crews is deploying an interesting narrative strategy in these passages, one that consistently centers the commodification of the female body within the field of consciousness of a male character rather than simply in the voice of the controlling narrator: as Joe Lon watches the beauty contest, his gaze is riveted on the young Rattlesnake Queen, "all flashing legs and rounded arms over rounded breasts over rounded hips" (146–7); we see Poncy "trying to act as though he wasn't watching [Susan Gender's] pumping hips and the fine vibrating flesh of her belly" (104); Joe Lon and Willard are transfixed by the "long-legged, black-haired cream-colored piece of ass" they soon come to know as Susan Gender (84); and at the Blue Pines, a local "farmer's nailhead eyes watched her [Susan's] little hard-nosed titties plunge against the fabric [of her blouse] as she jacked around to the music" (105). So when we discover the male gaze of Crews's characters fixing on the women before them, the scene unfolds from the perspective of the male gazer; that is, the center(s) of consciousness in these sequences is always that of one (or more) of the male spectators, not that of the novel's narrator. This is an important distinction, and not only for rescuing Crews's text—to some degree, at least—from charges of sexism. Part of the predatory nature of the novel revolves around this objectification/commodification of women characters and women's bodies. Teresa de Lauretis sees a similar dynamic operating in narrative cinema: "The woman, fixed in the position of icon, spectacle, or image to be looked at, bears the mobile look of both the spectator [for us, the reader] and the male character(s). It is the latter who commands at once the action and the landscape, and who occupies the position of subject of vision, which he relays to the spectator" (44). In fact, many of the women in the text—Susan Gender is a good example—are doubly possessed, doubly consumed, doubly commodified: "He [Deeter] enjoyed them looking at her. He *liked* them to want her. They wanted her, but by God Duffy Deeter had her" (*Feast* 85). We have already observed how characters feast on each other in the text; this male gazing, a feasting of the eyes, is still another example. It is also another example of the determining agencies at work in the novel. Mystic is nothing if not a patriarchal culture, the phallocentrism reinforced further by the often over-the-top serpentine phallic imagery. The male gaze so pervasive in the text serves to locate the women characters within this patriarchal order, to define them as sexual consumables.

Beatty points out that Susan Gender's name "certainly tips us off about her" (118). And, indeed, it does—as we have seen, she is quite literally defined by gender. In the scene which opens the second section of the novel, Deeter, having consumed Susan as an object of sexual desire, now finds her quite useless—and we see from him a different twist on the male gaze of desire, a different kind of objectification: "He watched her with a kind of ecstasy of loathing . . . Duffy thought that only something very dumb could eat apples like that. Only the most brutal kind of ignorance could talk the way she did" (*Feast* 81). Similarly, Elfie's physical deterioration renders her useless to Joe Lon: ". . . she turned around and she was a disaster. Those beautiful ball-crushing breasts she'd had two years ago now hung like enormous flaps down the front of her body. And although she was not fat, she looked like she was carrying a basketball under her dress" (9). Thus one of the few sympathetic characters in the narrative is figured, through Joe Lon's consciousness, as an object no longer worthy of desire, a commodity now lacking exchange value. Lottie Mae, who, as Beatty points out, is the only female consciousness we enter in the narrative (116), finds herself trapped by a confluence of many cultural forces. Poor and poorly educated, Lottie Mae is defined by both gender and race. She is raped and sexually intimidated by Buddy Matlow, who, of course, defines her through his gaze—"the minute I laid my eyes on that little jacked-up ass of yours I known I was in love again" (*Feast* 36). And she is reminded by Buddy that ethnicity is another agency shaping her fate: "Look at you. Ever time you show that black face in the world you got trouble" (36).

But in Crews's world, "everthing is eating everthing else," and the women characters, trapped though they are by patriarchal efforts to define and consume them, are, in most cases, as brutal and predatory as the men. Candy Sweet, shortly after threatening a fellow majorette—" 'You want you ass kicked, do you?' " (6)—takes genuine pleasure in watching Joe Lon's rattler strike and eat a rat. Later, she and Susan Gender first join in the persecution of Poncy, and then come to a near violent confrontation over their informal baton twirl-off. Even Beeder and Lottie Mae, the most victimized of Crews's women, are fascinated by the violence they see on television, and, of course, both, in a sense, are complicit in Buddy's death. Clearly, then women characters are operated on in the text by the male gaze, as well as being defined by—and, in many cases, eagerly participating in—the brutally competitive milieu Crews's novel posits. Thus, in the end, we see that what might be taken for sexism in *A Feast of Snakes* is actually a working out of the pessimistic determinism of Crews's naturalistic novel.

This recurring issue of pessimistic determinism brings us back to Joe Lon and a question we left unresolved earlier in our discussion. Is Joe Lon responsible for his actions? As with so many naturalistic studies of the criminal mind—Dreiser's *An American Tragedy*, Wright's *Native Son*, Mailer's *The Executioner's Song*—we are left, in many ways, with sympathy for the criminal. In fact, the naturalistic crime novel, in its classic form, seeks to explain why someone like a Clyde Griffith or a Bigger Thomas or a Gary Gilmore runs afoul of the law and becomes an enemy of so-called civilized society. Crews's novel doesn't really do that. Despite the predatory violence infesting *A Feast of Snakes*, few readers are prepared for Joe Lon's violent outburst in the final scene. We've seen the determining forces shaping Joe Lon's character—his family situation, his alcoholism, his football background, his saturation in a brutally competitive culture—but there is a mysterious indeterminacy behind Joe Lon's decline—something slippery, shadowy, unnamable, something that violates the often scientific examination of causality typical of so many naturalistic narratives. Perhaps this indeterminacy is what urges critics like Michael Spikes to insist that Joe Lon could have disentangled himself from the web of forces that seemed to be driving him over the edge. A postmodern rethinking of naturalism may help us unravel the question of how predestined Joe Lon's final rampage really is.

June Howard points out that one of the misconceptions about naturalism of any era is the sense of causality and determinism shaping the characters and events in the narrative. Forces in naturalistic novels are not always clearly observable in obvious patterns of causality; instead, an "indeterminacy," an "incalculable complexity" often characterizes the determining agents in a naturalistic text (Howard 49). Paul Civello asserts that this problematizing of the forces of causality is radically transformed in the postmodern era. In the postmodern period, Civello argues, "humanity's conception of an order in the material world" has utterly collapsed (124). The first literary naturalists responded to the death of God and the advent of Darwinism. But in the science of their period there remained an important residue of foundationalism, a scientific view of the cosmos as a knowable phenomenon structured by linear causality. Subsequent discoveries in quantum physics and the field theories that emanated from them have reconfigured our conception of the universe. Our world is no longer a mechanistic system, but rather an "open system" which "defies causality;" and man is no longer a helpless victim of chance, but rather an agent "interacting with his environment" who "determines as well as is determined" (121). The scientific world view that gave us traditional forms of naturalism is no longer a valid paradigm; and literary naturalism's essential "deterministic causes—heredity and environment—are now merely two factors in a warren of factors" (123).

The implications of this for literary naturalism, and for Crews's text, in particular, are considerable. Postmodern and/or contemporary naturalistic texts often consciously subvert linear causality (Civello 123). I am not suggesting that Harry Crews is a postmodern writer, as such; but that sense of indeterminacy we have discovered in Joe Lon's character frustrates our efforts to determine empirically whether Mackey can control himself. Joe Lon does not really know why he abuses Elfie, but we are told more than once that although he "didn't like it, . . . [he] couldn't help it" (*Feast* 12). In reflecting on his failed life, Joe Lon speculates that "he had done *something*" to "*deserve it*," and that "he would never find out what it was" (57). Clearly, Joe Lon does not know what is happening to him—and although we can speculate and tally up the forces conspiring to drive Mackey to mass murder, we, no more than Joe Lon, can be sure of what we know. For Crews, there are no easy answers, no simple formulas for explaining the violent universe around us. David K. Jeffrey observes that in Crews's essay on mass murderer Charles Whitman, he will "have none of" any medical explanation (a brain tumor) for Whitman's behavior (50). Instead, Crews insists that "[we] all have our towers to climb;" some of us resist the urge; some of us, like Whitman, like Joe Lon, do not ("Climbing the Tower" 213). So, again, is Joe Lon responsible for his actions? Crews's novel offers a most frustrating answer: we do not and cannot know. In an interview with William Walsh, Crews explains, "Our lives have been so abstracted from us, taken from us by our being intertwined with so many things that we have no control over it. It doesn't hurt be [sic] aware of what we have done to ourselves and what we are busily doing to ourselves. My fiction would probably be better if it were not written out of such a sense of anger and outrage" (129). And perhaps that is what is so unsettling, so disturbing about Crews's version of naturalism.[3] The forces that shape our lives—and our deaths—are more bewilderingly complex and aloof than we can imagine, and yet so close to us—perhaps emanating from within us—that we don't even realize they are there—until a Joe Lon Mackey or a Charles Whitman remind us.

HAVING A HARD TIME OF IT

Women in the Novels of Harry Crews

Elise S. Lake

H arry Crews writes about people on the margins of society. His characters, the poor, the deformed, cling desperately to dreams of success despite their incapacities. Although men are the focal points for most of Crews's works, some of his most memorable figures are women: women with high (perhaps unrealistic) aspirations, women with complex (and sometimes perverse) motivations, women caught in the conflicting demands of traditional and modern society.

Interpreters of Crews's work typically focus on the male characters from whose perspectives his stories are often told. Some critics, such as Patricia Beatty, dismiss his female characters as simplistic stereotypes— sexual superwomen, man-threatening monsters, or passive victims. In a harsh critique of Crews's portrayals of women in his earlier novels, Beatty imputes misogynism and immature sexuality to Crews himself (112).

I am not interested in Crews's sexuality, immature or otherwise. In- stead, I look to Crews as a social reporter and critic, who embeds his fictional women in uniquely Southern sociocultural contexts. These contexts are in transition, and change creates difficulties—for both sexes. There are stereotypical women in Crews's novels. There are also extraordinary women who attempt to control their lives, who strive to overcome disadvantage, who try to cope with the madness around or within them.

In this paper, I draw upon Crews's autobiography, selected essays and novels, and critiques of his work, to examine his portrayals of women and address several questions. How do critics view Crews's women characters? What are Crews's professed beliefs about women's roles, and how might these beliefs shape his fictional portrayals? Finally, what do Crews's female characters contribute to his vision of the modern world? Are the sexes really so different in their illusions, their ambitions, and the obstacles they encounter in trying to achieve success?

THE CRITICS ON CREWS'S WOMEN

Interpreters of Crews's work point to his fascination with the grotesque (Shepherd, "Matters" 53; Shelton, "Man's Search" 22–23), and his obsession with violence (Long, "Naked Americans"). Some readers see dark humor in the novels; others find them repellent (e.g., Blackburn). Reviewers have identified recurrent themes, including the demise of traditional communities and standards, the isolation of modern people, and the costs incurred when people aspire to levels of success that they cannot possibly achieve (DeBord and Long; Shelton, "The Poor Whites' Perspective"; Long, "Silences").

Most of those who write about Crews's work make only passing references to the women in his fiction. Typically, they note that in Crews's novels, female sexuality has the power to ruin men's lives. Donald Noble contends that Hester, in *The Gypsy's Curse*, illustrates Crews's less than affectionate view of women: "Hester ruins life at the Fireman's gym. Her powerful sexuality and her innate evil destroy the men she comes in contact with. Is she a typical Crews heroine? Does she represent Crews's 'attitude toward women'? Some will think so" (16). Casting a spell over the disabled and damaged men of Fireman's Gym, the beautiful Hester uses her power to make them all believe they can compete and win. Hester exploits others to relieve her own boredom and pain. Ultimately she wants to find a man who will love her enough to take her life. Her quest for thrills and death destroys the self-sufficient interdependence at the gym, and leads to one man's death and another's imprisonment.

Noble does not argue that the "typical Crews heroine" destroys men. But he does call Hester innately evil, and implies that her character may indicate that Crews sees women as threatening. For Crews, Noble suggests, modern women are a problem: "Crews seems to have difficulty with the contemporary, self-conscious feminist" (16).

Two interpreters examine Crews's female characters in greater depth. Patricia Beatty and Angela Weaver find sexism in the novels, but identify different sources for it. For Beatty, Crews himself is a sexist, whereas Weaver locates sexism in the kinds of men Crews portrays.

Beatty argues that unlike Crews's male characters, who generally are multidimensional and sympathetically presented, the female figures are poorly delineated cliches: "Women in his novels are seldom fully realized personalities; if they are not *Playboy* centerfolds, they are devouring monsters or pathetic victims of abuse" (112). In these characters, Beatty finds symptoms of Crews's psyche: they manifest Crews's macho hostility and fear of females. Arguing from a Jungian perspective, she suggests that male-female relationships in the novels represent archetypal struggles between the adolescent male ego and the "Great Mother" of the unconscious. Beatty attempts to show how female figures, representing terrifying goddesses, imperil the more humanly written male characters.

Beatty's analysis seems inadequate. She seems to assume that Crews is hostile to women, and that she can fathom his state of mind, even demonstrate his pathology, by superimposing a framework of myth and Jungian principles onto the texts. Her diagnosis reduces Crews's cultural critique to a manifestation of personal psychopathology. She ignores female characters in Crews's earlier works who are strong, fully drawn, and who fit neither Jungian interpretation nor cultural stereotypes. (It should be noted that Beatty's analysis predates the creation of some of Crews's more interesting women figures, such as Shereel, Earline, and Marvella in *Body*.)

Weaver offers a more balanced interpretation in her analysis of male-female relationships in three novels: *A Feast of Snakes*, *Body*, and *Scar Lover*. For Weaver, sexism in these works reflects the beliefs of the central male characters in the stories, not Crews's personality: "the female characters often become objects rather than people in the eyes of . . . [male characters], things to be conquered or else avoided. The women serve largely as foils, . . . [that is,] how the narrative presents a woman is less of a comment on the character of the woman herself than it is a revelation of the inner workings of the male psyche to whose point of view the novel's impressions are limited" (10). Women, as "Others" set in juxtaposition to men, define male characters, not only to the reader, but to the men themselves. Through interaction with women, men become self-aware and find their identities. Weaver suggests that in *Body*, Crews demonstrates that the reverse is also true: through relationships with men, women discover themselves.

CREWS'S COMMENTARIES ON WOMEN

Crews has commented on women's roles in an interview (Lytal and Russell), and in his essay, "The Unfeminine Mystique." In Lytal and Russell's interview, Crews claims sympathy with feminism (547–48). He admires women's survival in the face of hardships imposed upon them: "I know what a struggle women have had. Women couldn't own land, for God's sake, in this country. . . . And all the bullshit women had to go through to be able to vote. A woman went from being the property of her daddy to the property of her husband. Women had a hard time of it. It strikes me as ironic and really curious that they should have had such a hard time of it, when it is manifestly true, at least to me, that they are so much stronger than men are" (548). Crews's esteem for these "steel magnolias" should not be read as a statement of conventional feminism. A skeptical reading, informed by his commentary in "The Unfeminine Mystique," implies that his understanding of the term may depart from that of most feminists.

In "The Unfeminine Mystique," Crews decries feminist oversensitivity to labels. He describes two incidents in which he was criticized for "politically incorrect" talk. In one case, a bit of sexually-tinged banter between him and a woman bartender of his long-time acquaintance was overheard by another woman—a stranger—who chastised him for making sexist comments. In another incident, he referred to the wife of a friend as a "woman;" she took offense, preferring to be called a "person."

These incidents inspire Crews to rail against the hostility he has encountered from feminists. Why, he seems to argue, should we impose standards of public exchange, of universalism, on private interactions? Personal relationships achieve closeness through the exchange of intimacies, the recognition of individual differences, the negotiation of identities. When we eliminate particularism, relationships—including those between the sexes—become stilted, sterile. Lost are the markers of friendship. When men are confused about whether terms carrying specific connotations (such as "lady") will be deemed demeaning, they resort to bland, impersonal inoffensiveness. They call women "persons." Crews refuses to do this: ". . . [P]erson is one of the most anonymous, bloodless, faceless, characterless words in the language" (125). Although Crews acknowledges the goal of equality, he contends that feminist hostility toward men will not foster it.

More insights can be found in Crews's autobiography, *A Childhood: The Biography of a Place*, a description of his "grit" roots in Bacon County, Georgia, during the Great Depression. In this world, where men and women *were* different, sexual equality would have seemed unnatural and absurd. The centrality of this difference was apparent even to children, who learned early on of the necessary—and risky—attraction between males and females: "The mystery of little girls stood at dead even with the mystery of God. See, little girls had *it*. None of the little boys had *it*. We had to go through all kinds of things—fights, gifts, lies, whatever—if we wanted *it*. And little girls could give us some of *it* if they wanted to. As well as being unpleasant, the whole thing was scary" (167). What little power women could *overtly* exercise in this male-dominated world derived in part from sex.

Culturally defined as the leaders of rural southern society, the men of Bacon Country often lacked the material and social resources with which to command authority. Women were a stabilizing force—the carriers of ritual, the mainstays of family and community organization. Women held their families together when men were incapacitated, absent, or irresponsible. Crews's own mother had to cope with the early death of his father due to overwork. Later, to protect them all from the drunken violence of her second husband, she moved herself and her children to Florida and took a grueling job in a cigar factory. In Crews's portrayals of his mother and other women, his appreciation of their strength and centrality to country life is apparent.

In the community, women were the guardians of ritual, repositories of the lore of the spirit world. In one story from *A Childhood*, Auntie, an old, black, self-proclaimed "conjure woman," instructed the young Harry Crews in the ritual way to bury the eyes of the possum they had just eaten for dinner. Lest the possum come looking for the people who consumed him after they too were dead, the eyes had to be buried looking up (72–74).

It was the women who told cautionary tales about the human condition as they understood it: "The stories that women told and that men told were full of violence, sickness, and death. But it was the women whose stories were unrelieved by humor and filled with apocalyptic vision. . . . [W]omen would repeat stories about folks they did not know and had never seen, and consequently . . . the stories were as stark and cold as legend or myth" (101). Women's stories and the rituals they tended helped give people what little sense of control they felt in the precarious world of Bacon County: "[E]very single thing in the world was full of mystery and awesome power. And it was only by right ways of doing things—ritual ways—that kept any of us safe. Making stories about them was not so that we could understand them but so that we could live with them" (97–98).

In Crews's nonfiction, then, sexual difference seems a persistent theme. For the young Crews, the power of women lay in the mystery of their sexuality, their knowledge of nature, and their stamina in the face of adversities that incapacitated men. But Crews never does suggest that these strengths justify sexual and economic equality. Instead, he rejects the blurring of differences into a "universalistic personhood." Women are "the Other," simultaneously attractive and threatening in their difference from men. Similar themes can be found in Crews's fictional portrayals.

WOMEN IN THE NOVELS

In the novels published by Harry Crews since 1968, female characters are more varied than critics typically acknowledge. A partial list of "types" would include feisty old ladies, whores (both straight and lesbian), cheerleaders, sexually liberated graduate students, entrepreneurs, traditional homemakers, Caribbean conjure women, suburbanites on the make, and assorted madwomen. Sheer variety disputes the notion that Crews stereotypes women narrowly. Given this diversity, it is possible to find support for almost any assertion about Crews's stance toward females.

Objects of Lust, Objects of Rage

Several female characters support the claim that Crews sees women as inferior adjuncts to men. In *A Feast of Snakes*, sexy cheerleaders and downtrodden victims of male rage are important primarily for the actions they inspire in central male figures. In *Feast*, women set in motion turmoil and tragedy, but most of them remain enigmatic figures, incompletely drawn, their thoughts and motivations largely unknown.

With their transparently evocative names, Susan Gender, Berenice Sweet, and her sister Hard Candy are cheerleaders, objects of male lust in *Feast*. Elfie Mackey is a pathetic victim, acquiescent to her raging husband's demands. Of the cheerleaders, Berenice is primary, the former girlfriend of the novel's main character, Joe Lon Mackey. Her return from college for a rattlesnake roundup adds to Joe Lon's rage about his sorry life, which includes a dead-end job and his sweet but worn-out wife, Elfie. Once a high school football star, Joe Lon lost the chance to play college ball because he could not read. Anticipating Berenice's return, Joe Lon brutalizes Elfie during sex while calling out Berenice's name. Later, he has sex with Berenice while his humiliated wife waits outside their trailer, knowing full well what is taking place in the bedroom.

In different ways, Berenice and Elfie contribute to Joe Lon's desperation, and help to provoke his self-destructive act of mass murder. Both women are catalysts for male action and passive victims of Joe Lon's rage, but their characters are undeveloped. The other cheerleaders, Susan and Hard Candy, play only peripheral roles.

Characters such as Berenice and Elfie could cast Crews himself as misogynist troglodyte, endorsing roles for women that are secondary and male-focused. But Angela Weaver argues these characters are used by Crews to define his male figures—the sexism is in *their* eyes (10). In her reading, Crews is exonerated, merely a chronicler of misogyny within the contemporary American South.

The Passive and Not-So-Passive Aggressives

Other women characters are more adversarial in their relationships with men. In *Feast*, Joe Lon's long-dead mother, his sister Beeder (generally regarded as crazy), and a young black woman named Lottie Mae use extreme measures to cope with the insanity about them and to challenge male domination. It is not hard to feel sympathy for them.

For years, Joe Lon's mother had had an affair with Billy, a traveling shoe salesman. Abandoning her children and her hard-drinking husband for true love, Joe Lon's mother ran off to Atlanta with Billy. In the note she left behind, she said: "I have gone with Billy. Forgive me. But I love him and I have gone with him" (119). Her husband, Big Joe, was unimpressed by love. A believer in duty and discipline, he traveled to Atlanta and brought her back home. Joe Lon's sister Beeder came home from cheerleading practice to find her mother sitting in a rocker, dead, a plastic bag fastened over her head with Big Joe's necktie. Pinned to her chest was another note: "bring me back now you son of a bitch" (120). To escape her dead mother and the violence of her father, Beeder retreated to her room permanently. Now, eight years later, with her own feces smeared on her hair and face, Beeder watches television constantly, even after the stations sign off. She turns the volume up to drown out her father's voice as he calls through the door inquiring if she's all right, and to mute the yelping of the pit bulls Big Joe is training to fight to the death: "Beeder lay back on the pillow, thinking how peaceful everything was. . . . [S]he had found a place every bit as good as her mother's. Sometimes she thought it might be better than her mother's. But most times she did not" (72). Other characters in *Feast* think Beeder is insane, but her talk and thoughts suggest her behavior is an intentional escape from the madness of normal life in Mystic.

Lottie Mae, who helps keep house at Big Joe's, is the victim of a sexual predator, Sheriff Buddy Matlow. Buddy jails young women as "sporting women" unless they have sex with him. In the jail, Buddy rapes Lottie Mae, threatening her with a live rattlesnake to overcome her resistance. After her release, Lottie Mae is obsessed with snakes—she dreams of snakes, feels snakes in her mother's touch, sees snakes entwined in her mother's hair. At Big Joe's house, she tells Beeder she is afraid it will rain snakes. Beeder advises "be handy to you razor" (71) so Lottie Mae can kill the snakes if need be. Later, Buddy picks up Lottie Mae in his squad car, and shows her his lap, where "a snake rose straight as a plumb line" (129). Realizing this is the moment for which Beeder has prepared her, Lottie Mae reaches for the razor wedged in her shoe and strikes at the snake—Buddy's penis sheathed in a rattlesnake-patterned condom—and cuts it off.

For Beeder and her mother, retreat from the world is the solution to male control. Yet their masochistic responses are simultaneously aggressive, causing pain to the men around them. When Big Joe sees Beeder's face, so like his wife's, he can't help but picture his wife with the bag over her head. Joe Lon chugs half a bottle of whiskey in one gagging gulp trying to erase the image of Beeder smearing shit in her hair. For both men, Beeder is a constant reminder of the older woman's act of self-determination.

In Lottie Mae's response to Buddy Matlow's rape, there is no ambiguity. Even with her mind clouded by visions of snakes, her purpose is clear, and the meaning of her action is unequivocal. Her behavior stands in sharp contrast to that of the novel's other victim of male violence, Elfie, who tolerates her mistreatment almost willingly. At the end of the novel, after Joe Lon starts shooting into the crowd amid the snake-obsessed anarchy at the rattlesnake roundup, it is Lottie Mae and Beeder who seem victorious as they watch the chaos around them. Beeder has emerged from the bedroom where she has spent years, and Lottie Mae's assault on Buddy has led to his death. Both of these "madwomen" seem more sane than the violent "normals" around them.

In the small-town southern setting of *Feast*, the options open to women like Elfie, Beeder and her mother, and Lottie Mae, are limited. They can endure male domination passively, as Elfie does, or they can challenge it, and pay the price. For Beeder and her mother, the cost of aggression is retreat into suicide, or into a reclusive social suicide. Lottie Mae directly retaliates against her oppressor. For her, the cost of aggression—perhaps prison, or worse—is left to the reader's imagination.

However, it is not only the women in Mystic who have limited options. Joe Lon and his father are also trapped. Despite his high school triumphs, Joe Lon has been reduced to tending chemical toilets for the roundup and selling moonshine whiskey. Big Joe has turned his frustration inward in drunkenness, and outward in violence—he has castrated one man and scalped another. Joe Lon's frustration takes similar turns in his heavy drinking, his battering of Elfie, and his murderous violence. A dead-end world destroys people.

Hard Cases: Hard-Headed, Hard-Hearted, and Hard-Bodied

Other female characters in Crews's fiction are better developed. Harder and more aggressive, these women have aspirations—for financial success, social status, physical perfection. And all are thwarted, sometimes by the restraints of a male-oriented world, sometimes by their own inadequacies or conflicting desires.

With characters such as Dolly Furgeson, Gaye Nell Odell, and Shereel Dupont, Crews shows us the difficulties that ambitious women can face. In their failures, one might read an antifeminist message. However, the similarities of their strivings—and their failures—to those of the male characters suggest that it is not hostility to independent women that Crews intends to convey. Instead, he may mean to demonstrate that success itself is a delusion—for all people.

A central figure in *Naked in Garden Hills* is Dolly Furgeson. Dolly has grown up poor in Garden Hills, a nearly abandoned town in a phosphate mine pit, once owned by the mysterious Jack O'Boylan. Her only asset is her beauty, which won her the title of Phosphate Queen. Dolly dreams of success, but there is little chance of parlaying her looks into status in Garden Hills. The only wealthy man in town, Fat Man, has rejected her advances. So, Dolly trades on her sexual desirability by taking quarters from men who wish to touch her. With the money, she escapes to New York and becomes a go-go dancer, still guarding her virginity. In New York, she futilely searches for Jack O'Boylan to discover his secret of success. Eventually Dolly makes her own success by returning to Garden Hills and opening a discotheque in the empty phosphate processing plant. She sells the illusion of sex for tourist dollars.

As the money rolls in, Dolly is still unfulfilled. Success—as she defines it—requires losing her virginity to Fat Man and taking her place alongside him as the Queen of Garden Hills. But Fat Man can't be seduced; he longs for a homosexual relationship with a college friend. So Dolly changes her strategy: she will displace Fat Man as the wealthiest person in Garden Hills. To humiliate him, she isolates him from those on whom he depends to cope with his obesity. She hires away his household employees, cutting off his transportation and food. When Fat Man goes to the discotheque to beg for help, Dolly lures him into a golden go-go cage with food, then raises him to the ceiling as a freak in her sideshow for tourists.

Dolly is ambitious, "a determined virgin" (153). Initially, she uses a traditional feminine approach—snaring a rich man—to try to improve her status, but she chooses the wrong target, Fat Man. When she turns to the "masculine" strategy for success—business—she becomes rich, ruins Fat Man, and gives up being a woman simultaneously. Through Dolly, Crews seems to indict the modern woman who, in her drive to succeed, passes up traditional roles. Dolly has spurned other men in her material quest, yet her pursuit of Fat Man yields neither love nor status. She has become the Immaculate Virgin Dolly, her "iron hymen" sanctified but still intact (180). Judged against her original goals, Dolly's achievement is limited. It is costly to Fat Man, now an object on display, and to herself. She has put her feminine assets at risk: her beauty is fading, her capacity for compassion lost. The price of her wealth is her humanity.

But Crews's critique may be broader. Equally ruthless in the pursuit of profits and revenge is Jack O'Boylan. O'Boylan has given Fat Man the played-out phosphate mine in order to avoid taxes. In transferring the tax burden to him, O'Boylan takes revenge on Fat Man's now-dead father, who refused to sell land to the company for a low price. By showing the damage inflicted by both Dolly's and O'Boylan's crusades for wealth, Crews indicts American acquisitiveness. Both sexes become cruel and exploitive when the drive for affluence is all-consuming.

In *Karate Is a Thing of the Spirit*, Gaye Nell Odell is driven to achieve in two realms. A devotee of martial arts with a brown belt in karate, Gaye Nell is also a beauty queen, preparing to defend her crown. Gaye Nell's mother, the quintessential stage mother, was a contestant in the Miss America Pageant, binding the signs of her pregnancy with Gaye Nell in order to compete. She lost when the binding failed catastrophically during the swimsuit contest. Now, on the eve of her own pageant, Gaye Nell believes herself to be pregnant by John Kaimon, a new convert to karate. In an extraordinary encounter, she had raped him while his injured arms were encased in plaster casts, using her physical prowess to draw him into her and force him to climax. John now believes he loves her.

Because pregnancy threatens Gaye Nell's preeminence as both karate expert and beauty queen, she attempts unsuccessfully to dislodge the embryo by subjecting herself to repeated kicks in the stomach from the karate master, and by having strenuous sex with John. At the end of the story, the beauty pageant canceled by a plane crash and a riot, she gives up her goals for love, and runs away with John. Given her ambitions, this capitulation seems puzzling.

It is tempting to read Gaye Nell's behavior as Crews's repudiation of the powerful woman. In her are represented dualities: masculine and feminine, sex and violence. At the beauty pageant, she drives the crowd wild: "It was pussy and violence. It was an unimaginable fuck in the same black swimming suit with certain death and mutilation. And the crowd couldn't stand it" (183). When Gaye Nell isn't intimidating the men of the *karateka* with her mastery of karate, she is taunting them sexually, then humiliating them when they succumb. But confronted with pregnancy and love, Gaye Nell must yield, must surrender to a "true" feminine nature, as though her ambition has been an aberration. Perhaps Crews is arguing that the combination of masculinity and feminity is unsustainable. However, this interpretation is risky: John Kaimon too abandons his quest—karate mastery—for love. If Crews's message were strictly traditionalist, we might see Gaye Nell giving up her aspirations in order to have the child, while John Kaimon continued to pursue his martial arts development.

In Lytal and Russell's interview, Crews is asked why John rejects karate. Crews responds that men and women do such things because they love each other: ". . . flesh seeking flesh, two fleshes making one flesh, two beings making one being . . ." (544). If this represents Crews's genuine belief (and is not merely a retrospective defense of an apparent contradiction in John's character), then an antifeminist interpretation seems less supportable. *Both* sexes give themselves over to love, to sex; "the blood-pull . . . the race-of-man pull" (544) transcends karate for both.

Reading Gaye Nell's inexplicable capitulation as a commentary on modern gender roles may be risky for another reason. Perhaps the ending of *Karate* is merely weak, a collapse into unconvincing romance. The sudden renunciation of ambition seems to betray the characters of *both* Gaye Nell and John. The happy ending seems untrue to the logic of the novel.

It is in *Body* that Crews addresses women's roles most directly. Shereel Dupont is a bodybuilder, aspiring to the championship title of Ms. Cosmos. She has transformed herself from a rural girl named Dorothy Turnipseed into a world champion with a new name. She has done this under the tutelage of her trainer, Russell Muscle, with whom she has an alternately adversarial and supportive relationship. Russell sees her as *his* creation, and prides himself on creating the perfect female body without the use of male hormones, and without mimicking the male physique. If Shereel wins the championship, Russell will use her as a figurehead to promote his chain of health clubs.

A threat to Shereel's aspirations comes from Marvella, a hugely muscled black woman who used steroids to create her own kind of perfection, more masculine than feminine. The world of female bodybuilding is at war over what constitutes the ideal female form—the feminine figure as represented by Shereel, or the masculine version in the figure of Marvella. Shereel faces another threat as well. Her family and her fiancé Nailhead have arrived to reclaim her. If she loses the competition, she is expected to revert to Dorothy Turnipseed and to marry Nailhead.

A counterpoint to Shereel's story is that of her sister, the obese Earline, who has an associate degree in "Problems of Living," but no prospects for marriage. While Shereel steels herself for the competition, Earline falls in love with Billy Bat, a bodybuilder who eschews eating fat in order to compete. Billy Bat loves fat women; through them he vicariously indulges his appetites.

Although Shereel wins her weight class, she loses the overall competition to Marvella. Shereel's independence ends with the competition. Faced with the inevitability of a future that she does not control, she kills herself. On the other hand, Earline realizes her dream. She wins a man who loves her and wishes to marry her and raise a family.

In *Body*, Crews creates contrasting women's roles, and juxtaposes Shereel against two very different visions of womanhood: Earline, who longs for the traditional role of wife, and Marvella, who strives to remake herself in the image of man. Shereel seems to occupy a middle ground—strength in femininity. Unlike the ambiguous *Karate*, *Body* more clearly suggests that women can't have it all. For Shereel, the futility of this quest is finally apparent: she cannot play either role, the traditional woman or the male clone. Whether she wins or loses, her future is determined by the men in her life, Russell or Nailhead. Her only route to self-determination is self-destruction.

In Shereel's failure, Crews may be making a clear statement about gender difference: for Shereel, like Gaye Nell, the combination of masculine and feminine in one person is problematic. However, Crews shows us that Shereel's dilemma is not only one of gender. Shereel has, within the narrow confines of the bodybuilding world, improved herself. She has lost not only her old name, but also her old status. On the competition stage, she is something special, uniquely in control of her own destiny. Off stage, away from bodybuilding, she will be at the mercy of others—not only because she is a woman, but also because of her "grit" background. She lacks the education and connections needed to succeed in the modern world. All she knows is bodybuilding. Having lost the competition, even the route to an ambiguous success is no longer open to her.

MIXED MESSAGES

For critics who wish to cast him as hostile to women, Crews provides ample ammunition. At times, the language he uses regarding women is crude and derogatory. Yet, to label Crews a misogynist because of his language ignores his use of the spoken word to define identity. In his interview with Lytal and Russell, Crews says he uses dialect to convey his characters' "grit" roots (541).

Where crude language about women appears in the novels, it is usually in the talk of "grit" males. In *Scar Lover*, Pete Butcher and the Jamaican Rastafarian George discuss women while they load heavy bundles of cellophane into a boxcar:

George said: "Try dis. I smell pussy on ya when ya walk in de car today, mon. Ya *heavy*, ya *ranking* wih pussy. Sign bad."
Pete laughed nervously and kept swinging the bundles of cellophane. "I wished to God I had been into some pussy. I could use me some, but I been as dry as a dying dog in the desert." (30)

In the talk of Crews's men, women *are* objectified as objects of desire, frustration, and occasionally dread. The sheer rawness of the gypsy's curse in *Gypsy*, a Spanish phrase translated as "may you find a cunt that fits you" (65), suggests a repulsion and fear of enslavement that accompanies men's attraction to women. Such talk fits Crews's males, who often use disparaging terms to refer to people different from themselves: blacks and ethnic minorities, homosexuals, the physically disabled. Intolerance is common in Crews's lower-class characters. Their conversation reflects the casual sexism and racism of their culture.

Crews also provides ammunition for misogynist charges in depicting women as sex objects whose physical perfection exists for the gratification of men. These women represent the adolescent male fantasy of the ideal female: young, lean, leggy, tanned, and perky-breasted. Stereotypes *are* easy to find among the cheerleaders and beauty queens.

And yet, Crews can show empathy in describing women's relationships with their own bodies. This is evident in *Body*. Earline has been plagued by fat since childhood.

Although she believes her obesity makes her unattractive to men, she sees beauty in herself. When she studies herself, naked, in the mirror, she appreciates herself:

> She stared a long time at the slightly reddish triangle of hair where it grew thick and curling at the base of her belly. How lovely and silky it was. . . . It made her feel pretty.
> And she did not often feel pretty. The slightly reddish hair seemed to glow not with reflected light but with a light of its own and it made her feel pretty even if both her breasts were under her arms and her dimpled thighs cleaved one to the other all the way to her knees. (92)

Earline's appreciation for her physique is enhanced by Billy Bat's attention, but does not derive solely from it. Crews's depiction of this obese woman, so far from the "ideal," is never derisive, and rather sympathetic.

Critics who focus on Crews's more dangerous female characters infer that the author believes women endanger men. But the risks such characters pose are not solely to men. Hester, in *Gypsy*, does disrupt the cozy masculine community of Fireman's Gym. But it is not clear that her destructiveness results from hatred for men. Instead, it seems to grow out of her madness, out of a perverse need to stir things up, to relieve boredom. She is also cruel to her parents and she hopes to destroy herself.

Another figure who seems to be man-destroying is Charity, in *The Knockout Artist*. Charity has been terminated from a doctoral program in psychology, yet she persists in writing the ultimate treatise on madness. With a tape recorder running nearby, she interviews her "subject," a boxer named Eugene Biggs, while they have sex, when he is most vulnerable. Promising confidentiality, Charity coaxes from Eugene his deepest secrets and fears. Eventually, Eugene discovers her deception; she intends to publish the humiliating material using his name. Like Hester, however, Charity does not pose a threat to men *per se*. Late in the novel, she turns her sexual and research attentions to Jake Purcell, a lesbian who prostitutes herself to men. Charity has the potential to ruin women as well.

In Crews's novels, the sexes *are* different. As "the Other," women attract and threaten men. Men's language often bespeaks a deeply-rooted sexism. Against this background, Crews's avowed sympathy for feminism seems disingenuous. But the novels are not patriarchal tracts. Not all women are completely dominated by men. And while men frequently abuse women, they are not confident that abuse is justifiable. (In *Feast*, for example, Joe Lon beats Elfie but is ashamed; he hides the abuse by claiming she is clumsy.) Crews's women are often unabashedly sexual, uninhibited. Unconstrained by traditional morality, many of them control their own sexual expression. Still, they use sex for conventional ends—to manipulate men. Ultimately, they are not independent of men.

When Crews's women seek success in masculine domains (bodybuilding, karate, business) they fail, in one way or another. Perhaps Crews accepts a gender-based "natural order" in which women must "revert to type." But another interpretation is possible. For *most* of Crews's characters, hopes are unrealized, goals are unattained. Success is illusory, and self-determination is elusive for both men and women. In modern society, *people* fail. Attempts to overcome poverty, to surmount cultural barriers, are frustrated. Emphasizing individualism and unrealistic goals, modern society defeats both sexes.

Harry Crews's Home Place

An Excursion into Wiregrass Country and the Carnivalesque

Jerrilyn McGregory

W iregrass Country haunts Harry Crews's life and fiction like the specters and ghosts its residents deliciously conjure up as a quotidian part of their lives.[1] Harry Crews entitled his acclaimed memoir, *A Childhood: The Biography of a Place*. Bacon County, Georgia, is his birthplace, and it is situated within a little known region of the South, Wiregrass Country. This region historically deviated from much of the Deep South. Unlike the Black Belt, it was predominately white and its economic and cultural development originally was shaped more by yeoman farmers and frontier attitudes than by King Cotton, plantations, slaves, and aristocrats. Bacon County is located near the nucleus of Wiregrass Georgia. To attribute the eclecticism of Crews's prose to mere Southernness misses its specific articulation of place. Harry Crews is a son of the Wiregrass region, a land steeped in its own aberrations.

The Wiregrass has long been a marginalized space within a larger liminality. Significantly, no Civil War battles occurred within this vast region. Even the harbinger of the New South, economic exploitation came late. Agricultural diversification became its theme as this part of the South momentously turned to other market crops besides cotton. Farmers began to produce peanuts, tobacco, or even pecan trees. The tobacco farm—which ultimately claimed the life of the writer's youthful father, Ray Crews—is representative of this diversity trend. His father faced the stress from relatively unprecedented economic hardship in comparison to his predecessors. When sharecropping came to the region, it replaced a tradition of land ownership.

These proud but poor sons of landowners became dependent on a single cash crop in a changing economy, which made the acquisition of a traditionally designated home place more of an impossible dream. In *Childhood*, Crews, himself, assesses the *home place* "as vital and necessary as the beating of your own heart. It is that single house where you were born, where you lived out your childhood, where you grew into young manhood. It is your anchor in the world, that place, along with the memory of your kinsmen at the long supper table every night and the knowledge that it would always exist, if nowhere but in memory" (14). Thus, as descendents of yeomen farmers, the disillusioned Wiregrass sharecroppers' fate merged belatedly with the shared experiences of many other southern poor whites.

Crews's literature is a by-product of his own sociocultural inheritance. Frank Shelton presents Crews best, taking into full consideration his social position. Shelton identifies Crews as being "absolutely unique among Southern writers in that he writes about life from the perspective of the poor white" (47). William Moss, in "Postmodern Georgia Scene," argues for Crews's unique contribution, differentiating him from Southern grotesque literature. He perceptively writes that "Crews departs significantly from the tradition; he shares the vision neither of Caldwell nor of O'Connor" (39). Unlike Crews, Erskine Caldwell and Flannery O'Connor were born in the historic heartland of Georgia. As this essay stipulates, Crews's departure is a matter of a distinctive regionalized and social class identity.

While some literary critics struggle to position Crews within the paradigm of the southern gothic-grotesque school of fiction,[2] others point out the distinctiveness of his use. Walter Sullivan, in a 1969 review of *The Gospel Singer*, for example, comments that Crews asks his grotesque images "to carry more symbolic weight than [they] can comfortably hold." Similarly, Allen Shepherd in *Critique* remarks that "self-indulgent grotesqueries" (60) mar the typical Crews novel. In the *Dictionary of Literary Biography*, Shepherd also indicates that typically Crews's novels are criticized as "gratuitously violent, generally heartless, and occupied exclusively by freaks" (69). Here, he enumerates some of the excesses of carnival. To deconstruct a monolithic reading of southern literature, one might suggest that Crews's fiction is not just grotesque, but carnivalesque.

In accordance with the Russian literary theorist, Mikhail Bakhtin, Crews's images exist in polar opposition to all that is refined, pretentious, and doctrinaire (3).[3] As the region's major scribe and tradition bearer, Crews restores the carnivalesque principles of the culture of folk humor, relying foremost on images of grotesque realism. Crews's vision is indebted to folk cultural expressions. In *Childhood*, he writes, "I had already learned—without knowing I'd learned it—that every single thing in the world was full of mystery and awesome power. And it was only by right ways of doing things—ritual ways—that kept any of us safe" (90). It is as a result of this background that Crews's writing works against bourgeois cultural forms. Bakhtin likens the carnivalesque in literature to the kinds of activity that often takes place in the carnivals of folk culture, particularly the overturning and lampooning of traditional hierarchies and values by mingling "high culture" with the profane. An assault against conventionality, then, represents the essence of Crews's creative imagination.

Moreover, Medieval European carnivals developed out of a pagan past. The Renaissance writer Rabelais recaptured carnivalesque culture of the medieval world; and, in his literary studies, Bakhtin simultaneously commemorated the freedom of the Russian Revolution in opposition to Stalin's reign. Today, it is Crews amassing a folk cultural domain specific to the Wiregrass region to disrupt official American institutionalized value orientations. Forms like the novel provide a space for such carnivalization, and as a result allow for alternative voices within the text. This, for Bakhtin, is the site of resistance to the authority of literary culture and the place where cultural, and potentially political, change can take place.

In opposition to bourgeois cultural forms, Crews depends on aspects of folk humor endemic to his regional identity and particular social class. In *The Politics and Poetics of Transgression*, Peter Stallybrass and Allon White explicate Bakhtin and how carnivalesque activities readily fall within the cultural domain of a segment of the populace deemed vulgar, superstitious, and crude (9). For uninitiated readers, Crews is likewise deemed crude. A Bakhtinian reading of his two most popular novels will elaborate the role excess plays. Beginning with *The Gospel Singer*, Crews's first novel, the title character assails piety, also the target of carnival activities. As Bakhtin accentuates, religion constitutes one of the formal institutions that carnival forms parody (7).

The Gospel Singer records the exploits of an unnamed protagonist, who relies on his angelic appearance and inherently rich singing voice to escape the fated life of a

Wiregrass pig farmer. Yet, it is his ritualistic visits which seal his fate. "He didn't like to think of why he returned again and again to Enigma, more or less on the half-year mark" (51). Wiregrass Country is a locale, too, where the all night gospel sing has a long continuous history. Communities like Waycross, Georgia, fill football stadiums and convention centers to capacity for sacred music performances. Crews carnivalizes these events. Bakhtin indicates that degradation is a principle element of grotesque realism, which translates into diminishing all that is usually elevated including the spiritual (19).

The Gospel Singer's chauffeur-driven Cadillac, ranch home purchase, and other gifts to his family speak to the protagonist's achievement of a material sense of reality, while insinuating a spiritual one to his followers. In actuality, his carnival disguise masks an insatiable satyr. As another carnivalesque motif, the body attains freedom in pleasure normally withheld. For each carnal act, the Gospel Singer must pay a penance, repetitively sing a sacred hymn. The penance, humorously rendered as allocated by his murderous chauffeur Didymus, denotes the singer's "Saving Graces." For example, as characteristically accomplished, "He took off his clothes placed them neatly on hangers, and put them in the closet. Then he got into the closet with them, naked, and closed the door. He knelt between his coat and trousers. He opened his mouth and let out his voice" (71). This representation of a religious travesty is consistent with the carnivalesque spirit.

The novel's setting is in a Georgia town called Enigma, which signifies the quandary of those readers who expect the canonical, grotesque southern images only to confront Crews's Freak Fair and other carnivalized representations. Images of the grotesque concept of the body forms another constitutive element inherent to carnival. Grotesque body imagery, Bakhtin establishes, traditionally represents "why all that is bodily becomes grandiose, exaggerated, immeasurable" (19). Literally, a carnival-type Freak Fair travels in tandem with the public appearances of the Gospel Singer. Its proprietor, Foot, is described as being "fully twenty-seven inches high and eighteen inches broad under the toes" (203). Crews in true carnival form privileges the lower bodily stratum (feet, knees, legs, buttocks, genitals, belly, and anus). Some of the other wonders include: the Thing who "had arms that looked like legs and legs that looked like arms and a short square head jammed so deeply into its body that half its face was hidden behind collarbone" (36); and a Geek who "can eat a live chicken in three minutes, feathers and all. Peel a snake like a banana and eat it before you can say boo" (42). Crews's freaks, then, are a required part of a larger carnivalesque impression.

In addition, Crews consistently employs a literary technique dependent on structural inversion commonly associated with carnival. Another constitutive element of carnival is the depiction of a topsy-turvy world turned upside down. In the reversible world inscribed by Crews, pigs inhabit the private domain of humans while the gospel singer's followers, who are camped outside, wallow in the mud. Ironically, the Gospel Singer's sanctification occurs because his arrival in town coincides with a deluge of rain, which breaks a longstanding drought. His presence at his parents' upscale ranch-style home draws local residents on a pilgrimage in which they camp-out in the downpour, while inside, Didymus comments "They've got hogs in the seventy thousand-dollar house" (70). Furthermore, the town's proclaimed virginal spirit and his first convert, MaryBell Carter, is his whore, whom the Gospel Singer personally has trained to perform every act of sexual perversion. Crews writes, "And just to the degree that her sexual outrages with him became more numerous, the more her reputation for virtue in the community seemed to grow" (156). Upon his final ritualistic return, the Gospel Singer learns that Willalee Bookatee, (an African American who bears the name of Harry Crews's personal boyhood companion) is accused of her murder and is already resigned to the certainty of being lynched.

Not merely "gratuitous violence," but Southern folk justice reigns supreme. The Wiregrass region holds no special patent on violence but is prone to it in keeping with its isolation and frontier past. Bacon County, Georgia, possesses a single town, its county seat, Alma. But communities with names like Scuffletown typify the region. As my research discovered, reportedly, one "could identify his friends by the sound of their pistols as we identify now by the honk of automobile horns. Men carried pistols to town, parties, and to church" (70). Within such a context, violent acts are normative. *The Gospel Singer* articulates how much geographical and socioeconomic space remains outside a universalizing utopian fantasy of a homogeneous America.

The scenes leading to the denouement authenticate the innate resistance of the culture of folk humor to degenerate into innocuous revelry. A festive atmosphere permeates the novels as street vendors, the freak fair, and a television crew invade Enigma: "Hiram's brother Cash, who owned Enigma Seed and Feed, had sent out to Tifton for a cotton candy-making machine and across the street from the Funeral Parlor children sat on the edge of the wooden sidewalk eating tall pink sugar cones" (167). Additionally, over two-thirds of the audience are outsiders, more representative of Bakhtin's "official culture." Crews writes "And of the entire audience, at the moment, they were the angriest. They were wet, their good shoes were ruined, they were tired. And none of them was sure the Gospel Singer was going to prove to be a large enough entertainment to offset their uncomfortableness. They could have gone to a nice dry movie or stayed home and watched television" (231). Yet, when the sacred context turns profanely violent, the visitors become one with the "carnivalesque crowd."[4]

Lynching constitutes a time-honored Southern ritual act, a sort of grotesque cleansing operation. Although the term "lynching" is organically used to describe these extralegal acts of violence, a more sanitized hanging, shooting, or beating seldom comprised the extent of the ordeal. As in the case of Willalee's castration, "Blood poured from a wound between his legs" (238). Southern lynchings speak to another kind of symbolic action, the social drama.[5] Law enforcement officers like Sheriff Lucas knew their perfunctory, duplicitous roles well: "The boys gone treat him [Willalee] like he treated Marybell. And they subject to treat anybody that gits between them and him the same way" (189). This comment is froth with irony, the Gospel Singer, himself, succumbs when "He turned on the people of Enigma," (235) both literally and figuratively. He rejects the form of reaggregation they demand—his sanctification. Instead, ironically, it is his lynching that supplies the necessary balm. As historian Frank Tannenbaum avers, "After the lynching the community settles back to a state of quiet. . . . It helps one to come to grips with the world; it stabilizes the existence of the unfortunate community" (26).

Some aspects never change but may be transgressed in a racialized America such as the archetypal castration and lynching of an alleged Black rapist. As manifestations in a world chock full of grotesqueries, Crews's representation of African Americans rarely distances them from past literary stereotypes. These stereotypical notions stand to give definition to those "naked Americans" who perpetuate them.[6] Crews's narrators inevitably maintain a dehumanizing social discourse about African Americans, but actual events commonly belie them. A reluctant evangelist, the Gospel Singer is deified into a savior and could literally save Willalee by giving supportive testimony, which ironically never comes. Crews's African American characters typically lack agency and, by inference, must humanize themselves. The defrocking of the Gospel Singer and the synchronous lynching of him and Willalee conform to the noncanonical text which is carnival.

In *A Feast of Snakes*, Crews relates how rattlesnake roundups also have a special place in the Wiregrass region. For instance, Claxton, Georgia, on the second Saturday in every March, promotes its event as "the beauty and the beast" competition. The main events take place in a tobacco warehouse where snakes and beauties are simultaneously judged. A calculation of the snakes rounded up and the coronation of the queen occur concurrently. The objectification of both are powerful symbols in the context of the Biblical Eden. Moreover, Crews embarks on a carnivalesque course, by which current versions pale in Wiregrass Country. Present-day examples are more tame but still form a semiotic relationship. Covering one long weekend, Mystic, Georgia's Annual Rattlesnake Roundup offers a descriptive catalogue of carnivalesque motifs.

At this year's roundup, Hard Candy Sweet is dethroned by a new Miss Rattlesnake queen. Crews is disparaged for his depiction of women in his fiction,[7] and most are routinely portrayed as beauty queens. Once again, as my research on Wiregrass festivals indicates, allowances must be made for a regional obsession (109–11). Claxton's Rattlesnake Roundup Parade, for example, features over a dozen pageant queens, who had variously won titles such as Miss Gum Spirit and Turpentine, Miss Georgia Sweet Onion, Miss Liberty County, Miss Coastal Georgia, Miss Pinewood Christian Academy, or Miss Forestry Queen. These pageants signify the intensity of interest in regional, state, and national beauty competitions in this region. Given the status and roles of women in the region, for some, such titles represent the pinnacle of success, another carnivalesque inversion. This elevation of self, of course, is dependent on the objectification of one's self.

Crews's depiction of the constitutive elements of rattlesnake roundup can be explained in Bakhtinian terms: "As opposed to the official feast, one might say that carnival celebrates temporary liberation from the prevailing truth of the established order; it marks the suspension of all hierarchichal rank, privileges, norms and prohibitions" (109). Poncy is an example of structural inversion involving the collapse of hierarchies. A retired sales director, Poncy enters into a sadomasochistic relationship with the festival in-crowd. Taken on a madcap ride in the backseat of his own car that makes him nauseous, "Poncy, sitting with the little green puddle in his lap, tried to say something authoritative to them about abusing his car, after all he was old enough to be their father and there was no reason for him to take all this and not let them know what they were in for if they wrecked his Porsche or hurt him" (102). In true carnival fashion, Poncy's degradation continues inside the bar as he cannot control his bowels on the dance floor. Since no carnival revelry is complete without allusions to filth, the novel's early references to Johnny-on-the-spots should signal our entree into this world of folk humor. Scenes involving vomit and excrement are heavily sanctioned.

In *Popular Culture in Early Modern Europe*, Peter Burke delineates "three major themes in Carnival, real and symbolic: food, sex, and violence" (186). *A Feast* reveals their interlocking relationship in keeping with the forms of exaggeration that Bakhtin characterized as essential to displays of grotesque realism. He cites "for instance, gigantic sausages [being] carried by dozens of men" (63). Likewise, Crews presents a spectacle of crazed revelers displaying countless varieties of snakes adding to the carnivalesque tonality: "Almost everyone had brought pet snakes to the hunt. Mostly they were constrictors and black snakes and water snakes. They carried the snakes around with them, passing them from hand to hand, comparing them, describing their habits and disclosing their names" (52–3). Snakes and sausages represent edible cuisine while simultaneously alluding to a phallocentrism that portends violence. Such scenes operate as normative within the festive world and are emblematic of events to come.

The book's title manifests itself literally as a gloss for another sacred parody, the feast of fools. According to Bakhtin, "The feast of fools is one of the most colorful and genuine expressions of medieval festive laughter" (78). Hours before the hunt, Joe Lon graphically skins these reptiles to be cooked for a snake steak supper with his soused retinue of friends. The snake steak supper interrogates the ubiquitous banquet imagery endemic to depictions of festive forms. Bakhtin elaborates on the roles eating and drinking play as salient features pertaining to the grotesque body (281). Joe Lon devours the snake "without being devoured himself," (281) but he is being eaten up by his own ennui. He is "choking on both snake and the thought that he had spent his time and life selling nigger whiskey and watching Elfie's teeth fall out" (114).

Outside of pulp fiction, few literary works parallel the ubiquitous act of sexual perversion Crews prepares on the heel of this "last supper." Joe Lon's guests, by distracting his wife, Elfie, aid and abet his act of adulterous debauchery with his ex-girlfriend, Berenice, while his children sleep nearby. In a scene which can best be equated with the promiscuity and fervor of carnival, Joe Lon cynically expresses that *true* love, "goddam *true* love is taking it out of your ass and sticking it in you mouth" (121). In conformity with his concept of the grotesque image of the body, Bakhtin highlights the centrality of the gaping jaw to all the main organs and physical acts (339). Contributing to Joe Lon violently running amok, Elfie later misreads his abusive act with Berenice and yearns to prove her "true love." As Bakhtin contends, the fusion of abuse and praise are core elements of the carnivalesque language (415).

In addition, Stallybrass and White point out that "It is in fact striking how frequently violent social clashes apparently 'coincide' with carnival" (14). Excess rules. As part of the subtext, the town sheriff, Buddy Matlow, a physically mangled Vietnam War vet, usurps his power and sexually assaults women prisoners. However, he expresses "true love" for Lottie Mae, an African American woman, whom he has incarcerated. She cracks under the pressure of having to make the nightmarish choice between sharing her cell with a snake or Buddy. Buddy responds, " 'Ain't it a God's wonder what a snake can do for love?' " (38). Encouraged by Beeder, Joe Lon's reclusive sister who is a psychotic victim of an unrestrained patriarchal system, Lottie Mae is admonished to "Kill it" (70). Buddy's practically last glibly spoken words are "these goddam snakes already about run me crazy" (127). Such irony is bound to be lost in the carnivalesque mood of a reversible world in which a white man suffers castration by a razor wielding African American woman. Phallic symbols lose their subtlety by the time Buddy exposes himself: "It was the snake she had been waiting for, that she had been preparing for since that morning in Beeder's room" (129).

When festive revelers require official constraints, a triumvirate of drunken jocks—Willard Miller, Coach Tump, and Joe Lon—emerge as town leaders. Representing in Bakhtinian terms a "hierarchy of fools," this motley crew alludes to the inversion of the power structure in many small Southern communities to include those elements that only ascend during carnival elsewhere. Making a "fool of himself" (16) comprises one of Joe Lon's abiding fears in the hours leading up to the roundup. When bedlam erupted during the beauty pageant, Joe Lon abdicates his role and departs while the others "kicked and stomped and gouged and by God made sure Novella Watkins was crowned just like everbody known she ought to be" (153). Here, Crews lampoons those, of a "lowly" nature, who are elevated in hierarchical rank by default.

All the foregoing acts coexist within a sustained humorous tone. In his autobiography, Crews writes, "No matter how awful the stories were that the men told they were always funny" (94). Literary critic Shelton describes forms and functions of this mode of carnival laughter—"the laughter is directed at a corrupt so-called normal society" (48). Depending largely on irony, much of what Crews writes generates what Bakhtin calls "reduced laughter" (135). The most genuine laughter, however, comes at the expense of the elites, especially the town doctor and Shep, Berenice's preppy college sweetheart. For example, despite his condition, Buddy manages to drive to the doctor's residence. "In a little voice that was cracked and whining, Shep said: 'Somebody's cut his dick off.' He turned to the doctor for his statement to be denied but the doctor was already sliding to the floor in a faint" (136).

In the Bakhtinian sense, death constitutes a "funny monstrosity" (51). From the moment Shep arrives at the site of the dog fight (another ludic roundup event) to deliver Buddy's dying words to Joe Lon, who's one of the dog handlers, images of grotesque realism virtually erupt. As the result of a culmination of incidents, "Joe Lon started to howl" (159). Meanwhile, Big Joe (his father) and "the other dog owner were on their feet and Big Joe was calling to Joe Lon not to go crazy like his sister did" (159). In a miraculous recovery, Joe Lon resumes his official duties the next day at the rattlesnake hunt, where he encounters Poncy who masochistically proclaims, "'I'd rather be here on this hill with these snakes and you,' he said, 'than anywhere else in the world'" (175). In accordance with Bakhtin, hell comprises the most terrifying grotesque image, being representative of "the world which swallows up" (91). Thus, when Joe Lon's metamorphoses into a mass murderer and is hurled into the devouring snake pit, his death epitomizes a form of victory over fear. The final inversion being Joe Lon's sinking from his manly height to a level of hysteria long associated with women. Beeder and Lottie Mae "watching" bear witness to his fall (177).

In his own way, Crews operates as an active tradition bearer of the culture of folk humor via his literature. Bakhtin describes the carnival-grotesque form as fulfilling several functions: "to consecrate inventive freedom, to permit the combination of a variety of different elements and their rapprochement, to liberate from the prevailing point of view of the world from conventions and established truths, from cliches, from all that is humdrum and universally accepted" (34). Allon White cautions against the propensity to locate the carnivalesque within bourgeois cultural forms (109). One would be asinine to situate Crews within the prevailing hegemony, which seeks to suppress competing points of view. He, like Rabelais, garners authenticity by positioning his fiction within the "carnivalesque crowd" in opposition to the status quo.

Until acquiring an author like Crews, Wiregrass Country abounded with oral storytellers but lacked literary scribes. Although the South has more regions than any other part of the country, the Wiregrass is certainly the least referenced of them all. Harry Crews sallies forth as a local raconteur, weaving cautionary tales about contemporary lives devoid of meaning. When literary critics deploy the term "grotesque," in the context of Crews, now they must liberate its usage and allow for more carnivalesque interpretations.

THE GRIT ÉMIGRÉ IN
HARRY CREWS'S FICTION

Matthew Guinn

A s one of the foremost contemporary practitioners of the southern grotesque, Harry Crews presides over a literary terrain that seethes with tension and the constant threat of violence. As an artist who has known the South as a land of both rural poverty and Sunbelt opulence, Crews deftly chronicles the cultural shift of a region through the voices of a people left behind by prosperity. The result is a sprawling Rabelaisian vision that combines keen urban satire with grotesque frontier violence.

Yet as a young writer, Crews's struggle to discover his own literary voice was more arduous than most. As he revealed in a 1976 article for his "Grits" column in *Esquire* magazine, Crews found that his literary aspirations clashed with his humble origins. Writing of a period in the nineteen sixties when he was still unpublished, Crews relates staring in desperation at boxes of rejected manuscripts—five novels and hundreds of short stories—and realizing that he was, in his words, "a twenty-four karat fake" ("Television" 128). Ashamed of his background as a tenant farmer's son in "the worst hookworm-and-rickets part of Georgia," Crews had been working at a body of fiction written, he says, "out of a fear and loathing for what I was and who I was. It was all out of an effort to pretend otherwise" (128).

Crews terms the insight that followed "the only revelation of my life," the "dead-solid conviction" that "All I had going for me in the world or would ever have was that swamp, all those goddamn mules, all those screwworms that I'd dug out of pigs and all the other beautiful and dreadful and sorry circumstances that had made me the grit I am and will always be. Once I realized that the way I saw the world and man's condition in it would always be exactly and inevitably shaped by everything which up to that moment had only shamed me, once I realized that, I was home free" (128). Crews's revelation was a fortunate one; in the years since his epiphany he has produced fifteen novels and four collections of nonfiction that authoritatively explore the demesne of the lower-class southern white, and created an artistic viewpoint Frank W. Shelton has called "absolutely unique among Southern writers" (47).

Indeed, Crews's success as a novelist has hinged upon his relationship to the term 'grit'; rather than viewing the word as an epithet, he has accepted the moniker with pride. By drawing on his origins as the catalyst for his fiction, he has given voice to a people represented in previous southern literature solely by outside observers as varied as George Washington Harris and Erskine Caldwell. As Shelton notes, Crews writes "from *within* the class, not by observing it from without, the traditional perspective of white Southern writers" (47). And Crews's firsthand experience entails an immediate sympathy. Consider his comment in a recent *Georgia Review* interview: "what the rest of the country call 'rednecks' I call 'Grits.' . . . And in my lexicon, anyway, they have a great respect for values, for family, and for whatever virtues you wish to name" (Lytal and Russell 540).

Crews's discovery of indigenous source material for art seems to echo Faulkner's inexhaustible "postage stamp of native soil" (Meriwether 225). Yet one must keep in mind that for Crews, the rural experience is tainted with failure and consequently, mobility. In contrast to Yoknapatawpha County's role as a geographical locus, the Bacon County, Georgia, of Crews's childhood was a sort of jumping-off point. Farmers worked the land in Bacon County precariously, and when crops failed (as they often did), they traversed the roughly one hundred miles south to Jacksonville, Florida, to seek work in the city. Crews's family was no exception. After his parents separated when he was six years old, he accompanied his brother and mother to Jacksonville so that his mother could find work in one of the factories there. As

Crews relates in *A Childhood: The Biography of a Place*, such a journey was almost anticipated: "I knew absolutely, without knowing how I knew it, that something called the Springfield Section of Jacksonville was where all of us from Bacon County went, when we had to go, when our people and our place could no longer sustain us" (128). Thus for Crews Bacon County looms as an imaginative terrain, a formative amalgam of land and people which retains its power not in a tangible presence, but in the domain of memory.

Throughout Crews's fiction, these concerns are explored by means of a recurrent character type, which I will call the grit émigré. Like their author, many of Crews's characters are dislocated agrarian figures who migrate from various fictional locales in south Georgia to the Sunbelt industrial centers of north Florida. These grit émigré characters perhaps best represent the tensions that characterize Crews's work in general. As strangers to the urban setting, the rural emigrants embody the outsider perspective that colors his fiction as they attempt (like Crews himself) to reconcile their status as "grits" in a changing cultural landscape. Like the "freak" characters for which Crews is notorious, the grit émigrés struggle with the anxiety of separation and dislocation. Disconnected from the familiar rural landscape, they find themselves in alien urban situations and struggle to adapt themselves effectively. This struggle is often abortive. With no cultural antecedents as guides to behavior, their attempts to adapt to new environments often devolve into grotesque violence. As members of the dramatis personae of Crews's grotesque southern landscape, the grit émigrés form a trenchant example of the author's fixation on the convergence of the pre- and post-industrial South.[1]

Crews's fascination with the interstice between the rural and the urban is apparent in his first published novel, *The Gospel Singer* (1968). The novel centers upon the nearly-universal desire of its characters to escape the rural poverty of Enigma, Georgia. The Gospel Singer himself has been driven to success by "the prospect of getting out of Enigma"—a dream that has "sweetened his life and cheered his soul" (94). From the pinnacle of his successful career, the Gospel Singer realizes that the people of Enigma "were not his kind, and had not been since he had found the gospel singing voice and probably were not even before that" (51). One character phrases the problem in larger philosophical terms: "There are Enigmas all over this country, all over the world, and men everywhere are struggling to get out of them" (207–8).

The ambivalence the Gospel Singer feels on his return to Enigma would become one of the central dramatic tensions of the grit émigré novels to follow. As Crews has developed and refined his treatment of this ambivalence, his characters have become more sophisticated, and his treatment of them more uniquely his own. The emergence of the grit émigré character, building on the model of Crews's first protagonist, seems now to have been concurrent with Crews's own relinquishment of artistic influence: the grit émigré began to appear at the same time that Crews began to move out from the shadow of Erskine Caldwell and others.[2] And as Crews's fiction has improved from early, flawed novels such as *This Thing Don't Lead to Heaven* (1970) to the later works, the grit émigré has been central to his development. The evolution of this character type has been as important to Crews's work as was his early discovery of the importance of his grit heritage. It has been the means by which Crews has harnessed an artistic talent which, like the Gospel Singer's voice, threatened to separate him from his origins. It is Crews's adherence to these origins, and his continuous exploration of them, that has been the source of his unique perspective in southern letters. Crews's unlikely literary career has been a model for a second, younger generation of lower-class white authors such as Larry Brown and Dorothy Allison; it is difficult to imagine this career enduring without the grit émigré.

The earliest of the grit émigrés, George Gattling of *The Hawk Is Dying* (1973), appears to have made a successful transition to urban life. An emigrant from the "rickets and hookworm" town of Bainbridge, Georgia, George's life in Gainesville, Florida, is far removed from his dirt-poor origins in south Georgia—he owns a large home and a thriving automobile upholstery business.

Yet George finds his existence in the city to be pervaded by abstraction, and he views his material success as little more than "the incomprehensible paraphernalia of his life" (21). George feels no sense of connection or purpose in Gainesville; removed from the farming culture of his youth, he senses that urban life is a pointless series of unessential motion. Unlike the concrete existence of the farm, life here is complex and alienating. He sees his upholstery business as ludicrously unimportant, and he feels himself "pushed here and there willy-nilly, without purpose" in an environment he cannot understand (106). When his nephew drowns in a freak accident, the anxiety that has been growing in George "slowly like a secret cancer for years" erupts into despair (20). George thinks: *"I'm at the end of my road. . . . Work hard, they say, and you'll be happy. Get a car, get a house, get a business, get money. Get get get get get get get. Well, I got. And now it's led me here where everything is a dead-end"* (70–71). As a newcomer to the city, George has adopted the urban ethic of acquisition. But faced with a family tragedy—and consequently the re-emergence of his former connections—he relinquishes the urban.

George throws himself into his hobby of capturing and training hawks with a new passion born out of desperation, aware now that it is the only means of rekindling a link with his agricultural past. Like farming, the ancient art of hawking, with its equal measures of brutality and precision, counteracts his anxiety by reducing experience to absolutes. Driven to desperation by the apparent mendacity of urban life, he believes the tangible pain and controlled violence of manning a hawk to be "the only thing . . . that could be reckoned as meaningful" because the pain of it "was real. It was not something you could call by another name" (21, 103). As George observes, the brutality of the manning process is anti-abstraction itself: "This pain was directed toward an end he could understand, and therefore it was bearable" (88). Further, the manning process exists outside of any economic or commercial sphere. As George observes, "It was not reasonable. It was not sensible. It made no money. . . . It did not get you ahead in the world" (199).

The immediacy of hawking echoes the rhythm of the agricultural labor of George's youth as he returns to a personal interaction with nature. When he turns to making leather hoods for the hawk, he finds himself "focused on the hawk in a way that he had never been focused on anything before" (217). An employee suggests that George sew the hawk's hoods on the industrial machines of the upholstery shop, but George will not have his labor abstracted from him and performed on machines. Instead of crafting Naugahyde into seatcovers, he works leather with his own hands into a necessary product, returning to the tempo of craftsmanship. If the purpose of his work is no longer for physical survival (as with farming) it is a necessary means of avoiding spiritual extinction in the city. As an austringer, George affects a symbolic return to the cadences and meaning of agricultural labor; he comes to understand his place in a natural relationship as regenerative and transformative. After weeks of training, he finally flies the hawk over his nephew's grave, forging for himself a return to blood and nature, to vitality and freedom.

The Knockout Artist (1988) continues Crews's exploration of the city as an alienating environment. Like Crews himself, Eugene Biggs had left the family farm and done "what the people in South Georgia had been doing since the Great Depression. . . . He got on the Greyhound bus and went to Jacksonville, Florida" (18). The prize fighting career that Eugene begins in Jacksonville culminates in a crushing defeat in New Orleans, where Eugene, deserted by his trainer, remains. Capitalizing on his own glass jaw, he learns to knock himself out, and begins to exploit the last vestige of his former prowess for economic survival. His bizarre act is popular with the New Orleans underworld; he commands high prices performing for the subculture he calls "the stinking, hairy underbelly of New Orleans" (78). In a grotesque inversion of the boxer's performance role, Eugene becomes the object of voyeuristic perversity—the once-transcendent athlete as sideshow freak.

Eugene's perception of New Orleans is typical of the grit émigré's response to the metropolis. The city is as alien to him as a foreign country, and in his letters home he relays anecdotes to his father as if writing from an exotic culture. He experiences the city as an outsider, marveling at its international tourists and commercial excess, the seedy subculture of Bourbon Street, and the effects of industry on the Louisiana landscape. He observes smoldering chemical plants on the Mississippi River; the pollution in "the calm, lovely cobalt water" of Lake Pontchartrain provokes him to think of fish "cancerous with chemicals, their scaly backs spotted with open, spongy ulcers" (237). Like so much of what he has encountered since leaving Georgia, the lake contains a repulsive underside pregnant with possibilities for grotesque meditation.

The corruption Eugene perceives in his surroundings elicits in him a sharp nostalgia for his agrarian childhood, and he frequently seeks out connections to home. He enjoys New Orleans beignets because they evoke poignant memories of his mother's kitchen and the Sunday afternoons of his childhood, and he writes home habitually. He is drawn to the New Orleans Farmers' Market because the familiar produce and tempo of the place console him, even as he contemplates its close proximity to the seediness of the French Quarter. His slow walks through the Market remind him of the crops he harvested in the past, producing lyrical internal monologues in which he longs to be "back on the land," where "people talked straight and where things were what they seemed, where he could see unfolding plants break ground in spring and grow green and lush until harvest" (92). The pastoral language of Eugene's reverie is powerful.

But Crews's hardened realism prohibits a romanticized notion of farm life, and Eugene is snapped back into reality by his father's letters. The marginally literate letters the elder Biggs writes denigrate the Arcadian image, and remind Eugene and the reader of the hardscrabble reality of agricultural life:

Dear Eugene
Your brother broke his arm an is off work til it is heeled up if it ever does and its been no rain here for so long I bout forgot what it looks like. the crops is burning up on the feeled an you ma has been sick in bed near bout 2 weeks with the female

trouble. 4 of the calfs has got the scours an two of them have shit there selfs to death.
eugene we are all of us fine an hope you are the same.

....

mebbe it will rain soon an you brothers arm will heel up if it ever does and your ma
will git over the female trouble but I guess them two calfs that shit theirselfs to death
is gone forever.

love daddy. (54)

Hardly the correspondence of a gentleman farmer, Mr. Biggs's letter awakens Eugene
from his nostalgia. He concludes that his fantasy of returning to Bacon County and
buying a good farm is "just so much bullshit." He has "become someone else" in
the city, a process he sees as "irreversible" (92).

As a transformed grit émigré, Eugene views a return to the land as untenable—he
is too much changed by urban life to return to the farm. Yet he chooses to leave
New Orleans and repudiate his knockout act. He settles on the single word "No"
as the perfect reaction to the city as he has found it in New Orleans. A "huge, warm
cocoon of a word, wrapping and holding, serving to affirm and deny in the same
instant," the simple negative expression undercuts the entire abstraction of city life
and the knockout performance and connects him to a realism that can accept his
concrete, flawed humanity (262). Finally Eugene has discovered something legitimate that is solid and self-determining: "He only meant No. It was one of the few
utterly clear moments in his life when he was able to say exactly what he meant,
exactly" (261–62).

"No" is significant to the evolution of the grit émigré theme because it directly
addresses the industrial ideology that confronts the rural emigrants in the city. The
word stands in sharp contrast to the rhetoric that George Gattling had largely inter-
nalized, and Eugene's rapturous discovery of the word differs sharply from the anxiety George feels pervasively. Importantly, the word "No" is free of external
influences—it belongs solely to Eugene—and it represents a decision made by the
individual acting outside of urban ideological influences. While George's philosophy
of the work ethic is imposed on him by external forces, Eugene's simple word
hearkens back to the absolutes of rural existence and pure survival. Stripped of empty
rhetoric, it is the necessary step toward autonomous action, toward leaving the city
behind. Even though his departure from the city lacks the specific objectives and
promise of George's work with the hawk, his exodus is tentatively hopeful. By putting him in uncharted territory, it suggests possibilities not limited strictly to the
rural or the urban, an existence in the irresolute present with a consciousness of the

past. The redemptive quality of "No" lies in its search for alternatives; "No" confirms the existence of other options.

The urban carnival of *Body* (1990) posits a rural emigrant at the center of a struggle for identity as Shereel Dupont, a grit émigré from Waycross, joins other bodybuilders at the Ms. Cosmos contest in Miami. Here she finds herself at the pinnacle of her athletic career, for in the years since leaving Georgia she has shaped her body in anticipation of taking home a world title at the event. Her goals resemble those of Crews as a frustrated young writer: she hopes to join an international culture, but her ambivalent attitude toward her rural background confuses her. Without the benefit of precedent, she is working toward the unknown. The arrival of her family at the event threatens an intrusion of her grit past into the glamorous world of bodybuilding, however, and she feels herself at the center of a tense convergence between two disparate cultures. Her struggle for a reconciled identity becomes the novel's central conflict.

Shereel's bodybuilding career has been marked by the cultivation of a new post-grit identity, the eradication of her background and the creation of an idealized self worthy of the abstract title "Ms. Cosmos." Her trainer, Russell Morgan, has forced her to lose her Georgia accent and he has changed her given name from Dorothy Turnipseed to Shereel Dupont. As Russell says, "Nobody named Dorothy Turnipseed could ever be Ms. Cosmos" (20). Indeed, the clash between the names Dupont and Turnipseed is a strong one, and it emphasizes the difference between Shereel's old and new identities. "Turnipseed" evokes agricultural images of the less bucolic variety, but "Shereel Dupont" is highly suggestive; the "she" in the first name implies a universal feminine appeal, while "Dupont" connotes a parallel to the archetypal industrial company, the epitome of big business—and thus to commodity. "Shereel Dupont" is less a name than a title or brand name, and Russell and Shereel craft an appropriate model bodybuilder without a past or any other connections except to bodybuilding. The ahistorical, commercial aspect of Shereel's stage persona approaches the abstract to such a degree that one character asks in disbelief, "How can Ms. Dupont be related to something called a Turnipseed?" (50).

Shereel's organic origins—flawed and humble despite her athletic achievements—resurface with the arrival of the anachronistic Turnipseed clan. The Turnipseeds' appearance at the contest signals an irruption of the past into Shereel's carefully ordered competitive world, a threat to her new identity. By reminding Shereel that her bodybuilding persona is an artificial construct, the Turnipseeds illuminate the disparity between urban and rural cultures, the fantastical and the actual.

They are confounded by Shereel's new name, and in true grit fashion, they view it as a betrayal of blood relations and historical connection. Her fiancé, Nail, is particularly disturbed by the stage name; he remains unconvinced that the new personality is harmless. He maintains the importance of tradition, and says, "We talkin' blood. Your mama and daddy ain't named you no Shereel Dupont" (65). Shereel tries to placate him about the change:

"Names don't mean a thing. I'm the same girl."
"Names mean everything and you ain't the same girl," he said. "But I guess that's just something else you'll have to learn the hard way." (125)

Shereel will find that names—and titles—do mean everything. The spaces between Turnipseed and Dupont, and between Shereel Dupont and Ms. Cosmos, are chasms to her, dangerous intervals without sure footing.

The bodybuilding competition brings her identity crisis to its crescendo. Shereel's "whole future, the rest of her life" rests solely upon the outcome of the competition (228). As she competes on-stage with her main rival, Shereel considers the magnitude of her devotion to the contest. Her thoughts cohere around the mental image of a ledger: "On one side of the ledger was winning and its consequences. . . . Shereel Dupont, Ms. Cosmos, was somebody, somebody to reckon with. As Ms. Cosmos, she saw her name on gyms, on food supplements, on sportswear. . . . On the other side of the ledger was the alternative to winning. And she did not know, could not imagine, the consequences of not winning. That side of the ledger was not only blank, it was dark . . ." (228–29). Shereel perceives that her commitment to an idealized, manufactured identity as Ms. Cosmos has been monolithic; as the novel's title implies, the singular pursuit of "body" has left no room for the cultivation of the soul. Unlike George Gattling and Eugene Biggs, she has no alternatives. The binary construction of the ledger symbolizes a complete break from the past, an utter lack of options. Her defeat in the Ms. Cosmos contest, her failure to attain the abstract self by which she has defined herself, leads her to suicide. Nail's observation about Shereel and the contest proves to be prophetic: "It's some hereabouts thinks she's a Dupont, whatever the hell that is" (65). With her historical connections severed, Shereel's inability to establish an identity ("whatever the hell a Dupont is") is devastating. Her self-destruction stems from the challenge that Crews surmounted as a young writer: the struggle for post-agrarian identity.

Body is the first of the grit émigré novels to end in defeat. It is also the first of these novels in which Crews's tone (barring the comedy of Mr. Biggs's letter) approaches condescension toward his rural personae. Crews makes much of the Turnip-seeds' Snopes-like mannerisms, at times rendering them in the same appalled tone that his city-dwelling character Russell Morgan uses. And the novel's conclusion seems to confirm the sense of mocking desperation in Crews's prose. Nail's final act of murder-suicide is a gesture of retribution against the city that has ruined Shereel, but it also results in the destruction of himself. It would seem that by 1990 Crews had given up on the project of integrating the country and the city in his work, that his new technical approaches to the grit émigré in tone and denouement indicated the end of this phase of his career—that Crews's own post-agrarian survival ultimately demanded the immolation of his persistent character type.

But the 1992 publication of *Scar Lover* signaled a more positive, and perhaps final, resolution of the grit émigré's struggle. While much of the novel conforms to the patterns I have already outlined, its conclusion merits attention. For Pete Butcher's actions differ from those of his predecessors: he ultimately forms a community of émigrés *within* the city. He does not isolate himself from family like George Gattling or strike out for new territory like Eugene Biggs; neither does he reject his connections in the manner of Shereel Dupont. Instead, he re-integrates himself with the people he left behind, joining himself to the community of displaced countrymen who have also migrated to the city. And unlike any of his predecessors, Pete begins to feel "totally at one with himself and the world" because of this new community, suggesting the beginnings of a new existence unbound by geography or sociology (273). Pete discovers that the true domain of the grit émigré lies beyond place. He comes to occupy "a place where blood is joined . . . where the blood that beats in one heart beats in another heart" (129). The conclusion of *Scar Lover* is a fitting end for the odyssey of the grit émigré; it is a confirmation that the value of rural culture lies within the broad expanse of the human heart.

Crews's artistic journey with these characters has been the most effective channel of his own brand of social commentary, the vehicle by which he has best expressed his keen perceptions of social change in the contemporary South. The grit émigré character has allowed Crews to go beyond the vision of his predecessors in southern letters—to bring Tobacco Road into the city. Through their migrations, the grit émigrés dramatize the dynamic interval between a waning southern culture and a new one. Thus the rural emigrants occupy a space similar to the "crossing of the ways" Allen Tate observed, but with economic hindrances that prohibit them (unlike the Nashville Agrarians) from making a nostalgic return to the land—allowing for a completely new perspective in southern fiction. The interval they occupy, rife with combustibility, carries the potential for horrific violence—a rejection of the new culture—or a refined regional consciousness. For Crews and his grit émigré characters, the necessity of cultural transformation is irrefutable, yet the change is tempered by a sense of loss, the transition a poignant exodus from what Crews calls "a way of life gone forever out of the world" (*A Childhood* 4).

HARRY CREWS'S AWAY GAMES

Home and Sport in A Feast of Snakes *and* Body

Scott Romine

In his autobiography, *A Childhood: The Biography of a Place* (1978), Harry Crews describes the lack of a "home place" as a determining factor of his life:

> And in that very fact, the importance of family, lies what I think of as the rotten spot at the center of my life or, said another way, the rotten spot at the center of what my life might have been if circumstance had been different. I come from people who believe the home place is as vital and necessary as the beating of your own heart. It is that single house where you were born, where you lived out your childhood, where you grew into young manhood. It is your anchor in the world, that place, along with the memory of your kinsmen at the long supper table every night and knowledge that it would always exist, if nowhere but in memory. (13–14)

"[T]here is nowhere I can think of as the home place," Crews continues, "If I think of where I come from, I think of the entire country" (14). Crews's protagonists are likewise exiles. From John Kaimon in *Karate Is a Thing of the Spirit* to Shereel Dupont in *Body*, they are far from home psychologically as well as geographically. Their place of exile is, significantly, often associated with a game. In suggesting that Crews's games—from karate and bodybuilding to football in *A Feast of Snakes* and boxing in *The Knockout Artist*—are *away* games, I mean to indicate a recurring opposition between "game" and "home" in which games do not so much *cause* exile as respond to its existential ubiquity. Situated within their respective agons, Crews's protagonists use games as coping mechanisms, as ways of confronting a baffling, hostile world without the protections of a home place. While games are always being played, they are never playful. This essay examines the desperate games in two of Crews's most important novels, *A Feast of Snakes* (1976) and *Body* (1990). After briefly examining some of the literary traditions, especially antebellum southern humor, that precede and inform Crews's representation of gaming, I consider how, for both Joe Lon Mackey and Shereel Dupont, the tension between game and home leads intractably to annihilation.

As several critics have observed, the frontier humor that flourished in the South during the antebellum era acts as a kind of collective precursor text for Crews's fiction.[1] One important point of comparison involves the relationship between games and culture. In an interesting essay on the role of games in antebellum humor, Michael Oriad shows how the fluid, transitional social order of the frontier emphasized games as an individualistic, egalitarian means of establishing hierarchies and social relations (6–7). But while games serve an important social function as a "buffer against chaos" (11), they are consistently opposed to more corporate, hereditary modes of social organization. The tension between games and civilization is pervasive in antebellum humor, perhaps most notably in Augustus Baldwin Longstreet's *Georgia Scenes*, where Lyman Hall, Longstreet's gentleman narrator, recounts and occasionally participates in several games involving primarily the lower classes. At the conclusion of "The Fight," Hall comments negatively on the scene of masculine "barbarism and cruelty" he has just described, claiming that such episodes presently exist only in "some of the new counties" due to "the Christian religion, to schools, colleges, and benevolent associations" (70). To be sure, this hostile perspective changes as Hall synthesizes the opposition between frontier individualism and class hierarchy, but the resulting tension never disappears entirely. Nor is this tension always or even usually resolved in favor of "civilization," which acquires in many works a feminized, unmanly connotation. As the stable, constrictive structures of class and family interrupt the fluid, individualistic negotiation of status via games, the former are often gendered female and personified in the figures of the "charming creature" (Longstreet's term for the overly refined, socially pernicious woman) and the dandy, the feminized upper-class male whose "city airs" make him the butt of many a prank. Although occasionally, as in William Tappan Thompson's *Major Jones's Courtship* and William Gilmore Simms's "How Sharp Snaffles Got His Capital and His Wife," the tension between the masculine world of sport and camaraderie and the feminine world of marriage and family is resolved satisfactorily, the more common relationship is one of sustained opposition; to be a "good fellow" *and* a good husband is a rare feat indeed. The recurring theme of failed courtship, especially conspicuous in the works of Charles S. Robb, involves the protagonist's exile from a feminized civilization to a strictly masculine space, a shift that usually privileges the homosocial bond of sport over the heterosexual bond of marriage.

Several similarities between Crews's fiction and antebellum humor with respect to gaming will no doubt be apparent. First and most obviously, games are closely related to social hierarchies; to be good at a game is to possess status. A second, related similarity involves the nature of that status. Because the status conferred by games is contingent upon winning them, it tends to be more unstable that the status conferred by class or familial position. Crews follows his antebellum precursors in locating games at the margins of "civilization": games act both as a site of social cohesion and as an anti-social practice; they both create order and disrupt it. That the frontier in which antebellum gaming flourished is but a distant memory in Crews's world only exacerbates the deep tensions contained therein, since heading west, the archetypal American response to the overbearing constraint of civilization, no longer offers itself as a viable alternative for Crews's frustrated protagonists, many of whom, one feels, would have managed had a frontier been available. Like Nathanael West in *The Day of the Locust* (a novel whose texture of rage prefigures works like *A Feast of Snakes* and *Car*), Crews explores the sense of claustrophobic enclosure that results from the closure of the frontier as reality and metaphor. Third, Crews follows antebellum humorists in investing games with the high stakes of survival: in both instances, winning the game can be a matter of life and death. As Oriad points out, "in a contest between civilization and wilderness, between a man and an agent of the wilderness, the reward is survival in its bluntest, most unambiguous form" (8). Although Crews's corresponding survival motif is altogether more ambiguous, the absence of a literal wilderness does not reduce the stakes of game. In fact, the opposite may be true, since the imperative to "win" as a way of asserting the self in a hostile, antagonistic world—a wilderness of sorts—is not diminished when the agent of that wilderness fails to appear in a discrete, coherent form. To put the matter another way, the game metaphor pits the Crews protagonist against a "world" hypostatized *as* an opponent, although the precise nature of this opposition usually remains ambiguous, and often involves metonymic displacements between an oppositional "world" revealed to be the authentic opponent and the literal opponent of the game. A final relationship between Crews's fiction and antebellum humor involves the bifurcated image of woman as sex object and as wife. For a man so driven by appetite as George Washington Harris's Sut Lovingood, women such as Sicily Burns are systematically reduced to a collection of sexual characteristics: "Sich a buzzim! Jis' think ove two snow balls wif a strawberry stuck but-ainded intu bof on em" (69). The context of such backwoods *blasons*, examples of which abound throughout the genre, is typically the hunting camp or some other homosocial space in which whiskey flows freely and from which the category of "wife" is excluded precisely because wives are embedded within "civilization." Because the masculine world of gaming lies outside those systems of social obligation, women tend to be viewed as physical bodies and little more.

The opposition between sex object and wife is central to *A Feast of Snakes*, a novel whose protagonist, Joe Lon Mackey, is situated precariously between the worlds of adolescent gaming and adult responsibility. A former high school football hero enshrined locally as the Boss Snake of the Mystic High Rattlers, Joe Lon is trapped with a wife whose physical body is in decline: "Those beautiful ball-crushing breasts she'd had two years ago now hung like enormous flaps down the front of her body. And although she was not fat, she looked like she was carrying a basketball under her dress. Two inches below her navel her belly just leaped out in this absolutely unbelievable way. . . . Her teeth had gone bad. The doctor said it had something to do with having two babies so close together" (9–10). It is not merely a wife's body disfigured by childbearing that makes marriage so intolerable for Joe Lon, whose response to the dark parody of domesticity is to "trembl[e] with anger" and feel "like slapping somebody" (10). It is that marriage precludes the structured diffusion of violence that football had provided. Joe Lon has come home to his trailer from the Mystic High practice field, where he had watched the reigning Boss Snake, Willard Miller, "fake a grunion out of his shoes and then, after he had the boy entirely turned around and beaten, run directly over him for no reason at all" (7–8). His own "thigh muscles tick[ing]" as he watches the scene, Joe Lon attempts to repress the intolerable nature of his current situation: "Well, what the hell, all things had to end, both good and bad. There were other things in the world besides getting to step on somebody" (8). Precisely what those things *are*, Joe Lon has been unable to determine: hence his need to slap somebody. That this "somebody" is usually his

wife only exacerbates the situation, since Elfie is not, like the "grunions" ritualisti-
cally sacrificed to the Boss Snake, "fair game"—that is to say, a victim of violence
whose victimhood is legitimized as *part* of the game.

In Mystic, getting to step on somebody is imperative because violence is ubiquitous; indeed, it often assumes the quality of a physical presence, a contaminant. "It's
blood in the air," says Willard Miller as the rattlesnake festival reaches its feverish
pitch, "I can smell it. I can *smell* the goddam blood in the air" (145). It is precisely
this facet of violence, as Rene Girard shows in *Violence and the Sacred*, that makes it
such a threat to primitive societies lacking a judicial system. Such societies, Girard
argues, are protected through sacrificial rituals that "serve to polarize the community's aggressive impulses and redirect them toward victims that may be actual or
figurative, animate or inanimate, but that are always incapable of propagating further
vengeance" (18). Although not technically primitive, Mystic lacks many of the characteristics associated with modernity. Insofar as the defining characteristic of modern
society is, as Girard suggests, the establishment of a sovereign judicial system that
removes vengeance from private hands, Mystic hardly qualifies: vengeance remains
exclusively a private matter, while Sheriff Buddy Matlow, the primary representative
of the law in the novel, systematically arrests and rapes women whom he desires.[2]
Crews also emphasizes the fundamentally religious nature of the community, and
like Flannery O'Connor, another writer for whom violence and the sacred are intimately linked, is most drawn to primitive religious and quasi-religious practices.
Having established both the ubiquity of violence and the absence of modern meth-
ods of containing it, Crews foregrounds the primitive mechanisms of surrogate violence that permit the community's survival. Foremost among these are the snake
festival and football, the latter of which, insofar as it involves the ritualistic diffusion
of violence through surrogate victimhood, allows us to see in a new light the axiom
that, in the South, football is a religion. Gary Long's insight that "[v]iolence in
Crews's work is ubiquitous, but it is not gratuitous" (126) is therefore essential to
recognize, although violence, as we shall see, has a pronounced tendency to overflow
its normal channels.

If we divide responses to the ubiquity of violence into structures of repression
and structures of controlled expenditure, it becomes clear that the latter dominate
the corporate life of the community. Indeed, the only efficacious structure of repression involves the racial category of "nigger," which prevents Joe Lon's employee
Lummy, whose "job was to be the nigger" (149), from acting out his violent fantasies: "As soon as he was *not* around a white man, he quit being a nigger and thought

about many, many things that he did not ordinarily think about. One of the things he thought about was killing Mr. Joe Lon. Of course, as long as he was near him, he couldn't kill him, or even *think* about killing him. But when he was off by himself, or in the company of other black people, he not only thought about it, he often actually killed him" (149). In the end, even racial prohibitions give way as Lottie Mae, the current object of Buddy Matlow's sexual violence, castrates him with a straight razor. In Mystic, blood will out.

If even the massive prohibitions of race cannot prevent violence, there is little question that those associated with marriage can. Nevertheless, marriage retains for Joe Lon enough prohibitive force to create in him a sense of deep guilt over his treatment of Elfie. "Jesus, he wished he wasn't such a sonofabitch," he thinks to himself, "Christ, he treated her just like a goddam dog" (12). At root, *A Feast of Snakes* is a failed initiation story, as Joe Lon finds that he can no longer tolerate the domestic space—the "trailer where he lived in a constant state of suffocating anger" (8)—governed by rules that prohibit any sanctioned articulation of violence. The coming of the snake festival, with its carnivalesque suspension of normative rules, permits Joe Lon, accompanied by Willard Miller and Duffy Deeter, to reenter the homosocial space of play and surrogate violence. Yet even as he does so, he despairs at the regressive nature of the shift:

> It was Joe Lon's turn on the bench and he went under the weight in a sinking despair, thinking: *What am I doing here on my back? What is this I'm doing? I'm a grown man with two babies and a wife and I'm out here fucking around with weights. What the hell ails me?* . . . He had once had football to fill up his mind and his body and his days and so he had never thought about it. Then one day football was gone and it took everything with it. He kept thinking something else would surely take its place but nothing ever did. He stumbled from one thing to the next thing. From wife to babies to making a place for crazy campers bent on catching snakes. But nothing gave him anything back. So here he was lying under a dead weight doing what he'd done five years ago, when he was a boy. (101–02)

For Joe Lon, the adult world of work, marriage, and fatherhood fails to return his investment of libidinal energy—hence his desire to reenter an adolescent world that did. The crisis here is, more specifically, a crisis of masculinity: despite Jon Lon's dissatisfaction with "manhood" as it is conferred by adult roles, neither is he satisfied with "manhood" conceived as a prize contested among rivals. Crews is here working with a formula virtually as old as the American novel itself: the story of the man on the run. And as Leslie Fiedler shows in *Love and Death in the American Novel*, the "enemy of society on the run toward 'freedom' " and away from "civilization" and the "chafing and restrictive home" is typically "a pariah in flight from his guilt, the guilt of that very flight; and new phantoms arise to haunt him at every step" (6).

Joe Lon is no exception to this rule, as whiskey, weights, and the torture of Enrique "Poncy" Gomez reveal to him. A geographic and ethnic outsider ("It ain't our kind of people, is it?" Willard asks Joe Lon) and a physical weakling, Poncy meets the essential criterion for surrogate victims: he can be subjected to violence without fear of reprisal (Girard 13). But the violence Joe Lon and Willard expend upon him is indirect, as they first "help him to dance" by violently wrenching his back and then spin him "as if he was a maypole and each of his arms were streamers" (107). The game of Terrorize the Tourist thus conceals violence as "playfulness": "They were hurting him. But if either of them knew it they didn't show it. Their own faces were flushed, their lips peeled back in what was alternately snarl and laughter" (106). Neither is the violence arbitrary, since Poncy has "brought it on himself" first by unintentionally "mocking" their "grit voices" (99), and then, over-correcting that error, by using the hifalutin phrase "quite something" (107). The game thus responds to its own internal logic of playfulness and fairness. But for Joe Lon, the game is no longer a laughing matter. Lying in the back of Duffy's Winne-bago, he "thought about Poncy back there in the parking lot of the Blue Pines. He felt like he felt when he screamed at Elfie or hit her. He hadn't meant to hurt the old man, but he knew he had. He eased his hands down onto his flat hard stomach. Something in him was tearing loose" (108). Like O'Connor's Misfit, Joe Lon has gravitated from a philosophy of "no pleasure but in meanness" to one in which "it's no real pleasure in life."

Crews develops Joe Lon's liminal position between adolescence and adulthood, between game and home, by structurally situating him in relation to several other characters. Willard is clearly a younger, pre-initiate version of Joe Lon. Not only does he inherit Joe Lon's title as Boss Snake, he virtually inherits his girlfriend: his violent sexual relationship with Hard Candy Sweet replicates Joe Lon's relationship with her older sister Berenice. For Willard, violence still satisfies, rage still exhila-rates. In other respects, Joe Lon is doubled by Duffy Deeter. Like Joe Lon, Duffy has both a wife and an extra-marital object of sexual violence who moves effortlessly in the world of masculine gaming. But Duffy has established an equilibrium that eludes Joe Lon. A successful lawyer, he has mastered the world that baffles the younger man. Where Joe Lon is confounded by Berenice and the feminized domain of the university, Duffy dominates University of Florida graduate student Susan

Gender; where Joe Lon feels guilt over his treatment of Elfie, Duffy has left his wife behind with few regrets; where Joe Lon no longer has football to structure his world, Duffy continues to collect trophies in running, handball, and karate. In short, Duffy has successfully regressed to the homosocial world of violence from which Joe Lon has been irrevocably expelled. Significantly, it is Willard with whom he establishes the closest bond; the morning after a brawl from which Joe Lon conspicuously absents himself, Willard affirms to Joe Lon, "damn if I don't think I'm in love with this little fucker right here. You see'm last night? Worsen a pit bull when you git'm down in the dirt" (153).

The third and perhaps most important double is Buddy Matlow. His football career ended by an injured knee, Buddy takes refuge in sexual violence practiced upon black women and white transients whose marginal status prevents them from defending themselves. His surrogate victimization nevertheless acquires a certain pathological logic, for as an All-American prevented from a pro career by an injury and as a Vietnam veteran separated from a leg, "he'd paid his dues, and now it was his turn" (15). Buddy thus structures rape as a game. Besides being "fair," it has rules (Buddy forbids Lottie Mae from calling him "Mister" because he "loves her" [36]), and it is playful (on one occasion, Buddy offers her a choice between himself and a rattlesnake [37]). Unfortunately for Buddy, Lottie Mae refuses to play by his rules and castrates him with a straight razor. Mortally wounded, he tries to send a message to Joe Lon, but dies before he can do so. Although Crews withholds the content of the message, Buddy clearly offers it as an admonition, and, insofar as the novel permits speculation on the matter, it must surely have to do with a lesson that Buddy has had brought home to him with a vengeance: violence begets violence. As Duffy Deeter says of the incident, "What goes around comes around. . . . A guy that gets his dick cut off's got bad karma" (152). According to this logic, violence must be structured as a game—that is, it must be both "playful" and "fair"—lest it become random and infectious. It is precisely because Buddy's game meets neither criterion that violence contaminates him, gives him "bad karma." Joe Lon's situation is essentially identical; unable to configure his violence toward Poncy and Elfie as games, games themselves become tainted: "Joe Lon was bored with the game. Seemed it was one game after another" (113).

Buddy's castration also threatens to taint the collective game of the snake festival. Although Coach Tump worries that the incident will "put a damper on the whole thing" (152), the danger is actually in the opposite direction, for the violence loosened by the incident threatens to overwhelm the protections offered by the festival.

That this particular game is invested with mythical and religious significance—that it is, in short, a ritual—makes no real difference, since, as we have seen, the novel insists upon the essential commensurability of game and ritual as mechanisms of surrogate violence. Because, as Girard observes, non-human sacrificial victims typically observe a principle of resemblance to the object they replace (11), the snake serves as a likely choice, for it resembles the phallus, the generative source of violence within the community: in Mystic, sexuality and violence are inseparable. This equation is made explicit when Lottie Mae conflates snake and phallus and thus cuts off Buddy's penis *as* a snake (it is sheathed in a rattlesnake condom) and comes away "with the snake in her hand, its softening head with the needle fangs still showing just above her thumb and forefinger" (129). Recalling Girard's description of sacrifice as "an act of violence without risk of vengeance," we can observe that this displacement allows Lottie Mae to take revenge against a "snake" in a way that she could not against a white man's penis, where the risk of vengeance would be too great. Poncy enacts a similar displacement. The day after his degradation at the hands of Joe Lon and Willard, Poncy redirects his violent impulses toward a snake: "Poncy came closer and closer until he was looking right into the snake's eyes. Poncy hissed. From less than a foot away, he shot spit into the snake's gaping, fanged mouth" (174). It is an act of displaced revenge that allows him to understand and forgive his tormentor. "I don't care what you did in the bar," he tells Joe Lon, "I know why you did it. It's natural, and I don't hold it against you" (174–75). For Joe Lon, such displacements are no longer available. His tormentor is too massive and too amorphous: "And it was not any one thing that scared him. It was everything. It was his life. His life terrified him. He didn't see how he was going to get through the rest of it" (161). Without football to structure the violence within him, to provide victims within the limited arena of the game, his only alternative is to play the Game of Life (opponent: the world) according to the same violent rules. As he blasts away during his murderous rampage, his last and bloodiest act, "He felt better than he had ever felt in his life. Christ, it was good to be in control again" (176). And in a twisted way, he is.

II.

Games are always, in a sense, absurd; like manners, the rules of any game are finally arbitrary. And as with manners, it is precisely this arbitrariness that provides a check upon unrestrained passion and conceals the brutality of games' metaphoric referent, for, as Oriad says, " 'survival' is the stake of any game, from hopscotch to medieval jousts, though usually in subtle and refracted forms" (8). Check mate, we might say, is but a bloodless version of incipient regicide. Because Crews's blood sports involve only minimal refraction and no subtlety, they tend to offer little mediation of violence, little protection against the zero-sum logic that lies at their core. Because control *of* violence is so often related to control *through* violence, violence itself tends to resist control. As we have seen, games provide a deep metaphor of opposition that structures relationships in general for many of Crews's protagonists. For Joe Lon Mackey, a relationship based on anything other than hostility and dominance is virtually unthinkable; although opponents can be "maimed without malice, sometimes—even often—in friendship," love "seemed to mess up everything" (118). And because Crews's games cultivate and at best *structure* the abyss, civilization, conceived as a corporate attempt to repress violence, is inconceivable. For Joe Lon, civilization is so radically determined as a constrictive, suffocating space that its potential compensations never come into focus. The same cannot be said of *Body*, a novel that develops in greater depth the domain of home that stands in stark contrast to the world of the game. But for Shereel Dupont, who must leave Waycross, Georgia, to become a worldbeating bodybuilder, going home is no more an option than it is for Joe Lon, and like him she succumbs to a fate intimately linked to the game she plays.

Body is, on one level, a simple variation on the American narrative of ascent not dissimilar from *The Great Gatsby*, another novel that leaves its protagonist on the brink of obtaining the ultimate object of cathexis. Just as Jimmy Gatz must become "Oggsford" graduate Jay Gatsby, so Dorothy Turnipseed must become Shereel Dupont.[3] And like Gatsby, Shereel inhabits a world whose utopian aspect is sustained by simulations, surfaces, and appearances: "Everybody seemed perfect of his kind, teeth incredibly white, hair thick and wildly beautiful, eyes clear and shining with a kind of mindless confidence, as though the world would never die, could never die. Age and death seemed defeated here. They all conspicuously ignored one another as they moved in the contained monuments they had made of themselves. Their skins circumscribed their worlds, worlds they inhabited with obvious joy, contentment, and pride" (17). Death, of course, will not be defeated here: the novel moves relentlessly toward two suicides and a murder. But bodybuilding appears to offer a purely self-deterministic means of ascent for those with the "right bones" and the will to endure pain. Within the domain of the game, family is reduced to the level of chromosomes. As Russell Morgan, the trainer of the future Shereel Dupont, tells her upon discovering her at his Emporium of Pain, "You fell into a great gene pool" (23). Here, blood is a substance used to pump muscles, not a metaphor for kinship obligations. The utopian dimensions of bodybuilding, then, are contingent upon the erosion of social metaphors and categories, and the consequent emphasis on the sheer materiality of the body. Quite literally, skin circumscribes the world of the bodybuilder.

In that world between skin and bone—the two biological determinants of the game[4]—the possibilities are endless and intoxicating: "He'd made her somebody, made her hear thundering applause and shouts of approval, even love. He'd given her a cause in the world, a cause such as she had not known existed for anybody. And for that, she had done everything he had asked of her. And she was glad to do it, even to having her name changed" (23–24). Although the name of the cause is clear—winning the title of Ms. Cosmos—its referent is anything but. Indeed, the vague and evasive reference here to "a cause" is replicated throughout the novel; although Shereel names the more or less obvious desire to gain fame and fortune, her inability to articulate the precise nature of her quest suggests that fame and fortune are only peripheral. She begins to apprehend the true stake of the game when she finds, on the day of the competition, that she can no longer resist the notion that "[h]er whole future, the rest of her life, rested squarely on today": "On one side of the ledger was winning and its consequences. . . . Shereel Dupont, Ms. Cosmos, was somebody, somebody to reckon with. As Ms. Cosmos, she saw her name on gyms, on food supplements, on sportswear. . . . On the other side of the ledger was the alternative to winning. And she did not know, could not imagine, the consequences of not winning. That side of the ledger was not only blank, it was dark, like the thick dark of the convention center where the howling voice of the audience came from" (228–29). Even where winning is concerned, Shereel displaces the true stake of the game—becoming "somebody"—onto endorsements, and in so doing represses what is at stake where losing is concerned, which logically must be remaining or becoming "nobody." Losing, then, does not mean merely the loss of endorsements, but the loss of identity, the true stake of the game if and only if winning and losing are considered as absolute terms in no way limited by the game. In a zero-sum world consisting, as Russell says, of "the beater and the beaten" (59), to win is to become "somebody," to lose is to be annihilated.

The parameters of the game thus widen substantially. Stated in broadest terms, Shereel's quest—like that of Jay Gatsby, Thomas Sutpen, Willie Stark, and many another modern hero before her—is to bring the world to its knees, to make it conform to her desire. The game offers a mechanism by which a perfect return on her investment of pain and psychological energy can, ideally, be effected. The control offered by the game is the refore essential, as Russell emphasizes to his pupil: "Control is the name of this game. Control *everything*. *Believe* you can control everything. Believe it and you can *do* it. Believe it and it is the truth" (222). The seductiveness of Russell's vision depends upon two distinct factors: that the game actually offers this opportunity, and that the game offers it according to objective rules. Where corruption is an integral part of the careers of Gatsby, Sutpen, and Stark, the game makes it possible for Shereel to ascend, as Hemingway might say, *without cheating*. As is true throughout Hemingway's work, the domain of the game is perceived to be *pure* in a way that the world can never be. Russell, for example, "did not believe in luck—either good or bad—he believed in discipline" (87). Both Russell and his nemesis, Wallace Wilson, employ metaphors that endow the game with the precision of an economic transaction: Russell tells Shereel, "You've bought this and paid for it. Go pick it up and take it home" (221), while Wallace Wilson has tattooed on the bottom of his feet, "*Patience and perserverance is the price of mastery*" (79).[5] Within this disciplined domain, control—or at least the appearance thereof—is possible. But while the game can be pure, it must be significant. Here Crews departs from Hemingway, whose games typically involve an act of separation that produces "small" (even pyrrhic) victories in relation to a larger world perceived to be incoherent and ultimately unbeatable. Conversely, Shereel's opportunity to become "somebody" via the game, to become a "worldbeater," involves an implicit premise that "the world"—conceived as such and not just as a collection of opponents—can, like those opponents, be beaten. Thus, while the game permits competition that is "pure" and "clean," winning extends beyond the game to invoke metonymically a kind of mastery over the world.

Such, at least, is the game's utopian aspect, which Crews ruthlessly deconstructs. As we have already seen, opportunity is linked to risk. In order for control and mastery to apply outside the domain of the game, the boundary between game and world must disappear, one consequence of which is that winning—survival *in terms of* the game—becomes a literal matter of life and death. But perhaps more significantly, the domain of the game is itself tainted by indeterminacies that threaten to expose control as an illusion. Russell, for example, knows that while the "name of this game was supposed to be body . . . a woman needed a pretty face to win" (147). He is unsure whether "a name like Turnipseed would be enough to shoot a girl down" (147–48). And most importantly, there is no clear standard by which female bodybuilders are judged. It is not a question of whether Shereel or Marvella Washington conforms more closely to some platonic ideal of womanhood, but which of the two ideals they embody will win out over the other. It is here that the baffling nature of the world impinges upon the game, for the two ideals clearly respond to social imperatives. Wallace, Marvella's trainer, has "bet his reputation . . . on the side of unthinkable size" because "it was the American way," while Russell "knew in his blood that bigness was finished" (76): women who are "monsters to behold," he feels, cannot "be taken home to mother" (75). The contest will therefore *answer* the question "How big is the perfect woman?" (88), rather than presupposing an answer as a condition of the game. If the utopian dimension of bodybuilding depends upon the illusion that one can "control *everything*," Crews erodes that dimension by showing how the game is *like* the world, and connected to it, in the worst possible way.

Contrasted to the domain of the game in every significant respect is the domain of the family. Where the Turnipseed clan is concerned, not even the illusion of control is possible. Where the worldbeaters have bodies that are monuments to health and physical perfection, the Turnipseeds are physical grotesques. Earline and Earnestine could, according to Russell, "use the Morgan Dachau treatment for weight reduction" (35); Alphonse is "about the size of a retired jockey who might have been a bit consumptive" (37); Motor is a human hairball who causes Billy Bat to think (and not without reason), "If I ever seen a ruint gene, I'm lookin' at it right now" (134). But unlike the worldbeaters, the Turnipseeds are not *primarily* bodies; they are social beings whose status as such takes precedence over their material existence. Despite, for example, Motor's physical repulsiveness, Earnestine is able to love him as her child: "Motor was her favorite, hair and all. . . . The only thing was, his mother could not stand to touch him. He reminded her of a dog. But, good mother that she was, she kept it her secret, and her secret alone" (38). The family's flexible logic of concealment and repression stands in stark contrast to the game's inflexible antagonism. "Everybody here's an asshole," Russell tells Shereel, "It's those scumbags against us" (20). Where the game demands that the world be brought to its knees, the family is able to conform and adapt, and as a consequence, the ultimately baffling nature of the world is something the family can assimilate in a way that the game cannot. Thus, while the Turnipseeds may not understand Shereel's name change, they are willing to accept it—despite Shereel's prediction to the contrary (20)—as something other than a naked affront to blood ties. As she marches off to compete with the assertion that "Dorothy's dead. It's *Shereel* time," her mother is able to respond, "I don't understand . . . but you my youngun and I love you" (203).

Of the novel's three discrete domains—those of the family, the game, and the hotel—it is the family whose rules prove to be the healthiest and the most durable. During the course of the novel, each domain undergoes a disorientation in which normative rules are suspended. The Turnipseeds are, of course, tourists, as Earnestine observes: "We're off here amongst strangers," she tells her husband, "and I won't have them thinkin' this is a trashy family" (197). In this effort, she fails conspicuously: despite her attempts to project a respectable image by limiting foul language and dressing her family in outrageous J. C. Penney garb, the Turnipseeds are clearly out of their element. Indeed, their being so is precisely what disorients the other domains. The simulated perfection of the Blue Flamingo hotel barely survives the Turnipseeds. Dexter Friedkin, the toupee-wearing miracle of plastic surgery who manages the hotel, can think only to bribe them in an attempt to placate their unpredictable tendencies. Similarly, Russell views the family as a threat to his best-laid plans: "Them here at the Cosmos with you in a dogfight to win the world is a mistake. I can smell disaster. I can smell disaster coming off them from all the way up here" (41). Even Shereel, although not overtly hostile to her family, sees them as a distraction: "She wished with all her heart they had not come, and she had done everything possible to stop them, to head them off, short of telling them straight out they could not come" (128). From the perspectives of the hotel and the game, the family threatens the tenuous balance that keeps both domains intact. Curiously, however, both domains revert to familial roles in times of crisis. Confronted with a bleeding clerk, Dexter refers to him as "son": "He had never called Julian 'son' before. But then nothing of this sort had ever happened before" (71). Similarly, the night before the contest, Russell is transformed: "She felt something coming off him she had never felt before, off his voice, his hands, the heat of his body. And it was a shock to her when she realized it was the purest kind of caring, and concern, and love. And all of it untainted by anything sexual. It made her want to kiss him. And she knew she could have without doing violence to the moment. She could not help thinking it would be the kind of kiss she might give her father" (179–80).

If the game is seductive, then, the family might be said to be instinctive. The alternative provided by the family is clearly evident in the fate of Bill "the Bat" Bateman, the man with the worldbeating back who renounces the game to marry Shereel's sister Earline. Combining as it does equal portions of Erskine Caldwell and D. H. Lawrence, the relationship is bizarre by any standard: drawn to Earline's immense obesity, Billy wins her by posing as a professional "skin mechanic." When, after the consummation of their brief relationship, Earline annouces, "We married now," Billy "knew it was true, and he knew that she knew it was true. He had always been married to bodybuilding, but when he entered her, he got a divorce" (171). Although from the perspective of the game, Billy is "afflicted" (198), his choice responds to a more fundamental logic. The game "just don't mean what it used to" because family has taken precedence: "And once I get her up there where I come from, we'll see if we cain't have us some younguns. Man needs a family. Am I right or am I wrong?" (215).

Shereel's fate is a simple tragic inversion of her sister's comic outcome. *Body* traces in detail Shereel's increasing resistance to all roles that define her in relation to others. The roles of sister, daughter, and fiancé (or "fee*and*see," as Nail Head has it) are increasingly eroded as Shereel goes from protesting that "I'm the same girl I've always been" (115) to insisting that "Dorothy's dead." And it is not simply familial categories that lose their purchase on Shereel. In addition, she becomes less identifiable as a "southerner" (Russell demands "that she lose her Georgia accent" [11]), as a "pupil" (she increasingly resists Russell's leadership), even as a "woman" (she no longer has periods [11], her breasts have disappeared because "[t]its don't count in this contest" [67], and when Billy Bat asserts that men would beat women if they competed together, she "did not like the idea that anybody in the world could beat her, male or female . . ." [129]). No longer conceiving herself as being defined by these categories, Shereel is no longer constrained by them; neither is Marvella Washington limited *as* an African-American. Within the domain of the game, gender and race are rendered meaningless: body is all that matters. But isolation has its price as well its compensations. Warming up prior to the contest, Shereel "felt something move in her that was very nearly an audible *click*, a click that always felt like a bolt sliding shut, sliding shut and locking her in with herself and locking everybody else out" (218). This isolation enables the euphoria as she hears the wave of sound break from the audience:

Belligerent in its intensity, it did not even sound like applause as it came to her out of the vast darkness of the convention center and it joined her as vivid in its feeling as a raw nerve, joined her and lifted her with the certain, always startling knowledge: *They love me.* And the raw nerve of the audience's love forced her so deep inside herself that she felt if she wanted to, if she *needed* to, she could isolate every single cell of her body from every other cell of her body. . . . When her music ended as she hit the last pose and held it, she gave herself over to the thunderous applause that beat in her ears before finally beating with her heart in her blood. She was pure body, the bodiness of body, and in perfect control. (222–23)

It is only as a "pure body" that Shereel can achieve the perception of "perfect control," for bodies can be controlled in a way that, say, parents cannot. Parents, conversely, can love in a way impossible for a faceless audience. Indeed, it is the audience's "love" in a horribly mutated form—its "hysteria" for Marvella when she is announced as Ms. Cosmos (235)—that more than anything else annihilates Shereel. She is, as Donald Johnson says of Crews's athletes generally, a "victim of the very body that captivates [her] audience" (101). Connection is the obverse of constraint, and if the game permits the illusion of perfect control by stripping away the constraints associated with family, it also produces a radical and intolerable isolation. What Shereel might bear as a daughter or "feeandsee," she cannot as a body. Receiving the shock of the world at the end of her nerves, she is unprotected, and without family to protect her, she can only follow to its logical conclusion her earlier intuition that the loser of the game would "cease to exist" (217).

In a 1981 interview, Crews attributed to Ernest Hemingway the idea that "all stories end in death and that him that would keep you from that is no true storyteller" (148). If Hemingway is correct, then Harry Crews is a true storyteller, but the more interesting issue, I think, involves the implicit correlation between writing and sport that Crews borrows from his modernist precursor. For Hemingway, writing had rules, and those who broke them "cheated," an idea that Crews reiterates throughout his interviews.[6] For Crews, writing is a controllable domain structured by rules. And if one of those rules necessitates death, we can see how the equation of game and life doubles back on itself, for both games and lives point irrevocably toward a terminal moment. Facing that moment with grace—looking into the abyss with equanimity—becomes an imperative of the game. Both Joe Lon Mackey and Shereel Dupont resist cheating—Joe Lon by not intending to "go nuts trying to pretend things would someday be different" (170), Shereel by taking the last option that is her only option (238). But the trope of cheating death is meaningful only *in terms of* the game, and both novels in their different ways represent home as an unavailable domain inside which death is not an imperative. Here again, an autobiographical correlation suggests itself, for Harry Crews, as a writer leaving a "trail of mucus and blood and guts and everything else" ("An Interview" 151), cheats death no less than his characters. In the same interview, Crews claims that his "personal life is, and has been, as long as I can remember, a shambles. I don't live, I don't do it very well. But the one thing in the world that I can have some control over and shape and feel good about is whatever I can write" (151). It is the voice of a writer far from home.

THE PERFORMATIVE BODY IN
HARRY CREWS'S *KARATE IS A THING*
OF THE SPIRIT

Nicholas Spencer

The body posited as prior to the sign, is always *posited* or *signified* as *prior*. This signification produces as an effect of its own procedure the very body that it nevertheless and simultaneously claims to discover as that which *precedes* its own action. If the body signified as prior to signification is an effect of signification, then the mimetic or representational status of language, which claims that signs follow bodies as their necessary mirrors, is not mimetic at all. On the contrary, it is productive, constitutive, one might even argue *performative*, inasmuch as this signifying act delimits and contours the body that it then claims to find prior to any and all signification.

Judith Butler, *Bodies That Matter* (30)

D espite its cult popularity, the fiction of Harry Crews has rarely been studied by cultural theorists. Just as Marx and Engels regarded the unemployed lumpenproletariat of their day as reactionary, so too the white trash drifters and outsiders who people the work of Crews, Charles Bukowski, and other writers who are relatively ignored by cultural theorists are rarely seen as appropriate subject matter for the politicized critiques typical of cultural studies.[1] Unlike material treated by some cultural theorists, the cultural practices in Crews's work do not function in terms of marginalized groups' resistance, and as Patricia V. Beatty argues his writing may seem offensive or adolescent ("Body Language" 61). Moreover, Crews's writing often appears formally conservative and lacking in the kinds of textual surfaces that problematize issues of representation and identity. The linguistic innovation of Kathy Acker and William Burroughs is allied to a critique of subjectivity, but Crews, who can be identified with a "beat" or lumpenproletariat tradition in twentieth-century American literature that includes Acker, Burroughs, Nelson Algren, John Fante, and many others, writes in a naturalistic narrative style that does not seem to challenge hegemonic norms.[2] Nevertheless, for over thirty years Crews has been writing fiction that is often centered upon concerns such as the conjunction of the body and language, performativity and spectacle that are of widespread and growing interest in cultural studies. Analyzing Crews's fiction in terms of the cultural study of the body enables us to contribute detailed statements on parallels and varieties within contemporary American body culture and to establish a foundation upon which Crews's work can be considered in relation to the political critiques of cultural studies.

The representation of the body is one of the most consistent features of Crews's fiction. Most obviously, Crews often writes about freaks with deviant and disfigured bodies. Much criticism has been written on this aspect of Crews's work, and discussions of Crews's freaks have been central in the placement of Crews within the tradition of the southern Gothic, which remains the dominant critical paradigm for assessing Crews's work.[3] However, Crews is equally keen to portray the body in the context of the physical ordeals characters undertake, and an emphasis on such ordeals has implications for the generation of new critical paradigms for understanding Crews's fiction. Whereas the representation of freaks may seem to rely on a conception of the body's essential qualities, evocations of usually public ordeals treat the body as inseparable from social codes. The significance of the physical ordeals undertaken by Eugene Talmadge Biggs in *The Knockout Artist* (1988) and Shereel Dupont in *Body* (1990) is due to the systems of social rules that are reinforced, redefined and subverted. That the social coding of the body is a major facet of Crews's work is further indicated by the fact that Crews's freaks, such as Foot in *The Gospel Singer* (1968) and Fat Man in *Naked in Garden Hills* (1969), often appear in the context of public performance or spectacle. An equivalent distinction between essentialized and coded bodies is also apparent in the cultural theory of the body. Rosemarie Garland

Thomson discusses freaks in terms of "the semantic distinctions applied to anomalous bodies over time" (3), but as Judith Butler argues some feminist theorists posit the female body in opposition to categories of linguistic and social coding (*Bodies* 10).[4] While other feminist critics, such as Jeanie Forte (249–50), have argued that the body should not be viewed as a biological entity free of cultural construction, it is Butler who, through her concept of "performativity," has been most influential in generating a cultural theory of the body in terms of its social and linguistic coding.[5] In what follows I shall focus on the equivalent aspects of the work of Crews and Butler that emphasize the textualized body. To this end I shall offer a reading of Crews's *Karate Is a Thing of the Spirit* (1971), which, like other work of Crews's from the early 1970s such as *Car* (1972) and *The Hawk Is Dying* (1973), is less concerned with characters who have a freakish appearance than it is with those who negotiate crises of language and subjectivity by undertaking public bodily ordeals. It may seem peculiar to relate Butler's theories of gender trouble to Crews, who as Erik Bledsoe comments is often noted for his machismo (5). Yet the very excesses of Crews's work disclose the performative body as the social text of intersubjective relations and destabilize definitions of gender, sexuality and identity in ways that converge with as well as deviate from cultural theory such as Butler's.

The main narrative of *Karate Is a Thing of the Spirit* concerns John Kaimon's experience in a karate commune in Fort Lauderdale, Florida. An ex-member of a hippy commune in Mexico and a motorcycle gang in California, Kaimon is a restless beggar who is haunted by memories of his mother's violent death and his father's madness, and who has suffered hunger, imprisonment and repeated sexual abuse on the road. Devastated by physical suffering, Kaimon undergoes a crisis of subjectivity and looks for sanctuary. "My game is getting into other people's games," says Kaimon (330), and at the outset of the novel he is faced with the choice of whether to try to join the karate group he sees on the beach or accompany the two gay men, George and Marvin, in one of the beach's "homosexual meatracks" (14). By choosing the outlaw karate group Kaimon has found the sanctuary of a place to eat and sleep, but he must now endure a disorientating and demanding ordeal of ascetic diet, physical pain and linguistic confusion. Under the leadership of Belt and with the friendship of Gaye Nell Odell, Kaimon is trained through this regimen to become an adept and teacher of karate. Deliberate trials, such as the mutilation of Kaimon's hands by repeatedly striking a mackawari board, and unforeseen tribulations, such as the rape of Kaimon by George and Marvin, are used by Belt and Gaye Nell Odell to initiate Kaimon into the spirit of karate. The success of Kaimon's training is reflected in both the skillful karate moves that demonstrate his understanding of the karate spirit and his "move" (125) of reciting a letter to William Faulkner detailing the narrative of his experiences. However, the controlled environment of the karate commune breaks down as contingencies assert themselves. Gaye Nell Odell has sex with Kaimon as part of his training, but as a result she becomes pregnant. Kaimon and Gaye Nell Odell subsequently experience an emotional as well as sexual relationship, which enables Kaimon to overcome his long-standing suffering. Ultimately disillusioned with the karate commune because of it subservience to Belt's megalomaniacal plan to buy a mountaintop in Arkansas, Kaimon hot-wires Belt's microbus and accompanied by Gaye Nell Odell leaves with parenthood in view.

Kaimon associates the crises of his adult life with language. He tells Belt that he left his home town of Oxford, Mississippi, "because of Faulkner" (138), whom Kaimon describes as a "perverted degenerate" for his writing (141). As a result, his quest for sanctuary, as expressed in his initial decision to join the karate group's "game," entails a desire to transcend language and instead undergo a physical experience that will cause his identity to be recognized: "He did not know what he wanted to say. But he knew what he wanted to do. He wanted more than anything else to get in there and help them with the boy. He wanted to clean a wound. He wanted to rub a muscle. Most of all, he wanted them—all of them—to admit that he was in the world. To see him. To act like he was not air but flesh" (32).[6] Here, the opposition between language and materiality is absolute, and the latter is clearly privileged over the former as the site of subjectivity. As Judith Butler argues, the assumption that language and the body are wholly distinct has not only been used in western metaphysics to denigrate the body as "so much inert matter, signifying nothing, or, more specifically, signifying a profane void, the fallen state" (*Gender* 129), it is also central to the aforementioned feminist argument that criticizes the "linguistic idealism" (*Bodies* 10) of poststructuralism for reducing the subject and her world to discourse and thus of excluding materiality. Since Kaimon is mistrustful of language and seeks succor in the body, his perspective shares some features of the view of the essentialized body discussed by Butler. However, this clear opposition quickly gets complicated as the ability of karate to establish the body as a site of a performative material identity that is devoid of language breaks down.

Crews evokes the body as being shot through with linguistic and cultural categories in ways that approximate to Butler's concept of performativity. In developing this concept, Butler draws on J. L. Austin's influential distinction between constative and performative language, where the performative differs from the constative by performing an action (e.g., "Let the games begin") rather than simply naming some extra-linguistic phenomenon, and Jacques Derrida's critique of this distinction in "Signature Event Context" in terms of "citationality" and "iterability" (17).[7] Butler's definition of the performative undermines the integrity of Austin's distinction between constative and performative because constative references to the body are themselves performative in that they are an action that forms the body (and the performative is to some degree constative since actual bodies are sculpted by cultural and linguistic codes) (*Bodies* 10–11). Following Derrida, Butler argues that the performative involves the citation and reinforcement of norms that are hidden in the performative act. The body is thus the performative embodiment of cultural norms that are disguised by the constative metaphysics of the body as pre-linguistic referent. Butler uses the performative to debunk linguistic (poststructuralist) and materialist (feminist) idealisms by evoking language and the body as coterminous and mutually reinforcing. Butler's theorization means that the performative is a highly ambivalent concept because it both reinforces cultural norms that pass themselves off as the innocent referents of constative language and discloses itself to subvert those norms.[8]

At times Kaimon's quest appears to be successful. Kaimon's attraction to karate is social in nature—he wishes his identity to be recognized in his body. Belt's group provides a wordless physical sociality that is reduced to the observation of and contact with the karate body. For example, Belt deifies the midget Jefferson Davis Munroe for his demonstrations of karate feats for audiences (41). Kaimon achieves a form of illuminated recognition through such demonstrations. When he watches the ritualistic fight between a brown belt and a yellow belt he observes the interaction of their bodies and cries "That's a thing. . . . That's a real thing" (102). Here, Kaimon perceives the performative in the reactionary guise of constative metaphysics rather than as a self-referential (performative *as* performative) subversion. However, Crews evokes the karate demonstrations as semiotic performances that challenge any idea of the radical separation of language and the body. Most obviously, the karate encounter is coded by belt colors that signify levels of advancement within the discipline, but Kaimon's perception of the body itself is also described as a performative signification. In the aforementioned struggle between the yellow and brown belts Kaimon notices that the latter's "muscles under the skin were as sharply defined as if they had been etched by acid" (101). The "etching" of the body does not invoke the body as a *tabula rasa* that is then inscribed by culture (as in Foucault's theory that is criticized by Butler for its adherence to the notion of a pre-significatory body [*Gender* 129–30]), but rather suggests that the body is reiteratively (per)formed according to the same cultural categories that shape Kaimon's social perception of the body. In Butler's terms, the attainment of the body's muscularity is, no less than Kaimon's perception of it, quite literally a "signifying act [that] delimits and contours the body" (*Bodies* 30). Moreover, Kaimon realizes this bout is a "phantom fight" since the participants do not really strike each other. The sense of the battle as a *sign of battle* is underscored and extended by Kaimon's understanding of Gaye Nell Odell's subsequent "pantomime" (103) performance of it. Here, the social meaning of the body is not a fleshly a priori but is rather produced by the iterated performativity of a cultural code.

If the idea that the karate body is untainted by language is ruined by Kaimon's experience, so too is the belief that the karate commune provides identity recognition. As the title of the novel suggests, the true purpose of karate is to conjure the spirit rather than to affirm social identity. When performing their movements, the karate students are actually devoid of bodily sensation (17), and, as Gaye Nell Odell intones, the exercise of the body is undertaken to discover the body's unimportance: "Bowels, kidneys and blood are things of the world. Karate is a thing of the spirit. Breathe the world out and I will fill you full of the spirit" (96). Just as Kaimon momentarily attains an epiphanic recognition of the karate body, so too he successfully experiences the karate spirit beyond bodily recognition: "He was his own audience. He felt inside at last" (111). However, Crews erodes the sanctity of Kaimon's experience by suggesting that spiritual attainment is predicated upon the denial of the social marks of gender and sexuality upon the body. According to examples cited by Butler, the hidden law that performativity refers to is that of sexual difference, and the consequence of this iteration is the "repudiation" of sexualities and genderings other than the heterosexual matrix (*Bodies* 109). In *Karate Is a Thing of the Spirit* the performative karate body repudiates both homosexual and heterosexual identities by prohibiting their visual recognition in favor of the iteration of the norms of a self-absorbed spiritualized inwardness. If anything, it is the heterosexual gaze that is denied most vigorously by the karate body. Gaye Nell Odell beats up a yellow belt after he looks at her naked body, and, despite Kaimon's blandishments, the rest of the group stare blankly into the middle distance and refuse to observe the beaten yellow belt (31). However, from the beginning of the story, the karate commune is unable to sustain this prohibition. The novice Kaimon is conditioned to hit the mackawari board whenever he experiences sexual attraction to another's body as a means of eradicating such attraction (61). The fact that Gaye Nell Odell, an experienced brown belt, forces herself to transform her attraction to the male body into a desire for karate battle indicates how sexual identity must be repeatedly iterated through the performative body (15). Also, the peripheral characters that appear throughout the book compromise the purity of the karate commune's prohibition. Gaye Nell Odell may be able to punish the yellow belt's sexual gaze, but she can not prevent the uproarious attraction of the men in the nearby fireboat to her naked body (25). The most important sign of the triumph of sexual recognition over the karate group's asceticism is the heterosexual bond between Gaye Nell Odell and Kaimon, which, solidified by Gaye Nell Odell's pregnancy, enables Kaimon to over-come his crisis of subjectivity by rejecting the karate commune and its body fetish.

Since the heterosexuality that the karate group repudiates ultimately forces itself onto the text, Crews' novel appears as a heterosexual performative that presents the norm it resorts to as rebellion against organizational authority. The transgressiveness of the appearance of pregnancy in the beauty contests participated in by Gaye Nell Odell and her mother demonstrates Crews's attempt to represent heterosexual prac-tice and pregnancy as counter to the heterosexual performative. When Gaye Nell Odell tells Kaimon that she was on display in a beauty contest before she was born (as a fetus in her mother's uterus), she recognizes the priority of the heterosexual performative over the body (188). Despite the fact that pregnancy is thus figured as a subversion of this heterosexual performative, the centrality of sexual reproduction in the novel's conclusion undermines the potential for a critical performativity.[9] The opposition between good parental sex and the bad constructed sex of the beauty context fails to recognize the performative relatedness of the construction and prac-tice of heterosexuality. Moreover, the capitulation of Gaye Nell Odell, who had earlier tried to abort her fetus, to Kaimon's familial intentions suggests a misogynist aspect of Crews's assertion of the nuclear family and turn to a reproductive hetero-sexual performative.[10] Crews evokes Gaye Nell Odell and Kaimon as outsiders in the heterosexual world, who are aware of the heterosexual peformative. Such aware-ness reflects the "theoretical precociousness" and sensitivity to the codification of social behavior that Constance Penley, writing of the southern cracker culture in which she, like Crews, was raised, identifies with this white trash milieu (90). Yet the fact that the story ends as it does indicates the residue in *Karate Is a Thing of the Spirit* of what Butler, extending Monique Wittig's idea of "heterosexual contract" and Adrienne Rich's concept of "compulsory heterosexuality," defines as the heterosexual matrix (*Gender* 151).

The heterosexual normativity of Crews' novel is considerably qualified by the fact that homosexuality also asserts itself against the performative repudiations of the karate group. On one occasion a number of gay men stand at the bottom of the swimming pool where a karate lesson for children is taking place (108). Despite their best attempts to ignore this sight and focus on the lesson, teacher and students all look at the gay men. As a result, they hit the mackawari boards harder and harder to repudiate the consciousness of gay sexuality through iterated bodily performance. That the children are congratulated by their parents for this repudiation suggests they are iterating their bodies for sexual identity as well as karate proficiency (109). Whereas earlier karate appeared to repudiate heterosexuality, the iteration of a normative familial heterosexuality in this scene indicates that what was previously repudiated was uncontrolled heterosexual attraction. In the economy of the novel, therefore, homosexuality and the heterosexuality of Gaye Nell Odell and Kaimon have solidarity in both being repudiated by performative karate.

The centrality of homosexual identity to the linguistic performativity of the body in *Karate Is a Thing of the Spirit* is demonstrated by the association of gay men and language throughout the novel. When Kaimon first makes his decision to follow the karate people he is motivated by the desire to abandon language in favor of the body. He chooses not to accompany George and Marvin because "he had not come this long way to get involved with something he knew all about" (24). Language and gay men are the two things he knows about and initially rejects—yet both keep returning. As a means of preserving the spiritual vehicularity of the body against the taint of language, the karate commune denies linguistic referentiality and instead invokes acts of the spirit or will as the source of meaning. The commune's diet contains tasteless pills called "green leafy vegetables" or "red meat" (48). These monikers exemplify the division between language and the body that Kaimon is seeking: just as the self-contained body is free of language, terms such as "green leafy vegetables" refer to nothing other than themselves. Kaimon tries to "believe" (49) that the pills do taste like green leafy vegetables but he can not, and this signals the appearance of the problematic of language within his karate experience. Kaimon is as perturbed by a referential asceticism that denies language's connection with the world as he is by the correlative body asceticism that repudiates the influence of language. On one occasion he wills himself to eat masses of the tasteless pills (and this provokes an acceptable form of visual recognition in the karate commune as the others watch him), yet, like the instance when he wills himself into the isolated spiritual karate state, this is a desperate and transient occurrence (88). These two acts of will in language and the body are predicated upon the repudiation of gay sexuality from Kaimon's consciousness. His being accosted by George and Marvin is one of the thoughts he tries to repudiate when bingeing on the pills, and he achieves his karate spirit by repudiating the presence of the gay men at the swimming pool in his violent striking of the mackawari board. Both instances fail to prevent the problematic of language and its performative relation to the body from being visited upon Kaimon.

Given Andrew Parker and Eve Kosofsky Sedgwick's identification of the queer connotations of "etiolation," a term used by Austin to develop his theory of performative utterances (3–5), it is appropriate that in Crews's novel it is the gay characters who are the most significant agents of the return of performativity. We have already seen how Kaimon perceives the body in linguistic terms; through the gay characters Kaimon realizes how the linguistic categories of sexual difference determine the gendered perception of the body. This latter strain in *Karate Is a Thing of the Spirit* is particularly important because it returns Kaimon to the language of Faulkner that he originally sought to escape, and it reveals most clearly the ambivalent nature of the performative body. Butler describes the ambivalent nature of gay performativity in her study of the drag competitions in Jennie Livingston's *Paris Is Burning* (1991). Butler analyzes these competitions, in which black men in New York City compete in various drag categories, as simultaneously reinscribing and challenging the gender norms they imitate, such as those of ideal feminine types (*Bodies* 125). In approximating to the "realness" of categorized types (e.g., the executive woman, the Ivy League student, etc.), the competitors expose these "real" types as signs within a code of gender identity. In Butler's reading of Lacanian psychoanalysis, the assumption of the Symbolic order constitutes the subject according to the law of sexual difference. In other words, it is by being placed within a system of language that is based upon the apportioning of sexual difference that the subject is constituted. Butler's theory of the performative rewrites the Lacanian paradigm to argue for the primacy of gender norms of subjectivity, such as those reiterated in *Paris Is Burning*, that are not isolated in a linguistic system but must be continually proven through the iteration of the body. In Crews's novel and Butler's theory, iterativity is the source of the ambivalence of the performative: on the one hand, iterativity means that the performative lacks substantial foundation and can be exposed as such; on the other hand, iterativity may cause any attempted parody or subversion of the performative to become its realization.

Kaimon's experience of gender performativity occurs as an ordeal of linguistic disorientation similar to his bewilderment over the food pills. In a nightclub called The Iron Horse Kaimon goes to the men's rest room. Thinking of the labels "Set-ters" and "Pointers" on the bathroom doors, Kaimon is shocked to see a woman in the men's rest room whom, when he reveals his penis, is shown to be a man in drag. The shock is so great because as in the famous example of the rest room doors in Lacan's "The Agency of the Letter in the Unconscious, or Reason Since Freud," the public rest room is the sanctum of sexual difference, where the linguistic code of "men" and "women" most powerfully determines gendered perceptions of the body. Throughout The Iron Horse gender codes are self-consciously performed, inverted, amalgamated, and seemingly subverted. As Kaimon is told by Lazarus the bouncer, "Everything's in drag in here. Men dressed like women. Women dressed like men. And some dressed like both" (71). Working in The Iron Horse has made Lazarus regard the "normal" world as "strange" (72). The fact that he winks as he says this, as well as his comment that perverts who think they are normal are not allowed in the club, indicates that the notion of normality has not merely been relocated in "perversity" but has been radically problematized—nothing can really be normal if it is only (per)formed as such due to its position within a semiotic gender code. However, the subversiveness of such gender performativity is limited. Kaimon asks Lazarus why the man he saw in the men's room was not in the women's room. Lazarus tells him that the sign of the bathroom marks the limit of gender performativity. By telling Kaimon that men must go to the men's rest room and women must go to the women's rest room so that the tourists do not get upset, Lazarus admits the subservience of the performativity of The Iron Horse to a binary code of normality and tourism oddity that regards itself as pre-significatory and therefore does not recognize its own coded nature. This larger social binary inscribes the performativity of The Iron Horse as an oddball inversion of the natural reduction of gender to sex so that the authority of a constative bodily sex emerges triumphant.[11] As a result, the performative bodies of the club members, like the competitors in Paris Is Burning analyzed by Butler, reinforce as much as challenge gender norms, and Kaimon's realization of this is accompanied by relief: "When she pissed like that something let go in me and I could move again so I turned around and got the hell out of there" (70).

By declining to mention the sexuality of the man in drag Crews avoids the conflation of gender and sexuality, where, for example, women who take on masculine gender attributes are automatically assumed to be lesbian. Crews further avoids the overdetermination of the gender-sexuality nexus by using gay characters to show how the ambivalent effect produced by the gendered performance of the body informs not only overt acts of gender but also other performances of the body. When a group of gay men that includes George and Marvin take a karate lesson, this event is described as a gay signifying upon the karate body that exposes the latter as performatively textual rather than as a non-linguistic invocation of the spirit. However, in addition to illustrating how the performativity of gay sexuality can unmask the coded nature of the would-be constative body, this scene also means that the gay characters have assumed and thus reinscribed the constative bodily ideology of karate. Kaimon for one thinks that the gays took the lesson seriously, and this thought reflects his tendency towards not recognizing the performativity of the body that is apparent in his initial decision to join the karate group, his unproblematic assumption of heterosexual normativity, and elsewhere.

The crucial role of George and Marvin in drawing attention to the varied means by which linguistic performativity forms perceptions of the body suggests that Crews shares Butler's emphasis on the unmasking of the gendered performativity of the body by queer culture. As in the rest room scene, Kaimon's perception of the body when watching two erotic dancers in The Iron Horse is determined by gender codes. Kaimon assumes that the dancers are women who are objectifying themselves for the pleasure of the male gaze. He gets sexually aroused, but when he visits the dancers' dressing room they turn out to be George and Marvin. Kaimon realizes this when he recognizes in the dressing room the aluminum print of Faulkner on the back of his jersey. Kaimon had left his jersey with George and Marvin the moment he ran to join the karate group. This incident represents Kaimon's rejection of language and the association between language and homosexuality, and the recognition scene enacts Kaimon's inability to escape language either in terms of the codes of sexual difference that are disclosed by their drag performance or the influence of Faulkner. Like Butler, Kaimon appreciates the inseparability of language and the body, but instead of considering the body as a performative gender text, he comes to understand language self-reflectively as the physical act of authorship. During an argument with Kaimon, Belt proclaims some incredible physical feats performed throughout history, and Kaimon responds by describing Faulkner's writing feats as an equivalent physical accomplishment. Here, Crews opposes the unacknowledged performativity of karate's wordless bodily rituals of the spirit to a physical ordeal of writing, such as his own writing of *Karate Is a Thing of the Spirit*, in which a performative circuit of the disciplining of the body through its own production of language is recognized and endured.[12]

Despite Crews's turn towards a non-gendered treatment of language's performative relation to the body, the effect of his writing, such as a critique of the spirit

invoked by the karate commune, resonate with Butler's analyses. The primary consequence of mutilating his hands during his initial session on the macakwarai board is
Kaimon's inability to write: "Couldn't hold a pen. Couldn't type" (57). This exercise
in the spirit has therefore undermined Kaimon's ability to produce physical language.
In lieu of writing, Kaimon recites aloud a letter to Faulkner detailing the events that
led up to the reappearance of the Faulkner jersey in George and Marvin's dressing
room. Gaye Nell Odell overhears Kaimon, and she later tells him that this "move"
of reciting a letter to Faulkner marks the successful culmination of his karate training. Gaye Nell Odell thus concedes that karate is a thing of language as much as it
is of the spirit. However, Kaimon's experience of the constitutive function of language goes beyond Gaye Nell Odell's lauding of speech as the incarnation of "spirit"
or presence.[13] In the aforementioned argument with Kaimon, Belt counters by saying
that if Faulkner's writing was "perverted" (as Kaimon claims) then this means that
Faulkner himself was perverted: " 'If the heart is true the sword is true' means only
that the heart is manifest in the sword. The sword *is* the heart" (142, 143). Belt
reiterates Gaye Nell Odell's metaphysics of presence by claiming that Faulkner's
writing (sword) is reducible to his spirit (heart). Kaimon disputes whether this interpretation solves the "mystery" of Faulkner's writing, which is that it appears physically impossible yet is tangibly real. Belt insists that Kaimon should find the solution
to this mystery "in the spirit," yet the spirit is not real to Kaimon: "John Kaimon
couldn't really think of the inside of himself. . . . All that came to him were images
of veins and arteries and livers and other large damp organs that went squish squish
squish in places cast in the perpetually pink haze of blood" (143, 144). That it is
language that precludes the conjuring of the spirit is evidenced by the fact that on
another occasion Kaimon had failed to discover a "barren nothingness" within himself because he could not find any inner spirit or self prior to or more fundamental
than language: "*Barren nothingness.* The two words came back and hung in his head
like hooks. Barren nothingness? Where had he known that? Where had he learned
it?" (118).[14] Kaimon's understanding breaks out of the paradigms established by
Belt and Gaye Nell Odell by regarding language as irreducibly material in terms of
the physical act of writing and the material signifier that precludes the manifestation
of the signified spirit. When he leaves the karate commune, this is due not only to his
disillusionment with Belt's commercialism and his and Gaye Nell Odell's decision to
go through with her pregnancy, it is also the outcome of the incompatibility between
the understanding of language and the body in performative terms that Kaimon has

been exposed to and the karate commune's adherence, in Butler's terms, to the priority of the spirit over the body and of the body over language.

Yet even as the narrative concludes with an act that makes a spectacle of the karate commune's bogus attempt to pass the linguistic constitution of the body off as an unspeakable ordeal of the spirit, Kaimon goes on "believing" in the heterosexual normativity that his familial union with Gaye Nell Odell reinscribes. Kaimon describes himself as "the world's champion believer" (50), and Belt tries to replace Kaimon's belief-compulsion with a doctrine of the will. Kaimon demystifies the unacknowledged performativity of Belt's philosophy, but he reacts to this by returning to belief rather than the incredulity towards writing or karate accomplishments that he momentarily feels. According to Butler, gender is "a constructed identity, a performative accomplishment which the mundane social audience, including the actors themselves, come to believe and to perform in the mode of belief" (*Gender* 141). While there is no doubt that Butler's theory of performativity is ambivalent and perhaps even pessimistic, her conclusion to *Gender Trouble* suggests that it is possible to disbelieve the normativity that gender performativity iterates: "Genders can be neither true nor false, neither real nor apparent, neither original nor derived. As credible bearers of those attributes, however, genders can also be rendered thoroughly and radically *incredible*" (141). In returning to the mode of belief Kaimon becomes part of the mundane social audience. In the very act that represents his debunking of the karate commune's constative metaphysics of body and spirit, Kaimon performatively reinscribes an outlaw form of heterosexual normativity.

For all the freakery of its anomalous characters and aberrant practices, the narrative of Crews's *Karate Is a Thing of the Spirit* concludes in a very traditional manner. Along with Crews's blunt style that can seem offensive, such conservatism suggests why Crews has only rarely been discussed in terms of cultural theory that often challenges the constructed and performed bases of normative representations.[15] If this is so then the neglect is unwarranted because Crews's writing displays considerable subtlety in traversing issues of language and the body that are central to much cultural theory. Even though Crews differs from theorists like Butler in that he may dispense with the gendered emphasis on the performative body and reinscribe heterosexual norms, he represents the performativity of language and the body in ways that have similarities with Butler's work. Butler is highly ambivalent about the practices of performativity, and the inability of Crews's characters to break free of normative behaviors involves similar forms of ambivalence. In *Karate Is a Thing of the Spirit* such ambivalence is manifested in the experience of Kaimon, who resolves his crisis of subjectivity through the demystification of the performativity of the karate commune, an acknowledgment of the performativity of language and the body in his encounters with George and Marvin and his return to Faulkner, and the performative reinscription of behavioral norms that occurs in his final gesture of belief with Gaye Nell Odell. By thinking of fiction such as Crews's in terms of theory such as Butler's, we get a sense of the considerable overlap that exists among apparently disparate sectors of contemporary American culture. Crews's superficial machismo is often the vehicle for complex negotiations of language, gender and the body. Similarly, the apparently rarefied discourse of cultural theory often addresses the very real bodies of marginal social life. Whether as cultural theorists or literary critics of Crews's work, if we fail to comprehend such cross-currents we distort the map of our cultural terrain.

AN INTERVIEW WITH HARRY CREWS

Erik Bledsoe

The following interview was conducted on July 26, 1997, at Harry Crews's home in Gainesville, Florida. Like many writers who have been interviewed repeatedly, Crews has stock answers that he gives to frequently asked questions. I wanted to avoid asking the usual questions. In particular, I vowed not to ask him about the so-called freaks that populate his fiction. Entirely accustomed to the interview process, Crews did not wait for me to begin taping or even to ask a question before he launched into an "answer" about his writing habits. The interview begins as he discusses his efforts to maintain both his productive work habits and the physical condition of his body, weakened by years of hard living and age.

CREWS: . . . so I said, "Good Lord, let me see what kind of shape I can get into one more time before I die," so my normal routine is I get up at 4:00 and start to work, and work until 8:30, when my gym opens. And then I go to the gym. Whatever isn't written between 4:00 and 8:30 doesn't get written. And then I come back and do all those things you have to do around the house and then I revise. I have to revise. Whatever I wrote in the morning doesn't even look like it did.

BLEDSOE: So, you revise in the afternoon what you wrote that morning?

CREWS: Yeah. But of course you understand that it's just the way I happen to work. Some guys write the book, trying to find a narrative line of a story in any language. But I can't do that. I find the story out of the language that I use.

I recently threw away a hundred pages. It was a bus trip, and I have to say I liked the writing, and I sort of liked what went on on the bus, except it just didn't belong in the book. And I didn't know it until George [*his longtime girlfriend*] read it. And she just made a couple of low-key observations, she wouldn't go and tell me how to write it or something. And as soon as she said it, I thought, "Oh man, that won't do." So, I threw it away.

I do a lot of things that are not, I think, the best way to go about it. But as you know, every writer works a different way. Some writers can't work any way except starting to work when it starts to get dark. Work all night, sleep all day. I don't trust anything I write at night. I did when I was young. Because I had to. I had to go out and make a living. I worked ten years, writing as hard as I knew how to write, and I made one hundred dollars. Sold a story to *Sewanee Review*. Then I published *The Gospel Singer* in 1968. And I pretty much published everything I've written since then. I don't understand. I turned the corner. I'd also had migraine headaches, bad ones, up to that time. Published *The Gospel Singer* and never had another one.

BLEDSOE: How did you find a publisher for *The Gospel Singer*?

CREWS: Oh, God, oh God. Well, fasting and praying and watching small drops of blood break out on sundry parts of my body. I sent it to World Publishing Company because I saw that they—this is how innocent I was—they were having a, quote, novel contest for unpublished writers, unquote, and Herbert Gold, who later I got to know, was the judge. So I sent it up there, and in about a month I got this letter that said, "We're gonna publish your novel." And, God, I was overjoyed. To make it short, they kept it a year and a half. No contract. No money had changed hands.

And Donn Pearce, who wrote *Cool Hand Luke*, happened to live in the same town, Fort Lauderdale. I told him that and he said, "You're fucking crazy! What are you doing that for? Get your book."

I said, "No, no. They said they were gonna publish it. I can't."

And then he got me an agent in New York. And the agent wrote back and said, "This is crazy. You're crazy. Write me a letter. Give me authorization. Let me go and get your damned book back."

He did. In five days I had a contract from William Morrow, who published the first five books I wrote. That's the way it was. And then I left that agent after that book and went with John Hawkins and Associates, John Hawkins. He's been my agent ever since. Thirty years.

BLEDSOE: You left the first agent after *The Gospel Singer?* Or after the first five novels?
CREWS: No. The first five books were published by William Morrow, but I got a new agent for *Naked in Garden Hills*, John Hawkins.

And one day Hawkins called me—I think it's probably one of the really bad moves I ever made—John Hawkins called me and he said, "I was at a party last night and the guy that runs Knopf came up and said, 'I want to whisper something in your ear.' "

And he said, "What?"

And he said, "Harry Crews."

He said, "I'll give you some money"—it wasn't much, a little bit of money— "just for switching publishers, and we'll get the next book." And I had a book done.

And so I published two books with that publisher. The first book they took of mine was *The Hawk Is Dying*. Couldn't get along with that editor, though.

BLEDSOE: You've talked about growing up and you've told the story about the Sears, Roebuck catalog a lot. But making up stories about the Sears, Roebuck catalog is a world away from imagining that you can actually make a living writing stories.
CREWS: I didn't, I didn't, I never thought of it as making a living at it. Certainly back then I was just a little kid. I'm a storyteller, that's what I do. I just imagine that I'm back in the Stone Age and I'm squatting in front of the cave, and all my buddies with loincloths and wives and children and all are standing around, and we're eating saber-tooth tiger. And I killed that sabertooth tiger that day. And I'm squatting there, and I say to them, "That tiger, when I first saw it, he come charging and got me up a little spindly tree, so spindly that he couldn't climb it. So I was at the top of it."

Well, the obvious question the reader always asks is "What then? Why do we have the tiger on the fire and you're not eaten up?" So I gotta get out of that somehow; I've got to tell the story. And you don't tell stories by, oh God, making the novel the subject of the novel. Or whatever.

BLEDSOE: You've expressed your disdain for postmodernism before.
CREWS: I was gonna use that word, but I decided I wouldn't. But no, "disdain" is probably not too strong a word. It probably is not too strong a word, but I don't know. Disdain? It's just not my bag, man. It's just not.

BLEDSOE: How do you handle students in your classes who come in and that's what they want to do?

CREWS: Well, I don't teach anymore. Haven't taught for a while now. But there were never any "thou shall nots" in a writing class. You and I both know—hardly new to anybody—that you can't teach writing novels or stories. Maybe you can teach writing essays, but I doubt that too, [not] very good essays. You can teach form, but there won't be very much inside the form. There were no "thou shall nots," except you couldn't write horror stories, science fiction, or detective shit. You couldn't do that. But outside that, you could write anything you wanted to.

A writer can't be taught, but he can be coached. And we would have a conversation. Criticism should never be a monologue. It ought to be a dialogue. Mainly because you're trying to get a young writer—and sometimes an old, established writer—to see what he has done. He is so damn close to it, has lived with it for so long, that he can't see it anymore. And if nothing else, a good editor—and there are damn few of them left—he can get you to see what you've done, and sometimes in seeing that he doesn't even have to tell you. You see where you went wrong.

BLEDSOE: You've written that "A teacher must hold up a standard of excellence to his student and demand that he at least make every effort to meet the standard. But it has to be done in such a way that his spirit, his desire to excel, is not killed." How do you walk that line?

CREWS: Not easily. Not easily. And I know, as does every other teacher who will admit it, I know that I've hurt a great many students without meaning to. You don't want to take everything from the writer. Among other things, you want to give him a place to go back and work. A good class is where the writers can't wait to get home to their typewriters, and, as a matter of fact, about half the classes, they don't want to come to. They want to stay home and write. If you turn them into somebody who doesn't want to write, then you've just failed and hurt them.

I try as best I can to see what they've done, and understand what they're trying to do. And that can only come out of them; it can't come out of me. I help them to do that by talking to them. Talking about language. Writing is good to the degree that it is concrete and specific. And bad to the degree that it is abstract and vague. You know. I don't know what a soul is. I don't know what a spirit is. I don't know what your, your—my endeavor to soar among the—all that kind of writing. I don't know what any of that is. I know what a brick is. I know what steps are. Shoes. And, God bless me, ladies' panties. I know what they are. They're the stuff of the world; they're what makes our heart sing. A brick can make your heart sing. You know?

BLEDSOE: Out of any given class, how many students in there can really write?

CREWS: Man, I'll tell you, the last class—the last few classes—I taught, every one of them wrote really, really well. They *wrote* well. The problem was that—I'll just go ahead and say it—they didn't have anything to write about. I go to great pains to tell them that it was a great shock to me to learn that writing well was not enough. God knows, that's hard enough, but learning to write well is not enough.

You know, when the thing is put together in four or five hundred pages, it ought to mean something, it ought to be memorable, it ought to feel inevitable. The reason the stuff happens in the book the way it does is because it couldn't happen any other way. It ought to have that feeling. And it ought to hurt your heart. It ought to crush your heart with a living memory. And then you do remember it. Try to remember an episode of *Perry Mason*. Or any other of those things that purport to be drama on television. You can't. You can't. Not a single one can you remember. The highest rated thing on television is *Seinfeld*. Now, try to remember one episode. You can't. But books!

BLEDSOE: You said earlier that you thought that leaving Morrow was a mistake.

CREWS: Yeah, I do.

BLEDSOE: Why?

CREWS: Because I had a great editor there who—he had just started, he was younger than I was, and I wasn't very old when I published *The Gospel Singer*, but he was a *great* editor. The best editor I've ever had, Jim Landis. Who's no longer at Morrow. No longer in publishing. He's writing. Novels. That fool. [*Laughs.*] But anyway, I like Jim Landis a lot, and it genuinely hurt him when I left. I wrote him a letter, the kindest letter I could write. I said, "Hey listen, bud, when my work is in with me and the legal pad and the pencil in the room where I write, it's—I hope—art. Or at least I have pretensions to art. When it gets outside that room, it's a business. The guy offered me money, I need money. I got a wife and a kid, and I don't make much where I work."

BLEDSOE: Erskine Caldwell's widow once told me that she thought the greatest mistake Caldwell had made was switching publishers, because he didn't stay and develop a career with Scribner's, particularly with Max Perkins. Reynolds Price has told me that he was very conscious of staying with the same publisher throughout his career.

CREWS: Well, good for him. He's smarter than I was, that's all. I just thought that's what you did—you do what your agent tells you to do. That's why he's a ten-percenter; he's got ten percent of your life. And so he said it was a good idea, and I knew Knopf, I mean, damn, I thought they had—and they may have had at this time, they may have now—the best list in the country. I did what I thought was right and it wasn't.

BLEDSOE: I want to go back a ways to your story "The Player Piano."

CREWS: Way back.

BLEDSOE: That reminds me of Caldwell. It's got that same kind of sexual tension going on with one character not really being aware of the overtones that are being made. Were you reading a lot of Caldwell at the time?

CREWS: Yeah, and since you . . . you ever read a story of Caldwell's called "A Knife to Cut the Cornbread With"?

BLEDSOE: Yeah.

CREWS: You know, there it is. The guy's paralyzed and his wife is out picking cotton, and he's in there paralyzed in the bed. They don't have any meat to eat. Well, you don't have to go any further than that. He wisely left that off stage.

Here's sorta the way it went. The first writer I read all of was Mickey Spillane. *I, the Jury; My Gun Is Quick; Kiss Me, Deadly*—I could name them all. Well, I can't name them all because I stopped, and he's written some more, but reading, like water, seeks its own level. You get tired of that after a while. You run into something else. And, I admit it, I was in my early teens, and I just liked all those naked ladies and stuff.

And then, curiously enough, I went to Caldwell. I didn't read him all then. But I read a lot of it. And then I went to Somerset Maugham. Read all of him. I really did. And then I read all of Ayn Rand, *The Fountainhead* and so on. Well, Somerset Maugham's got one book. Well, you can give him more than that. *Of Human Bondage* is a fine book. The rest . . . He's an expert at cheating, particularly in short stories. The guy I studied with, Andrew Lytle, used to call him "that old whore of litera-ture." Ayn Rand, of course, doesn't write as well as Maugham does, and she writes thesis literature, which I've been accused of writing. I don't care. I don't believe I do or did. And a lot worse things have been said about me than that. But then some-where after Maugham I went to Greene. And when I went to Greene, man, I *did* read all of him. And I read him again.

I read a lot of stuff that's just coming out, but I also read a lot of things like—well, William Faulkner said he read *Madame Bovary* once a year. I don't do that, but

I read a lot of stuff back there. I read to steal. I read—if not to steal, you can say it a better way—to learn. It's not as though I go through there with a pencil trying to pick up lines. I don't. You get it through your skin. It's osmosis or something.

BLEDSOE: Your first published story, "The Unattached Smile," appeared in *Sewanee Review*.

CREWS: Yeah.

BLEDSOE: Lytle was the editor at the time?

CREWS: Yeah, he was.

BLEDSOE: Did he help you get that published? Did it come up in a workshop and he said, "I want this"?

CREWS: No, no. Mr. Lytle had left here and gone back up there to Sewanee to be editor of the *Sewanee Review* and other things, and I was here working with another guy, Smith Kirkpatrick, to whom *Naked in Garden Hills* is dedicated, probably a mistake, probably should have dedicated . . . I never dedicated a book to Mr. Lytle because I never thought I wrote anything he would want his name on. Mr. Lytle wanted nothing but perfection, in his work as well as yours, which he knew he couldn't have. But he wanted it anyway. But no, Mr. Lytle never saw that in workshop or in draft.

But once he accepted it at the *Review*, I went through about ten different revisions. He would just say little things, and you could see right off that he was right. And the little things would lead to other things. God, he would have made a great editor. If he had wanted to go to a house, I really do believe that he could have had the reputation of a Maxwell Perkins, or somebody like that. Man, when he read something of yours, the words were read right off the page. He didn't even have to look at the story when he was talking to you about it. He never looked at the story.

BLEDSOE: He died just over a year ago. How did that affect you?

CREWS: As though some rent had been made in my life or a big hole jerked in it that can never be replaced. Although he was no longer reading for me or . . . I still enjoyed . . . Mr. Lytle always . . . I enjoyed talking to him. Mr. Lytle tended to talk in essays. I mean, you'd ask him a question, and he would give you an essay back. And I certainly don't mean that in any pejorative sense. But he would.

But we were from very different Souths, and I don't think he ever realized that. His daddy sent him to France to study. His daddy was a planter that never touched a plow, never had his hands on a plow or stock. My family was the white trash way down at the end of the road from the big house. And, you know, he never understood that. I remember one time we were driving somewhere, and I brought up the white/black business. Well, anyway, I don't want to talk about . . . but what he gave me was an essay, essentially, out of the Middle Ages, where every man had his man, and God had the king, and, obviously, the poor shall always be with us there on the bottom rung. But somebody's got to . . . I don't know. I'm doing him an injustice, but I did get an essay back. And I thought to myself, "I love you, I love you, but that's all bullshit." I mean, it ain't right. It ain't never been right. And it won't ever be right. But it's probably always going to be with us.

BLEDSOE: As far as I've been able to find out, you only published three short stories before *The Gospel Singer*, and I think you've published one more since then in a recent anthology called *Little Deaths*.

CREWS: I'll tell you about short stories. This may be a very bad reason not to write short stories, but here it is. Okay, you write a short story. How many places are there to publish it? I mean, nationally. *Playboy* and *Harper's* and *Atlantic* and whatever. But you can name them all with two hands. And, okay, on top of that, how many people are gonna read it? Even when you look at Raymond Carver's short stories, you look in the front of a collection, half of them were published in little magazines that maybe two thousand people read. All right, a lot of people read Raymond Carver short stories. Well, that was Raymond Carver. How many people are gonna read a book of short stories by Harry Crews? I don't think many people. Because I'll tell you something else, I don't think I've ever sold ten thousand copies of a hardcover book in my life. I finally found an audience. France. France. The French love me.

I just said, "Well, if you're gonna read anything, you read novels." Short stories, they're too hard to write to not have anybody read them.

BLEDSOE: You joined the Marines at seventeen.

CREWS: Yeah, well, just before my eighteenth birthday, but yeah, I was seventeen.

BLEDSOE: Okay, so, about 1953?

CREWS: Yeah.

BLEDSOE: That was during the Korean War. Did you serve in Korea?

CREWS: No. My brother was fighting in Korea at the time I joined. It ended while I was on Parris Island. And we were, of course, all extremely disappointed. There's something—and this may be a lie, or a myth, or whatever—but it seems to me that when a war breaks out, all the southern boys run down as quick as they can. Probably out of ignorance. And also because, in many instances—as was true in my case—there's no jobs, and I had no skills. And my brother was in Korea, you know, so you run down and join up.

I joined the Marine Corps for two reasons. I thought if you were gonna go, that you might as well try yourself. And the other reason, I frankly admit, was to see if I could do it. I had polio when I was a kid, or something. They think now it wasn't polio. That was the only thing I was worried about was my legs, whether or not they were strong enough. And I got through, you know.

BLEDSOE: After the Marines you came back and attended the University of Florida.
CREWS: Straight in there, Well, not straight in there; I went to Jacksonville and worked that summer in a pulp mill. Then I went to the University of Florida. And why I went to the University of Florida instead of the University of Georgia, God only knows. If I hadn't been a vet, they would have never let me in. I was a very bad student in high school because I wasn't there most of the time. If I could, I read all night long, and then I slept through the day. That was when we were at Jacksonville. My mom had to go to the King Edward cigar factory and work, so there was nobody there to make me go, so I just slept. I never failed a course, but I made a lot of D's. I didn't take any science, I didn't take any math, I didn't take any languages.

The university to me was really easy. I was there about a week or two weeks, we had to take a test of some sort, and a guy called me over to the administration and he said, "Look, on the basis of these here scores on these tests, what you ought to do is drop out and apprentice yourself to a cabinetmaker or a plumber or something, because you're gonna fail here. Then you're gonna think of yourself as a failure."

And he was a good guy, he meant well. And I said, "Does that mean I have to leave?"

And he said, "No, no, you can stay if you want to."

And I said, "I think I'll stay. Just let me give it a shot."

I made the dean's list the first semester, and with the exception of Shakespeare and a little geology, and a little history, I was never assigned a book I hadn't already read.

When I was in Jacksonville, of course, I had access to libraries. In Georgia I never did. And, it was very hard getting old books. When I went to my first duty station, I found out there was a library, there was a library on every station. And if they didn't have the book, they'd get it for you. So I spent my time in the Marine Corps with a rifle in one hand and a book in the other.

BLEDSOE: You left Florida after two years and took the eighteen-month motorcycle trip.

CREWS: Yeah, at the end of my sophomore year. I couldn't take it. I had a brand new motorcycle and I left here with less than a hundred dollars in my pocket. Didn't know where I was going or how long I was staying. And I went from, to make it quick, here to Wyoming, up through Montana to Canada, from Canada back across to Salt Lake City, Salt Lake City to San Francisco, San Francisco back across over Monarch Pass—the highest pass in the Rockies—to Colorado Springs, from Colorado Springs west over Rathhome Pass in New Mexico down to El Paso, down through the desert to the state of Chihuahua and the city of Chihuahua, back up to El Paso. And then the longest trip I ever expect to make, from El Paso to New Orleans. Across the longest part of Texas. I thought I would *never* get out of Texas. And from New Orleans back into Gainesville.

How'd I do it on a hundred dollars? I'll tell you. And I think it is true to this day, although people may tell me otherwise. If you can cook or tend bar, you can work in any city in this country. It ought to take you about two days to find a job. I'm not saying you'll make much money, maybe a lousy bar, maybe a neighborhood bar, maybe whatever. It may be turning hamburgers. So that's what I did. I did other jobs too, cut straw, worked in a salt mine where they let the ocean in and let it evaporate. I worked in a lot of places.

BLEDSOE: You've called *Naked in Garden Hills* your best book.

CREWS: I think it is and I think it would run even a good critic, a critic's critic, the guys who do this for a living, I think it would run the best of them crazy trying to figure out the time sequence, which I think makes sense and works. I like the people in it. I just like what I did in it.

Two books, *Naked in Garden Hills* and *Car*, both of them I wrote in six weeks. But in those days I was young. I pretty much lived on amphetamines and when I got too wired, there was always the bottle. I had a Mason fruit jar full of amphetamines and a bottle of Wild Turkey, and if you get too wired, you just take a hit. I'd bubble the bottle a couple of times and be ready to work. Stay up, it's amazing how long you can stay up when you are young. I was real healthy.

BLEDSOE: Most of the characters in that book are called something other than their given names.

CREWS: Well, if you look through all of my work, I've got a screwy thing about names.

BLEDSOE: What's up with that?

CREWS: I don't know. I really don't know. It might be somehow connected with the fact that I consciously change the way I look, pretty much every day. People have made a lot out of this, and it was all making fun of me or saying something bad about me, but that's all right, I don't mind that a bit. That's fine, doesn't hurt my feelings.

If you look at that picture back there, the documentary *Guilty as Charged*. Now that picture was made ten years ago, eleven years ago, and I had that mustache for twenty years, and it really is that white. I've had a Mohawk haircut; I had my head shaved for about three years.

It was down to my shoulders, and I was living out of town on a lake, and I got drunk one night, and I had a girl there with me, and I said, "I wonder what I'd look like bald."

And she said, "I don't know. Let's," she was drunk too, she said, "Let's shave your head."

And I said, "Fine, let's do it."

I forgot I had to go to the university the next morning. So I walk into the English Department. Then I thought you've got to have the courage of your madness, so I kept it shaved three years. I don't know. Maybe it has something to do with that.

Maybe it has something to do with this, and this will blow you away and you'll think "Oh, you've got to be kidding because it's not true." Well, maybe, maybe not. I think that all of my books, everything I've written as a matter of fact, including the journalism, in one way or another is either about people searching for something to believe in, something that has to do with faith, or the nature of faith.

And hooked, it seems inevitably, with that is identity, because after all, monks— that's one extreme end—have an identity, but then so do the churches devoted to worshipping Satan in the hills of California. Those guys have an identity.

BLEDSOE: So in order to have something that you believe in, you must first know who you are? And tied up in that is naming?

CREWS: Yeah, I would agree with that. And connected to that—I've said this before, but I don't think I've ever written it—yeah, I have; I wrote it in the *Childhood* book in the front where I've got all those disclaimers. But I have never been sure of who I am.

I was in the university my whole working life; I was *in* it, but not *of* it. I wrote that somewhere; I've written everything I know somewhere. So somebody calling me "professor"—I don't have a Ph.D. I don't even have a master's, really. The English Department I taught in turned me down to work for an English master's degree, and I got a master's degree in education, which is no master's degree at all. I never even bought any of their books. You don't have to buy their books. I made up the bibliographies for papers I wrote. I made up the footnotes. I made up the authors. Nobody ever knew, nobody ever cared. I got a master's degree in nine months and didn't write a thesis, had no language. You figure it out. But it allowed me to teach in a junior college. The year previous to that I met a hundred and eighty kids every day.

BLEDSOE: Teaching in junior high?
CREWS: Yeah, and taught five different classes in five different buildings. And wrote a book that year. It's called *This World Uncommitted*, and you can tell from the title what it might have been like. It's a very bad book.

BLEDSOE: You called *Naked in Garden Hills* your best book; you've also referred to *This Thing Don't Lead to Heaven* as being the book you are the least satisfied with.
CREWS: You know, I did say that, and I've changed my mind.

BLEDSOE: Okay, why?
CREWS: I changed my mind because it was the third book I wrote, and it is dedicated to my dead son. James Boatwright, who was then and perhaps is now, was until very recently if he's not still down there, the editor of the *Shenandoah Review*, he reviewed it in the *New York Times*. Half a page review. Big, big review. He was not just unhappy with the book. He was unhappy that I was alive. About halfway through the review it just switched from the book to me. I just believed the guy. It was an early book and I believed the guy. I caught the virus. I got down on it.

Later, when he was on sabbatical and a poet was the guest editor, I published a piece in his journal, the *Shenandoah Review*, that won the Coordinating Council of Literary Magazines in America's award for the best nonfiction piece published in any literary magazine in the whole country that year.

BLEDSOE: What was that piece?
CREWS: It was a piece out of the *Childhood* book. It was the piece dealing with the scalding.

BLEDSOE: Okay.
CREWS: About that, let me just tell you this. Most people don't notice this stuff,

some do, some don't. I'd been writing really regularly a book a year almost, and then I got into dope and stuff and it was a book every two years, but the *Childhood* book . . . I wrote the *Childhood* book, and then after that I published *Blood and Grits*, but that book was already written, so you can't count that. So I wrote the *Childhood* book, and then there was a nine-year yawning silence. And it was simply because the *Childhood* book damn near killed me. I don't want to make too much out of it. But I thought, and maybe I've written this somewhere, but I thought that living through it again, remembering it all and writing it down in the most concrete, specific language I could summon, would be cathartic and I would no longer be plagued with the memories. Didn't work at all. So much for that.

I'm writing now, or I have a contract with Simon and Schuster to write, a book called *Assault of Memory*, which is another memoir after the fashion of *A Childhood*, but in this one I am starting out when I'm ten, my brother is fourteen, my mother is just going into a body cast.

BLEDSOE: Has this one been as difficult to work on?

CREWS: I've quit working on it. I wrote my agent and said I'm happy with what I've got. I've got about, I don't know, a hundred and eighty manuscript pages, but I just couldn't go on with it.

And I had a novel with me that I'd been working on for a long time; it was called *The Horsehog-Gator Connection* and then it was called a whole bunch of things. It was called just *Horse*, now it's called this, and it'll probably be called something else finally. But I've had it with me a long time, and I like it. So I said I'll just finish this novel.

I do think that if I live, and assuming they don't blow the frigging world up, that I'll finish *Assault of Memory* because I really want to write it, but, damn, it's ugly. And I just, you know . . . I'd much rather sit here and look at the trees—and just beyond, just right out where the trees start is a little creek. And it is clear, a really clear little creek. Poison, of course.

BLEDSOE: I know that you worked on several screenplays in the early eighties.

CREWS: Yeah, earlier than that . . .

BLEDSOE: Has anything ever come out of any of the screenplays that you've done?

CREWS: Money! I got paid for them. Larry McMurtry's told me he'd written, at that time, and this was a couple of years ago, that he's written twenty-seven screenplays, and I think he said three or maybe four had been made into films. That's generally the way it works.

I wrote a screenplay for *The Gospel Singer*. See, I sold *The Gospel Singer* outright to Larry Spangler. I'd already found the location to shoot the film, Tallahassee, Alabama. It looked just like the town I had described in Enigma, Georgia. But he got into some legal trouble, and he sold my screenplay to Tom Jones. I went to see Tom Jones, and he hit on my wife. That was fun, hit on her while I was sitting there. Sally was beautiful though; she's a very beautiful woman. Tom Jones hit on everything that moved. I'm surprised that he didn't hit on me. But he was on tour, and we went to see him on tour. Anyway, it got locked up in courts, between the two of them, and now it's tied up and nobody will ever make it, but I wrote the screenplay for it and got paid for that.

I wrote a screenplay for *Naked in Garden Hills* for Frank Perry. I learned what I know from him. And then I wrote a screenplay for *The Hawk Is Dying*. That fell through. Couldn't find the money. I wrote an original screenplay for Sean Penn. He took me out to his house in Hollywood for a week and introduced me to Ed Harris and some of his other friends. I was supposed to write a screenplay for those people to be in. Ed Harris is one of my favorite movie guys anyway. So, yeah, I've written some screenplays. I wrote a screenplay for Michael Cimino right after *Heaven's Gate* came out.

BLEDSOE: Who's doing *The Knockout Artist*? And is it far enough along now that it will be made?

CREWS: Francis Ford Coppola is the moving force behind it. A guy named Don Was, if you know anything about music, he's the guy that is directing it. Coppola was the guy that talked him into getting out of making videos and other things and into big screen. Coppola's company is doing the money part of it.

Francis Ford Coppola put in for me to write the screenplay for Kerouac's *On the Road*, which he's got the rights to. I didn't tell him yes; I didn't tell him no. I went down to the end of the street and bought the damn book and read it again, and said, "I don't want to write this." And I didn't. And I called him, and I said, "No, I don't think I want to write it."

And he said, "What do you want, more money?"

And I said, "That's not the issue. You know, you travel all the hell over in the book," and I named the city, and I said, "You know, I don't know the city, I don't know what it looks like this time of year, and I'd just be, I . . .

He said, "Hey, you rent yourself a big coach, get a couple of friends, put one in the driver's seat, just go, follow the route, whatever, do it that way."

I said, "Man, you know how long you're talking about taking out of my life? I mean, I'd be on the road for X number of weeks, then I'd be on the set."

See, I wrote a screenplay called *The New Kids*, about a boy and girl whose daddy was a colonel, and a big hero, and they lived up north. They'd lived all over, been overseas, army brats. Their daddy was flying to Washington for the President to pin a medal on him and the plane went down and crashed, and he and the mama died. Left the two kids. One's in the eleventh grade, and one's in the twelfth grade.

And the only relative they've got is an uncle, lives in Homestead, Florida, a cracker, and so they have to move down there to live with him. So, they've got to go, these two Yankee kids, into a redneck school.

The guy that made it, Sean Cunningham, his claim to fame is he made the first *Friday the 13th*, and got rich off it, and he's been making shitty pictures since. I was on the set of that film. I spent two days and two nights in a room with James Spader trying to teach him how to talk southern, because he was supposed to be a southern redneck. But he'd already had voice lessons in New York. I'd talk southern, and they only teach one dialect, the Delta dialect . . . "cah," you know, they call car "cah" . . . well, they don't call it "cah" down there, they call it "car," with a hard "rrrr," "carrrr." And he never could do that. But, we made the film.

All I can say is the money's good. And it was shitty work, but I liked Cunningham, I like his wife, they were down there, so it was all right. So, I've done a lot of that, and I've had the chance to do more. Had a guy that said, "Move to Los Angeles, I'll put you on salary and give you a great place to stay, and then when I got a project, then I'll pay you scale." I belong to the Screenwriters Guild, and—actually, it's the Writers Guild West, is what they call it. The least you can make for writing a screenplay is something like sixty thousand dollars; it goes up quickly from there. And it was really easy to say "no."

I'm gonna leave this? I ain't a screenwriter. I didn't start out to be a screenwriter; I didn't start out to work for *Playboy* either. I did it because my salary from the university went for alimony, so I had to make a nickel somewhere. And, so, that's what I did. I couldn't do it today. When I was younger, I stayed on the damn airplane, and in hotels, and dancing with people, you know.

BLEDSOE: During an interview while you were working on *Scar Lover*, you called it "the darkest, blackest book I've written." Yet many, most, reviewers have seen the ending as being kind of upbeat and affirming the possibility of love and family.

CREWS: Well, I guess I called it that. Naw. Obviously I think that if we polled a whole bunch of people who read this stuff, if we could find them, they'd say *Feast of Snakes* would be the blackest. But I don't know. I love the business of loving a scar because once it scars, it don't hurt no more. That's cool. You'd be hard pressed to name something on me that hadn't been broke, including my neck and my cheeks crushed, my nose broken. Anyway, so scars, I loved that.

But burning that guy, going in the freezer. I mean, I don't even know. Going in the cold storage and looking for the tag on his toe. Said, "The hell with the tag, look for one with four toes, cut one off in the chopping block" [*laughing*]. And the woman picking up the skull after it cools. She had her fingers in his eye sockets; it was like a bowling ball, and I wrote that and I thought, "man, damn, this is . . . where is this shit coming from? This is terrible."

BLEDSOE: *Scar Lover* and *The Mulching of America* seem to me to be a little bit different than your previous works in that . . .
CREWS: Outside the corpus . . . is that what they call it? Or whatever, oeuvre, or however you say that word. Yep, they seem to be outside and they are.

BLEDSOE: They are almost surreal.
CREWS: They are, they are. God knows, anybody with any sense of fair play knows that I am not full of myself; you can't mention Faulkner in the same breath with me, but it is a little like *A Fable* with Faulkner. Somebody gave him that idea; you know that. It's got it right in the book. "I'm indebted to so and so for this idea." Well, he should have gone and shot the guy who gave him the idea. I think, that's just my own opinion.

And truthfully, *Mulching of America* . . . um [*sighs*], *Mulching of America* just got away from me. It got away from me and I never could get it back. It has about it, certainly in the ending and in other places, the cardinal sin of any drama or novel; it is just totally unbelievable. It is painful to say these things, but, if it is the truth . . . It's like my ma said about the *Childhood* book, "If it's the truth, write it." So, the truth is that I wish I had the *Mulching* book back, and I would burn it. Although the French just bought it for, God bless them, I mean, I can keep my head above water for a while on what they paid for it. I don't know why. The French are curious people.

BLEDSOE: You've talked a lot in the past about writers that you've read that influenced you, who you think are good. What about the current crop of writers? Who do you think is out there writing right now that you think is good?
CREWS: Curiously enough, I think that Barry Hannah has the most distinctive voice

maybe in the whole damn country. He does things with sentences that I look at them and try to see what the hell he did with them to make them sound so memorable, so uniquely his own. I never can see. So I like his work a lot. One of the really new ones—well, he's been at it a while now, but it hasn't been too terribly long—Larry Brown is right up there. He lives right there by Barry Hannah. I don't know; people ask me questions like that and it's like asking "What books have you read recently?" and I can't name any despite the fact that I read constantly.

BLEDSOE: You've said before that "I'm a believer with nothing to believe." Could you elaborate on that a little bit?

CREWS: I am a believer. Natural laws just put you into a bind. Why does everything fall down instead of sideways? And why does sap rise at a certain time? And all that kind of thing. I mean, it just blows me away. And one famous theologian, whose name I can't recall, said the ultimate question to ask an atheist is "Why is there something instead of nothing?" And then you think about first cause. All right, some proteins came together and crawled up out of the sea, all right, but anyway, you know what I mean.

But number one, I have never . . . and I've tried, I really gave it a shot. I went to all of them practically that I could find, churches, organized religions, trying to find one that I could just . . . 'cause I think church is a really good . . . Going to church is really good for one reason: it is a place to go and sit down and contemplate the inadequacies of your own heart and just leave it there. But you could do that any-where. But I couldn't find anything like that.

And then secondly the whole business of—I mean, we've got Bangladesh and Bosnia, and there is supposed to be somebody or something somewhere that knows Harry Crews—Harry Crews?— and some kind of record is being kept? And we got mansions and streets of gold and, hell, I mean, really. Oliver Wendell Holmes, a confirmed atheist, said, "You'll have to forgive me if I cannot believe in your fairy tales."

But it's not so much believing. The Bible is a great book to read because there is just so much in it that is patently true. You can't go around coveting your neighbor's wife. It won't work. You don't necessarily need the Bible for that. But we live in a totally secular world. I mean the "God is dead" thing; of course, that goes back a long time, Nietzsche, even earlier.

But wouldn't it be wonderful, and I'm talking about me now, wouldn't it be wonderful for me if I did have something immutable, omnipotent, ubiquitous—all those other English teacher words—and that I could put myself into the keeping of that kind of power and knowledge. And He will, or She . . . It will provide. So, no, I believe, but there ain't nothing to believe. Said another way, the culture and, God help us, the economic system I live in has killed any semblance of anything that resembles or could resemble a godhead or first cause or anything like that.

If communism worked, if we really could "from each according to, to each according to," if it really worked . . . Property is theft. I really believe that. What am I doing in this house? Please tell me. When there are people sleeping in refrigerator cartons, boxes, pasteboard boxes, and starving to death, and my stomach is full. And I still got some money left. What the hell is that all about?

So, but for communism as Lenin and Marx and Engels, the stuff that all three of those guys wrote, for that to work you'd have to have an entire population of what Jesus is reported to have been. If you had everybody like that, then you could do it—somebody who would ride a donkey when he could get into a Cadillac. After all, if you can change water into wine, why not change water into Cadillac even back then? He could have just gotten himself some gas and tooled around. But he didn't do that.

BLEDSOE: Your comment about church being a good place to contemplate the inadequacies of your own heart actually sounds very familiar, very similar to some of the comments you've made about what effect you want to have on your readers. That you want them to look . . .

CREWS: I want my work to turn them back upon themselves and force them to look into their own hearts. And I think that if you can really get them so that they are so involved with, so enamored of, so outraged by these people that never existed—they don't exist, just little scratches on a piece of paper—if you can get them so enamored that they begin to make judgments, every effort of the writer is to make the reader make the judgments, the big judgments. You make the little ones—he was a little man—well, how little is little? What the hell does that mean? Well, let it go, you know, he was a little guy. Not those judgments. To make him make the big judgments.

The greatest of that kind of literature will change you, make you weep. Faulkner's short story "Two Soldiers"—if I want to tear up, I can just go read that. World War II has just started, and this guy says to his younger brother, "Well, I gotta go down and join up."

And his little brother says, "Yeah, we'll just have to go on down there and join up."

And he says, "Well, you can't go. You're too little."

And the little brother says, "Well, they'll have to have somebody to cut the wood and tote the water. I can go do that." And he follows his brother up to the recruiting station and pulls his knife—he's just a little boy—pulls his knife on the recruiting sergeant, but they finally sent him back home.

But there's a lot of places like that. Hemingway, as melodramatic and operatic as he can sometimes be, when Robert Jordan has broken his leg, right at the end of the book [*For Whom the Bell Tolls*], and he's running from the guys coming up the hill, and he's off his horse, he can't ride. Maria's still on the horse, and he says, "We can never go to Madrid together." And he's asking for a gun to hold them off as long as he can. And he and Maria are talking and she's got his baby, and interspersed all between this, which is just a stroke of genius, interlaced between this terribly touching thing between him and Maria, this fucking gypsy keeps saying, "Do you want me to shoot you, *Ingles*? It is nothing, *Ingles*. I could shoot you." He's not an Englishman, he's a goddamn American, but he calls him *"Ingles"* all through. You know, that's just a moment.

And that turns you always; it always comes back here [*pointing to himself*].

BLEDSOE: What was the last book that you read that had one of those moments that made you turn back in upon yourself?

CREWS: Well, I just got through with a book called *Suicide Blonde*—I wish they hadn't called it that—by Darcy Steinke. God, the paperback's got a naked lady lying on a bed lighting a cigarette—I wish that weren't there too—and it is, as George Garrett says on the back of the thing, aflame with sex. But it also deals with lust and love, and deals with how the promise of Eden can turn into a nightmare. It is beautifully written. It's about this girl that's living on the edge where there is no edge. She's looking right into the abyss. And she's not doing it to make a lot of money, she's not doing it to be famous, not for game, but really for the most ordinary human reasons. What kind of human reasons? Because she is lonely. Because she wants to be loved. Because she wants to save certain people she cares about from themselves. Just the kind of shit we all get caught in.

BLEDSOE: In *The Hawk Is Dying* you begin with an epigraph from Flaubert that I'll read . . .

CREWS: I can quote it.

BLEDSOE: Okay, go ahead.

CREWS: "Human language is" —I may get some words wrong, just let me say it— "Human language is a cracked bell on which we beat out tunes for bears to dance to while—while all the—something—we are longing to move the stars to pity." Which is just a long way around of saying that . . . anybody that writes a book and doesn't feel that it is a failure I am suspect of. It took Flaubert nine years to write *Madame Bovary*, but that don't mean nothing necessarily. The guy who wrote *Look Homeward, Angel*—see, I can't get these names. I know where the guy comes from and everything else.

BLEDSOE: Thomas Wolfe.

CREWS: Yeah. Thomas Wolfe's *Look Homeward, Angel* never would have been published if it had been left up to him. They gave him a little spot up in the Scribner's building and he was up there, goddamnit, rewriting the galleys, which you can't do. Jesus, it would cost a fortune to rewrite those sons-of-bitches. But he was. One time Maxwell Perkins sent him home to cut this piece, and he came back the next day and it was ten thousand words longer. Maxwell Perkins without his knowledge just sent the son of a bitch right on to the printer. Because, you know, he just couldn't get it right.

And all those times that Hemingway rewrote the ending to *A Farewell to Arms*. He rewrote it fifty-some-odd times.

They said, "What were you trying to do?"

He said, "Get the words right."

I always love answers like that. I mean, hey, don't ask me stupid questions. If I'd figured it out, I wouldn't have had to rewrite it fifty-three times, or forty-two, or nineteen, or whatever it was.

BLEDSOE: While you were working on *All We Need of Hell*, two excerpts appeared, both called "The Enthusiast," which was the novel's working title. One of those excerpts was in *Black Warrior Review*, but it is a very different-feeling piece than the published novel. It's about a writer named Harry Crews . . .

CREWS: Oh yeah, well, that now has become *Where Do You Go When There's No Place Left to Go?* Harry Crews is in that novel. And Belt is in it from the karate book. Margo the hotel whore is in it from *Car*, as is the boy that eats the car. Fat Man is in it from *Naked in Garden Hills*. The Gospel Singer is in it. He didn't die. He's got this purple scar around his neck. He can't sing anymore, but people can come up after he gets through preaching and they can hold his throat, and many times they are healed. But his voice is ruined from hanging on the rope all night. He can't sing anymore. And Didymus says that it's a miracle, but Harry Crews doesn't understand, because what would he know about miracles.

And it turns out, someplace in the book, Margo asks him, "Did you ever think about healing yourself or your ruined voice by holding your own throat?" And of course he holds his own throat, but he holds it so tight he ends up strangling himself to death.

It is a curious book. Those were curious times. I was starting things and not finishing them. And I was confused.

BLEDSOE: That's also about the same time that you started *Blood Issue*.
CREWS: Yeah, yeah, yeah, that was about that time. It's true.

BLEDSOE: But you didn't finish that until 1989 or so?
CREWS: Well, it was after I came back from Louisiana and I'd just sold *The Knockout Artist* for way and again more money than I'd ever sold any novel for. I sold it for more than I'd ever sold four novels for. And the Actors Theatre of Louisville asked me if I'd take fifteen thousand dollars' commission to write a play, a full-length play. And since I'd never written a play, didn't know the first thing about it, I said yes, just to see if I could.

The play got a standing ovation. There were seven new plays done there, and I got a standing ovation. It's been performed at several local places since then. I always threatened to keep working on it until I got it down; it's too damn long. I know now why playwrights are thought of as poets and why poets have been playwrights. Man, language—language is the gig. I mean, if Tennessee Williams wasn't a poet, what the hell was he? As a matter of fact, can I tell you this thing about Tennessee Williams?

BLEDSOE: Sure.
CREWS: I knew Tennessee Williams off and on and saw him here and yonder for many, many years. And Tennessee was down at this time in Key West, and the university was forever trying to get him to come up here and do something, anything. So finally he wrote and said, "Yeah, I'll come up if you let Harry Crews introduce me." They never let me introduce anybody because they were afraid of what I'd do. And so Tennessee and I were supposed to go to dinner, and we did go to dinner, but we didn't eat, we drank it. So we're both pretty well lit, and we are going back to the Reitz Union, that seats six hundred people. There were people sitting in the aisles and all the seats are full. And right in the front were the president of the school and all the bald-headed deans and vice presidents, all that bullshit.

Somebody introduced me, and it was long and terrible. And I said, "Thank you very much for that warm and generous introduction."

And then here is the introduction I gave for Tennessee, verbatim. I said, "Ladies and gentlemen, it is customary on these occasions to say where the writer went to school and where he was born, and the honors he has won. But who gives a shit?" You hear this collective gasp. "But who gives"—I'm staring right at the power structure of the school—"who gives a shit? If Tennessee Williams had not written anything other than the long lyrical poem that is *The Glass Menagerie*, it would be enough for us to come here and pay him homage. Ladies and gentlemen, America's greatest living playwright, Tennessee Williams."

And he made his way to the podium, and he just was kind of blinking and shaking his head, and in that lovely accent of his he said, "That's rather the nicest introduction I've ever had." And only because he said that I didn't hear a word from anybody about what I had said. If he hadn't said that, I would have been, first, in the chairman's office the next morning, and after that I would have been in the dean's office.

BLEDSOE: You begin *A Childhood* with "My first memory is of a period ten years before I was born."

CREWS: I can quote that sentence, too. Sentences like that don't just pop out of your head. "My first"—let's see if I can—"My first memory is of a time before I was born and takes place where I have never been and involves my father, whom I never knew." It's not antithetical, but it is classically balanced. I'm proud of the sentence. I was proud of the sentence when I finally got it.

I'll tell you, for whatever it is worth, and worth very little, I suspect, but I consciously try to write the strongest beginning, whether it is an essay or a novel or anything. I try to write the strongest beginning I can write and try to live up to it. You know, say, "All right, boy, that fucking beginning sings, Jack. You're from the Hell's-a-Poppin' School of Literature and that motherfucker is exploding there." I say that to myself whether it is or not. A writer's the worst judge of his work. The worst person in the world to ask about a book is the guy that wrote it. But then I try, as I say, *try* to live up to it. That's how that sentence came to be.

BLEDSOE: One of your favorite techniques is to bring characters from one novel to another one.

CREWS: Yeah, well, it's not so much as I bring them, as the sons-of-bitches turn up. I think it's because I already know them. I'll tell you, Tote Walker, in *All We Need of*

Hell, he really deserves a novel that's all his own. I think he's got one of the best hearts of any guy I ever met, the way he deals with the kid, the way he deals with the cops, the way he deals with Duffy. Know when to use it, and know when to lose it. It doesn't matter, that coke and shit; he shouldn't be doing it, but he does it. He deserves his own novel.

Do you know the book *Edisto?* Padgett Powell just wrote a sequel to that novel. If I'm going to write a sequel about anything, it would be *The Knockout Artist,* when the guy looks up and he says, "You want me? I got nothin', we got nothin'—we got nothin'."

And the Cajun kid holds up his fists, and he says, "We got dese."

And they're going away in a pickup truck, they're leaving New Orleans and they're getting away from Oyster Boy and all that stuff. And, you know, I wonder where they went and I wonder what they're doing. I don't know, but I can find out.

BLEDSOE: Like many writers, you speak as though your characters are a separate thing.

CREWS: I'll tell you something, man, the reason I gotta go back in there every morning is I leave my characters. Sometimes they are about to eat a meal, or sometimes they're coming down a ladder, and I've left them there. Jesus . . . that's no way to do! I mean, you gotta go get them down off the ladder, or you gotta feed them, or the guy has just cut himself bad, and nobody's even picked him up, he's gotta get to a hospital. And that bothers me. But, hell, if he's in a really good place, I want to know how much he's gonna enjoy it.

At first, you only have a name, Jim or John, or whatever, and then he's a cipher. It's nothing. But gradually that thing begins to get blood and bone and hair and bad breath and history and children and a mother, and he feels like however he feels toward his mother and where he's born and how he is and how he talks, and what he wants and what he is willing to give up to get it, and all of these things. It's impossible, it seems to me, that if you are writing honestly and hard, not to come to think of them as living, breathing beings. And so that's the way that is. You're absolutely right. I talk about them that way; I think about them that way.

BLEDSOE: The character of Russell Morgan, Russell Muscle, seems to be one of your favorites. He's been in four novels now.

CREWS: Yeah, well, he just keeps popping up. He's just got bit parts, cameo roles in the others. In *Knockout Artist,* he just introduces the fighters. But I know Lee Haney, who's won Mr. Olympia more times than Schwarzenegger won it. I have talked at great length to Schwarzenegger, out in California, at Gold's Gym. I know the Golden Eagle, and I know Franco Columbo, who won Mr. Olympia, too, and who's a chiropractor, and Sylvester Stallone's trainer. I've known those guys, and Russell Morgan just so reminded me of them. He works out like a house afire, and then he lies in a dark room and plies himself with these supplements and all kinds of other things.

Russell Morgan is just sweet and tragic at the same time. That business of his wife, his poor little wife and his little children, how beat down and brutalized they are. A guy that wants to do something that bad is willing to sacrifice anybody, including his mother. It's just the way they are, and it's the thing they make themselves. And you can't do it any other way than to do it that way.

There's an overwhelming fascination for me with people who are willing to pay the price, whatever the price is, to do what's in them to do. A twenty-eight-year-old Mr. America dropped dead of a heart attack from steroids. And you get into roaring rages. They pump enough testosterone in you and you'll attack an elephant.

So you say, "Well, why are these guys doing this?" Well, let me tell you something. When I was twenty-eight or twenty-nine years old, I'd been struggling all this time and losing, if somebody had come to me and said, "Harry, I've got a needle with some stuff in it, that I can just hit you in the ass with, but I gotta keep hitting you with it for a while, a month, or two, or three, and then you'll have a novel, and it'll be a fine novel." I would be to a novel what Lyle Alzado was to his position.

"But," the guy would tell me, "you might, you might not, but there's a fair chance that you will die early, or have some side effects that are rather dreadful."

I wouldn't have hesitated a second. I would have said, "Where is the needle?" That's how bad I wanted it, and those guys want it that bad.

BLEDSOE: You've used just the names of some people, like your childhood playmate Willalee, who . . .

CREWS: Willalee Bookatee was . . . Now, we know what "Bookatee" would have come from. That's Booker T. Washington. Willalee? I don't know what that's all about, but he was just called Willalee Bookatee. Little black boy, about the same age as me.

BLEDSOE: But I'm not just talking about in *A Childhood*. In *The Gospel Singer*, you have a character with that same name. He ends up being lynched at the end, and then Willalee's real sister was named Lottie Mae, right? And you have a character named Lottie Mae in *Feast*, and she's the one who is raped by the sheriff. That seems like a strange thing to do to your childhood friends—to use them to name your characters who suffer such horrendous ends.

CREWS: [*pauses*] I didn't even know I'd done that, until you just told me.

BLEDSOE: Really?

CREWS: No. Uh-uh . . . oh God. Well . . . well, I'm just glad that I won't be around . . . well, ain't anybody gonna pick over my work anyway. And if they do, I . . . I hope I'm not around to see it, or . . . I never read any reviews or stuff, and certainly I don't read interviews because I always sound like such a fool, and I get stuff wrong. When it's wrong, I say to myself, "I couldn't possibly have said that."

BLEDSOE: Were you hurt or angered by Sterling Watson's fictionalized portrayal of you in *The Calling*?

CREWS: He sent me the book, and he said something to the effect that he meant it as a tribute, or something, whatever. You know, Sterling Watson . . . I didn't do anything for Sterling Watson but buy his food half the time, buy him his whiskey, help him with his family—he had a wife and kid, he was a student of mine—and I taught him everything I could teach him. Hung out with him. Back in those days, we ran together, every evening and all that.

And he's not only got me in there, he's got my wife in there. My son was receiving death threats, not delivered with a stamp on it from the postman, but in an envelope in my mailbox. I never could find out who was doing it. But he's got that in there. He's got my dog in there, and there's just a lot of things he's got in there that are just . . . true. And the guy that reviewed it in the *New York Times* said, "This is supposed to be a *Roman à clef*, but you don't need a key. Anybody that knows anything about American literature knows that this is patterned after Harry Crews."

Sterling called me one time, and I said, "The only thing I've got to say is that this is a blood offense. And the only thing that satisfies a blood offense is blood." And that's where the matter stands.

I haven't seen him. There was a big literary fair down there at the school where he is, and every writer in the country was there. But he didn't show up anywhere around there. I didn't know quite how it would be if he did. It didn't bother me that much of what he wrote was true. What bothered me was the tone of it. The stance that was taken on it. How this was a guy that hurts people, that fucks over people, that doesn't care about people, that is a slobbering drunk that doesn't do anything but drink.

People say, "Well, you've stayed drunk and done all this your whole life?"

I just say, "Look at the work, man, you can't do that drunk, or any other way. You gotta be straight to do that. And, you can't do it with your head on the curb, or anything else."

So there's this perception of me, and I wish it weren't true. The word in the street and in the writing community, such as I am in the writing community—it's just all wrong. The guy in the *Tampa Tribune*, when he did that article, up at the top, it had "Tough Guy." Going way back, yeah, it's true, I hung out in bars, and you hang out in certain places, well, you ain't gonna fall off a ten-thousand-foot rock face unless you put yourself up there. If you put yourself in the right place, things happen.

But, going way back, when I was healthy and young, and a lot stronger than I am now, guys would walk up to me and tell me things I was supposed to be involved in, and I'd say, "No, man, no . . . whoever told you that, I wouldn't have been nowhere around that."

And guys would walk up to me and say, "Oh, you're so and so," and "You're the guy that thinks he's so bad."

And I'd say, "No, no, wait a minute. I don't think I am." And he'd be talking so loud, and I'd say, "Now wait a minute, man, I don't know you; you don't know me. We got nothing to say to each other. See that door over there?" I mean, I'm in the corner, the bar is here, the wall's there, and I got no place to go and he's between me and the door. I'd say, "You see the door over there? If you'll just let me get to the door, and walk out of here, then you won't have to bother with me any more, because I don't want it this way." But that's the wrong thing to say, too, because that just makes the guy think you're playing with him or something.

I wish that perception wasn't there. I think it comes from the subject matter of my books, and I think it comes from my mugging for cameras, which I do because it's the only way I can stand to look at a camera. I just can't do it. I feel so weird, and particularly if you've got six or seven guys with cameras, you feel like something in a zoo. So, you want something in a zoo, I'll show you something in a zoo.

It's a mistake I started making early, and I never knew it was a mistake until it was too late. So now it's stuck, and that's the label that's on me. Back when I drank so bad, when I went anywhere to lecture, or do something at a university, first thing that happened when I get off the plane is some guy handed me a glass. And the game was "Let's give Crews all the alcohol he'll take in his hand, and watch him get totally out of it and be a fool." Which is what all stone drunks end up doing 'cause they don't know what they're doing.

So that's part of it. But I suspect that it's not just writers. It's not unique to any given profession or avocation or anything else. Everybody's got a whole bunch of stuff that they think, "Gee, I know if I could have cut that out, or if I could edit this life, I would snip that out." Of course that really doesn't work.

BLEDSOE: Nearly everyone I told that I was coming down here to interview you had a Harry Crews story to share. Do you worry that "Harry Crews: The Legend" threatens to overshadow "Harry Crews: The Work"?

CREWS: Well, as far as that goes, I already do. I mean, more people are more interested, it seems, in talking about what I'm supposed to have done and what I still do than they are interested in my books. They read one book and they've read me or something. Hey, if you like my work and you read a lot of it . . . well, of course I'm glad. I mean, that's what I wrote it for. But if you don't, I'm not angry, I'm not sad, I'm not anything. Nobody's under any obligation to read any more than you want to read, or read any at all. It certainly doesn't worry me.

I worry a lot, but about the only thing I ever worry about is the next five hundred words. Because, I'll tell you, I can't understand anybody who tells me that they enjoy writing, that it's fun. Frankly, I don't believe them. It's certainly never been fun for me. What *is* a real rush, for me, is after you've done it, before you even send it to New York, and that's it. I know this is strange, but when you look at it, and you think, "Before me, this was not. Because of me, this is." Now that's a rush.

ASSAULT OF MEMORY

Harry Crews

CHAPTER ONE

I stood at the foot of the hospital bed watching my Mama die. The
bed was set up in the master bedroom of her house in the little
South Georgia town of Ashburn. Her mouth was stretched wide open,
the tendons standing like wire in her old, milk-white neck. Her jaw was
ridged and inside her obscenely black mouth her purple tongue rose at
odd moments, moved randomly, and then disappeared. Her teeth that
she had been so proud of keeping for all these years were the color of
tobacco, although she had never smoked in her life, and they were
chipped and cracked.

I was staring and knew I was staring, but I could not help it. It was
as though I was trying to memorize something or maybe just to believe
what I was seeing. And hearing. And smelling. Her breathing was irregu-
lar and had the curious sound a baby might make if it were strangling.

From across the length of the bed her breath had the odor of a diseased dog. And looking at the bed I could not help thinking that this was the bed that waited for all of us if we were so unfortunate as to live long enough for all the provinces of our bodies to revolt.

My brother, Hoyett, came into the room, fell onto his knees at the side of the bed and began praying to his God. Eugenia, our cousin, care-giver to any sick of the extended family, watcher over all blood kin in the final days and hours of their dying, was sitting on a ladder-backed chair at the head of the bed where she could wipe Mama's face with a cool, damp cloth and swab out her mouth and dampen her gums and tongue and lips, lips that by now were raw and cracked and dull pink in color like an old wound.

When my brother started to pray, Eugenia eased off the chair and went slowly and heavily to her knees, bowed her graying head, and remained silent except for, now and again, a random Yes counterpoint to Hoyett's exhortations to the Lord. His prayer had started softly but his voice had gone steadily louder, more strident, and sounded by turns angry, threatening, and full of violence, as he hammered at the ear of his God to take the old lady to a place of perpetual happiness, put her down on streets of gold, dress her in a white gown, and set her singing an interminable hymn of praise to the Crucified Christ.

His prayer, its sheer ragged, blood-filled volume, might have unnerved me, maybe even frightened me, but for the fact that I had heard it all before in other places, at other times. And not only over the dying or dead or even the seriously ill. My brother could get down with God, get down and do it, almost anywhere, on any occasion: on the eve of a long trip, on the eve of a short trip, at breakfast, going to bed, getting up from bed, or sitting utterly alone on the bank of a lake in the deep woods while wrapping and impaling an earthworm on the point of his fishhook.

While my brother and I had always lived within a few hours of each other all of our adult lives, we had seen precious little of each other over the past thirty some-odd years. But I had not forgotten his on-again, off-again love affair with Jesus Christ. Or the nature and violence of his prayer. It was not the sort of thing a man might easily forget. He could out-pray anybody I'd ever seen him come up against, and, as a young man I'd seen him matched against some pretty good ones. However, as sometimes happens, he had back-slid on and off all his life. But then he would be born again. He was born again more than any man or woman I have ever met. And every time he was born again, his roof-rattling, fire-and-brimstone, urgent need, and marvelously inventive ability to pray—each time hotter than the time before—would lay him low again. He was not an easy man to love or even to like, and he had done me hurts, especially in our early years, that I would never forget and could never forgive.

But there was another side to him too. He was savagely moral, savagely charitable, savagely loving, and savagely stoic. He was also savagely suspect of anyone who did not hold savagely to the same code of conduct as he. My brother not only did not suffer fools gladly, he did not suffer anyone gladly. And last and most important, you had to remember he was not a man with whom to fool around or to take lightly. Life was by God serious and his every gesture was calculated to let you know that he was himself at least as serious as God. You walked very softly around him, or you did not walk at all.

He was a hard man, a cold man. He kept his own council and was not given to seeking or following the advice of anyone else. The crucible of deprivation, pain and self-denial that had been Mama's life had been his as well. It had also been mine, but because of the sickness, accidents, and plain bad luck that had befallen me in the early years of my life, Mama had protected and sheltered me in a way she did not, could not, protect and shelter him. I was four years younger than he, and I was weak and clumsy, and I was her baby, which she never let me—or him—forget. God love her, she did the best by both of us she could, but it was always obvious that I was her favorite. I knew it and he knew it and all of our blood kin knew it.

When I got old enough to realize that my brother was carrying much of the burden that should have been mine, bearing much of the pain that I should have borne, it hurt me deeply because in the blind, profound way of blood, I loved him beyond saying in spite of anything he could think of to hurt me. Even as little more than a baby, I knew that how he treated me was not right, but there was very little I could do about it.

Did my mama's favoritism, in part, make him the bitter man he has become today? If it did not, it could have, and with justification, it probably should have. Was it mostly responsible for his unthinkably brutal behavior toward me as a child when Mama or nobody else was around to protect me? If it was not, it could have. Looking back, I cannot forgive him for marking me with memories that still jerk me from sleep, startled and shaking in the middle of the night. I cannot forgive him but I think I can understand, because there is no doubt at all that the world he had to scratch and fight his way through to manhood was unbelievably harder than the world I knew.

"Amen," Hoyett said.

Eugenia, softly: "Amen."

I said nothing. In the sudden silence, the sound of the strangling baby bubbled and gasped in Mama's throat.

They both stayed on their knees and looked up at me. Finally, Hoyett rose to his feet and Eugenia struggled to lift herself back onto her chair. My brother came to stand beside me and put his hand on my shoulder.

"Harry," he said, "have you thought about your soul today?"

I did not answer. I was used to the question. But apparently it was impossible for him to get used to an absence of a response from me, because he would not leave it alone.

He said: "All you need to know or to believe is John 3:16."

He started to quote the verse, but I half-turned, interrupting him.

"I know what it says."

"Could you try to believe what it says? Could you just try?"

"I've tried," I said.

"You ain't tried," he said, his voice suddenly going louder, and filling with heat. "Writing them books is ruint you mind. And if you ain't a heathen already you ain't far from it."

"This is no time for you two boys to be carrying on," Eugenia said in her soft, country-woman's voice.

Half turned from my brother I was looking at an electric fan sitting on a chest of drawers against the far wall. Mama always kept the fan out where she could see it. It was hardly bigger than a man's hand. It had once been painted green but time had turned it nearly black. The blades were thickly coated with grease and dust. To my knowledge, it was the only thing in the entire house Mama, for reasons known only to herself, did not keep spotlessly clean. It was from the time of her most terrible trial, and it was also, curiously, during that trial that I have the sweetest but also most devastating memory of my brother.

I pointed toward the fan. "You remember that?"

He glanced at it briefly. "Not likely I'd forget it," he said, and walked out of the room.

The fan had been all Mama had to try to stay cool during the sweltering summer she was in a body cast, a cast that extended from above her breasts to just above her knees. The fan could not have helped much. Perhaps it helped to cool her none at all. Maybe it was only the soft, droning sound of it that had helped her. Night and day she kept it turned on her face which was the color of chalk under her dark hair, heavy with sweat and plastered to her scalp.

It was the summer of 1945 and we were living at 1931 Ionia Street in the Springfield section of Jacksonville, Florida. The street was narrow and littered with trash of every kind: pieces of bicycles, worn out automobile tires, garbage that was rarely picked up but left to decompose where it was dropped, serving as thin meals for dirty, starved cats and dogs that roamed everywhere in surprising numbers and chased by equally starved and dirty children. The houses were cut up into tiny, airless apartments that housed families of Georgia dirt farmers and their enormous numbers of ill-clothed children, families who drifted down to Jacksonville for all manner of reasons to sell their backs and sweat.

I was ten years old and my brother fourteen. We lived in two rooms on the ground floor in one of the houses that fronted onto the neighborhood grocery store where I had once watched a man stab himself to death three years earlier when a minor catastrophe had driven us south to live for a while on Market street in an apartment nearly identical to the one we lived in now on Ionia. Everybody said the man, whose name nobody knew, was crazy. But I did not think he was crazy. I was standing only a few feet from him as he pounded the knife he had taken from the butcher's block into his chest. He had looked directly at me with calm, steady eyes and said that he was lonely and had nowhere to go, that there was no nail in the wide world where he was welcome to hang his hat. Not then but later, it seemed to me a terrible but an entirely reasonable thing to do.

We had moved down from Georgia this time because the old man who had helped us farm had become too feeble to work and we had no choice. None of the sharecroppers I knew who every few years—and sometimes more often—moved from Georgia to the Springfield section of Jacksonville had any choice either. When the rain did not fall or fertilizer became too dear to be had or the rain never stopped and drowned the crops or a mule died without there being money to buy another or a father was crippled cutting wood to cook tobacco or had a foot taken off by the blade of a cut-a-way harrow or any of a thousand other things that could and did happen happened, Jacksonville, which Georgia people—or the ones that were my people anyway—dreaded and feared second only to hell, was always waiting to take them in to places like the pulp mill on Talleyrand Avenue where when I was older I would work, or Merrill-Stevens shipyard on the St. Johns River where I also worked, or the Merita Bread Company on Main Street where I worked, or the Jacksonville Paper Company on Bay Street where I worked, or the King Edward Cigar Factory, billed at the time as the largest cigar factory under one roof in the world where my mama always worked and where I worked the summer I broke my neck one year before I joined the Marine Corps to escape Jacksonville.

Mama had no husband to help her now that she had finally rid herself of Pascal, who was my dead daddy's older brother and who was also my stepfather, a man who was by turns brutal, generous, kind, and always drunk when he could manage it. And so she was back working at the cigar factory, the job she had no choice but to take when circumstances forced us to board the Greyhound bus in Alma, the county seat of Bacon County, and head to the place we had been so many times before. Her job at King Edward's was piece work: the more cigars she rolled, the more money she made. If she could manage to roll 6,000 cigars a day we could keep a roof over us and food on the table.

Then an unheard of thing happened. Mama missed two days work, a Monday and a Thursday in the same week. She never missed work, not for sickness, not to go to a dentist, and most times not even for the funeral of blood kin. She never lost a day at her job because she could not miss work and still make enough money to feed us. The following week she missed another day's work, and that afternoon when I came home from school, I found her sitting on the side of her bed, her eyes very red and a look on her face that kicked my heartbeat high the moment I saw her. She took me into her arms, and in a voice that scared me, said she had to go into the hospital for an operation.

"What kind of operation?"

"Something's growing in my bones. Eating them."

"All of m? Is it something growing in all you bones?"

Something growing in my mama's bones conjured the most unreasonable image of horror that I had ever had in my short life. I saw, suddenly and plainly, furry little worms with huge teeth swarming through all the bones of her body eating out the marrow as they went. I had eaten enough marrow out of the bones of quail and dove and pigs and squirrel and goats to know that nothing could live without marrow in its bones.

"No, no child," she said. "It's my left hip and thigh." There were tears in her eyes and she was trembling and I could feel how terrified she was.

"How much will the operation cost?" I asked. "Is it gone be enough money?"

She violently pushed me away from her and held my shoulders so tightly that pain shot down both my arms and made my hands go numb. Tears were on her cheeks but her eyes were blazing and her face was a twisted mask of rage that I had never seen before. She turned loose my left shoulder and slapped me across the face with such force that I would have gone down had she not been holding me with her other hand. It was so much a surprise that I did not even cry, but my head rang like a bell tower.

"You little shitbritches," she growled in a hoarse, choked voice, "you better be asking if it's gone kill me. It's bone cancer, you goddamn afflicted idiot. Bone cancer. You understand??"

"Yes, mam."

But I did not understand. I had asked the question I had been raised to ask. In our world money was more important than death. It was the first and last question, the ultimate question, the answer to which you wanted most desperately in any crisis, in the face of any problem. And you knew before you asked that there would probably not be enough, and that there not being enough would inevitably bring down a long string of catastrophes. You might come home and find your bedding and few sticks of furniture out on the sidewalk in the rain. That had happened. There might be a week or more of meals when there was nothing on the table but a bowl of grits and biscuits, the biscuits made with nothing but water, lard, and flour. That had happened. In the dead of winter, the heater might be cold for days because there was no kerosene. The last of the hand soap in the house would be used up. You might be forced to steal buckets of water from a neighbor's outside spigot because the city had cut off the water to your apartment. The list of loss and humiliation was endless.

She shook me hard again. "Do you understand, damn you?"

"I do. Yes mam. I do now.

My head snapped with her shaking and I cried soundlessly, but I did not ask her for any kind of explanation, because I felt another slap was one wrong word away. And I did not understand. I had been slapped before and my brother and I had been beaten long and hard, usually with a belt but sometimes with a coat hanger or a broken broom handle or just about anything else that came to her hand when it was time to punish us. But she never ever caused either of us pain for no reason at all. We always knew why we were being whipped or otherwise punished. We knew as well as we knew our names the line she had clearly drawn and told us never to step over, and she had always given us the reasons why the line was not to be crossed. This time though, there had been no reason for her to slap me. I had done nothing but ask the question that would have come first to the lips of any dirt farmer's child from Bacon County.

But then as quickly as she had slapped me and rage had taken her face, the fire went out of her eyes and her thin, grim mouth started to relax and tremble and the mask of anger dissolved and I was looking at the loving, forgiving mother I had always known. She pulled me to her and I smelled the indescribable mother smell of her that I swear before all that is holy I can still smell as I sit here writing this. The smell that could quiet any agitation or exorcise any fear that ever took my heart, a smell that I always associated with her soft and generous and all-loving breasts with which—in good, country woman fashion—she nursed me long after she had any milk, nursed me randomly in all times of little boy hurt in the light of day or little boy terror in the dark of night right on up to the time my fourth birthday had come and gone.

With my face buried in her neck, she whispered, "Oh, my baby. My pore, pore little throwed-away youngun. We all gone suffer for what I ought to care by myself. I cain't care it though. And it ain't no way in God's world I can hep it. I didn't mean to hit you, son. I'm so awful scared to have to leave you boys."

"Don't you worry, Mama, not about us. We gone be fine, me and him. Everything's gone turn out fine, you gone see.

She took her hands off my shoulders and folded them in her lap and looked down at them for what seemed a very long time without saying anything.

And then finally, without looking at me, she said: "If everything is ever fine again for us, son, it'll be a long time coming. They gone put a cast on me.

"A cast." I said, making it a statement, not a question.

I knew well enough what a cast was but the only ones I had ever seen had been on an arm and maybe one or two times in my whole life on a leg. But as far as I could tell her arms and legs were all right and I could not imagine why she would need a cast and where they might put it.

When she did not say anything but only sat there silently looking down at her hands, I said hesitantly, "Uh, where bouts will they . . . I mean, which arm you think they mean to put it on?"

She looked up now, her eyes dry, her face composed, "They mean to put me in a cast. Called a body cast is what it's called."

I was suddenly trembling. "Oh, Lordy, Lordy, Mama. I wish, wish . . ." I couldn't finish. The vision that had flashed on me was of the mummies wrapped from head to toe I had seen in the movie serials on Saturdays when we were in Jacksonville.

"It's no good can come of wishing." She had her old strong, I-can-and-will-do-whatever-has-to-be-done voice again, the voice that did not admit of whining, hopeless wishing, or the thing that she had least patience with: wallowing about in pity.

"It's settled. It'll either work or it won't. It ain't no other way. The only thing we all got to hold onto is I wouldn't be going into a cast if it weren't the Lord's will. I've prayed on it. That's all I can do."

"A body cast," I said. "I never seen one. I cain't . . ."

"It goes from here." She held her hands just above her breasts. "To here." Her hands moved down to mid-thigh. "You can see it when you get a chance to come home from Alton's to visit." I started to speak but she shook her head and held up her hand. "They say I'll be flat on my back for three months, maybe more, so you have to go stay with your Uncle Alton. It's settled. That's the way it has to be."

"You mean me and Hoyett's going . . ."

"You're going. He's staying. He's got a job working at night. Him and me's been trying to get this fixed for some time now. *Somebody's* got to work. I'd ruther take a beatin than put this on him but I don't see no other way."

Work? Him? I couldn't imagine what she was talking about. He already had a *Times-Union* paper route that got him out of bed at four o'clock in the morning seven days a week and on Saturdays he bagged groceries at the A&P. How could he work at night too, and what in the world would he be working at?

"Where bouts did he get a job?"

"Getters Box Factory. I went over there with him and seen J. P. Hughes, the foreman, and he fixed it for us when I told him how it was. I known J. P. since before he left Bacon County and come off down here to Jacksonville more'n twenty year ago. Thank God I did and thank God he seen his way clear to hep us."

"But . . ."

"Hush, child. It's done, I told you. He goes to work Monday. You get on the Greyhound for Alton's Wednesday and I go into the hospital on Friday. "It's all settled and I cain't stand any more talk about it so it won't be none, not a word. You understand that, do you?"

"Yes, mam."

I knew where Getters Box Factory was well enough. I'd been over there hundreds of times because right behind the factory was a sawdust pile that must have been seventy feet high. It was the favorite place for my friends and me to play, struggling up the steep side of the pile, wrestling at the top, and then all of us but one would go rolling down, ass over elbow, playing king of the mountain.

But the factory itself was no place for boys to play. It was no place for boys to do anything at all, much less work. There was nothing but grown men going in and coming out of the huge loading docks, and without exception, all the men I had ever seen were sweated down, not a dry stitch of clothes on them, and their faces showed the bone-deep exhaustion they were carrying. There were a hundred questions I wanted to ask. Maybe my brother was going to be sweeping floors or picking up scrap paper and wood chips or some such thing. Any boy could do work like that, and certainly my brother could.

But I did not know for sure he'd get off that light though, and I wanted to know. But Mama had said the matter was closed and there would be no more talk about it. My brother was not given to talk much anyway and certainly he would respond to no question of mine, except maybe to slap me down if Mama was out of sight. Even though there were only four years difference in our ages, beating me and generally torturing me was his favorite pastime and he indulged himself when we were alone in the apartment, which was much of the time.

Until he went to work on Monday night we lived in the apartment like strangers. There was very nearly a total silence, even when we were eating. Beyond something like "Pass the biscuits," or "Is it any more of that rice?", we said very little or nothing at all. Mama had quit going to the cigar factory and spent most of her time sitting in the only rocking chair we had, slowly rubbing her hands, one over the other, and looking out the window at the house next door which was only about fifteen feet away.

Her hip was giving her a lot of trouble. She never talked about it, but she could not hide the pain that twisted her face and made her take her lower lip between her teeth when she had to walk. It would not occur to me until much later how badly she must have hurt before she let herself take a day off to go to a doctor. Even though she was only thirty-three years old, fear and pain and worry had aged her terribly. Her skin was leached of color, and she had lost weight, and her neck was mottled with a texture like crepe paper.

She had never slept well, but the few nights before I left on the Greyhound for my Uncle Alton's, I would wake up to find her sitting in the rocking chair staring at the darkened window. She sat completely still. Her silhouette, dark against the darker window, looked painted on the glass. The rocker appeared carved from stone rather than made from wood. In the morning I never spoke to her about seeing her in the chair, and neither did I ask her why she was doing it. I wish now I had because it affected me deeply, leaving me shaken and wide awake, sometimes for the rest of the night. The image of the utterly immobile chair and my silent mama as a one-dimensional, black silhouette is as clear in every detail today as it was the first night I saw her.

The tension in the apartment grew to the point where it seemed I could feel it on the surface of my skin. Maybe that was why my brother was never around. I don't know where he went but he stayed gone most of the time. He had quit his job with the *Times-Union* newspaper, and on Saturday he didn't go down to the A&P to bag groceries. I had no idea how he felt about Mama going to the hospital or his new job at the box factory or about me going to stay with Uncle Alton and Aunt Eva, but he had long since made it clear to me that if he wanted me to know something he would tell me; otherwise, I was to leave him alone. The penalty for not doing what he told me to do was severe.

Late Monday afternoon Mama and I stood on the steps of the apartment house and watched Hoyett walk off down the sidewalk with the sack of baloney-and-mayonnaise sandwiches Mama had made for him to eat at midnight in one hand and a pair of thick cotton work gloves she had somehow got for him sticking out of his back pocket.

"You think he's gone be all right?" I asked.

She did not answer, but only watched him as he neared the corner where he would turn and be out of sight. It seemed to me that his shoulders had started to sway in a kind of swagger.

"Look the way he's walking," I said. "He's trying to walk like he's grown."

"He's got ever right to walk any way he wants to," she said.

We were both waiting for him when he walked back into the apartment the next morning a little before nine.

It was only then that I learned he would be pulling a twelve-hour shift every night. And he looked as if he had worked twelve hours, too. His eyes were caught in a web of red veins and the way he stood, his feet wide apart, his shoulders slumped, made him look as though even his bones were tired.

"How was it, Son?" Mama asked. He watched her as though he had not understood, as though she had maybe spoken in a foreign language. "I've got you a good breakfast cooked. It's in the oven."

He said: "I'm gone go on to bed."

"How come you keeping you hands in you pockets like that?"

I had not noticed he had his hands in his pockets like he did and he did not take them out after she asked him the question.

"Them gloves you given me weren't no match for the job."

"How come, Son?" She had not stopped looking at his hands, which he still had not taken out of his pockets. "Anything ail them hands of yorn?"

"Hands all right," he said. "Hope them gloves didn't set you back too much, though. They didn't last long as a sneeze. Ripped to pieces before I hardly started."

"Ripped, you say?"

"They didn't last the first hour."

"How bad is you hands?"

"They been worse."

"If them gloves you had won't do, what kind is it you need?"

"Welder's gloves is the only kind'll last."

"Them what the othern got?"

"Some do, some don't."

"What do them that don't have'm do?"

"Without."

"Maybe we can get you some like you need."

"Welder's gloves is made out of leather. They don't cost but a arm and a leg. I can get by without'm. The men on the job say you hands'll callous up. If you can stand it long enough and soak you hands in salt water for a hour ever night."

"Son, it breaks my heart to . . .

"Sorry to break you heart," he said bitterly, interrupting her. "But when you ain't got no choice, seems like it makes everthing real easy. From everthing you told me, I cain't see as I got a choice."

He took a bath, left his breakfast in the oven, and went to bed. Mama sent me to the A&P to buy a pound of pork chops which she cooked for him to have with a plate of potatoes and all the biscuits he wanted for supper. His hands were red and his palms were a mass of scabs and he made no effort to hide them as he ate, but Mama made every effort not to look at them.

Whether it was because of his hands, which I had looked at over the supper table, or because I was leaving the next day on the bus without any real notion of how long it would be before I'd be able to come back to visit, I took it into my head to go to Getters where he was working. I didn't know what I wanted to see or what I wanted to say, but whatever the reason, the desire to go was so strong that it would not go away and I could not ignore it.

That night the box factory was flooded with light and there was no problem getting in as I knew there would not be. All the big doors to the loading docks were open and when I found one that had no trucks backed up to it or workmen standing about on the concrete apron, I walked in.

I had no idea where to look for him and it was sheer luck that the third long aisle I looked down, I saw him. And from my first look at him I understood why he seemed so badly beaten down when he came home from his first night on the job. He was in constant motion catching flattened pasteboard boxes as they came hurtling down a motorized belt from the floor above and stacking them on a dolly that must have been fifteen or twenty feet long. The boxes looked as if they were coming down the belt toward him at twenty miles an hour, which they may or may not have been, but that's the way it looked like. And, remembering his hands from the supper table, I immediately thought of how badly it hurt the few times that I had cut my finger on the sharp edge of a piece of paper.

His shirt and trousers were dark with sweat and his hair was plastered over his forehead. In a gesture that was already part of the rhythm of his working, he continually wiped at his eyes with the back of his hand.

I was no more than fifteen feet away from him before he saw me. He hit a switch and the belt stopped. We did not talk but a minute, but while we did, he constantly glanced at the stopped belt that was slanting down from the floor above us.

"What the hell you doin here?"

"I . . ."

"I cain't keep this thing stopped. Do, I'll lose this job."

I had just noticed his hands and I could not speak. They were not just cut and bleeding, but blood was actually dripping off the ends of his fingers.

"You get on out of here and go home," he said. "You ain't nothing but a kid." He hit the switch and the flattened boxes came hurtling down the belt, their rough edges slamming into his bloody hands.

As old as I was, what he had said had nearly made me cry. What a terrible thing for a bloody handed boy working a twelve-hour shift at a man's job to have to say to his ten-year-old brother.

You ain't nothing but a kid.

I knew before I ever got to the loading dock that I would never forget what he had just said, and I never did. Over the years, there was much I felt I had to forgive him because of what he had said that night and the circumstances under which he had said it. He banked a lot of coin when he made that statement, but he had spent every nickel of it before we were grown. That may say more about me than it does about him, but however it happened, that magnificent and courageous statement was eventually bankrupted.

When I woke up the next morning, Mama showed me a small green fan that I'd never seen before. And to this day I don't know where she got it.

"Maybe this'll hep to keep me cool," she said, "when they put me in that cast."

I walked across the room and picked up the fan, turned it in my hands, and set it back down again.

Eugenia said: "That little thing probably won't even run anymore. Wonder how come you mama to keep it all these years?"

"I don't know," I said. And I didn't.

Out in the living room, my brother was on the couch. I went over and sat in a chair by the sliding glass doors giving on to the back porch.

"I know what you think you gone do," he said. "You think you gone come up here and set on you ass and write. But you ain't."

I did not answer his . . . his what? Accusation? Threat? Whatever it was, I did not even look up. But this did not bother him. He was used to getting no answer from me because whatever he asked was more often than not unanswerable. *Had I thought about my soul? Was I planning to sit on my ass and write with my mama dying in the next room?* I had been trying to control the anger that had been building in me since late that morning, and my brother was doing nothing to help matters.

Here was what was threatening to drive me around the bend. Mama had always wanted to die in her own home, so she had been taken from a Tift Memorial Hospital bed in Tifton, Georgia, twenty-five miles away, to the privacy of her own home in Ashburn, Georgia, which had no hospital, so we could kill her.

Maybe I have overstated—or stated too harshly—what had happened and what would continue to happen until Mama was dead. It did not help a bit that we had the doctor's blessing. That it was legal did nothing to ease my anger and pain. To hell with the doctor and the law. She was the one who had suffered my passage into the world. And I knew or thought I knew, that for the rest of my life, I would be subject to sudden stingers of self-hatred and guilt of suicidal intensity for what we were doing. It would have been a far better thing if Mama had died where she fell on her living room floor before anyone could find her. But that would have been very nearly impossible in a small Georgia town where everyone felt personally responsible for taking care of the very old.

Mama had an appointment at the beauty parlor (yes, the beauty parlor) at eleven o'clock on Thursday. She didn't show up on time, which was unlike her because she was on time for *everything*. However, the ladies at the beauty parlor knew that Mama and her best friend, Rosa Fountain, who was eighty-nine years old herself, had shelled a bushel of peas the day before to start their canning as they always did every year, and the ladies in the beauty parlor thought that Mama might just be a little tired and would show up directly.

Chapter Two

When Mama had neither called nor arrived by noon, they called her. When she did not answer, they called the sheriff, whom Mama had known since he was a boy, and he immediately dropped whatever he was doing and drove to the house, a distance of a few blocks, the exact distance from my mama's house to the largest Baptist church in town, where the preacher would say the last words over her on Sunday July 23rd with the entire town—but for the sick and infirm—in attendance.

The sheriff called an ambulance, a service they kept in Ashburn because, lacking a hospital, people who were really sick or badly hurt had to be driven to Albany or Cordele or Tifton or sometimes all the way to Atlanta. Mama, who never regained consciousness, was taken to Tifton.

When I was called in Gainesville, Florida, I left without packing a bag or even taking a shaving kit. It was about a three-hour drive to Tifton, but I made it in two. My brother lives in Rome, Georgia, seven hours away, but he was at the hospital when I got there because he had started the trip to her house that morning intending to visit her for a week. It was to be a surprise for her. He was always an exceptionally good and dutiful son to his mother. He had brought his tools and planned to do some work on her house for her.

The doctor in charge of Emergency Medicine told us before we even saw Mama that she looked pretty bad from the fall she had taken, black eyes and badly bruised face. The fall was caused by a massive stroke, and there had also been brain damage. Since she fell, she had neither opened her eyes nor had she spoken. She might last for months, the doctor said, or she might die tonight. The odds were overwhelmingly against her coming out of the coma. But if she did, she would be unable to speak or to recognize anybody.

When they took us into her room, she had oxygen tubes in her nostrils and drips in her arms. The doctor was kind and gentle and unhurried, trying, I am sure, to ease some of our pain, talking on at length about her condition. He need have said nothing. Death was all over her.

When he was finally winding down, he said: "Finally, I can only hope you will not become waiting room casualties, yourselves. Too many people have loved ones in the condition of your mother and they literally live in the waiting room until they collapse. I hope you won't do that. If there's any change, you will be notified immediately. And . . ."

He went on like that for a bit and then left. My brother fell to praying and I went outside to think and to smoke, a habit I had started again on the drive up from Florida, after not smoking for three years. Strangely I had not shed a tear. I didn't even feel particularly sad. If I felt anything, I felt numb. I had always thought losing Mama would be the most traumatic event of my life. But now, after thinking about it, I wondered if perhaps nearly as difficult to bear would be the endless number of ill-prepared actors, of which I was one, ready to go through the motions of predictable cliches: The patient, the caring doctor; the God-fearing prayerful son; a mulligan stew of condolences, ranging from the mailman to the oldest members of blood kin who could either no longer remember what they were able to say, or could no longer say what they were able to remember; the preacher whose practiced face would hold the grief of the ages, or so he would think; and finally, the undertaker, the strangest actor in this most human of rituals that once, a long, long time ago no doubt meant something. The undertaker whose unctuous manner and soft, grieving voice would be filled with satin-lined, mahogany boxes to be buried to rot in the ground and flowers of every design and kind and a hearse that cost more than the dear old lady's house, a hearse to haul her the half-mile to bury her in a plot of ground too small to plant a garden in, but expensive enough to support many of the families of Ashburn for a year, a plot of ground in a place no longer called a graveyard, a word with some honesty and dignity if for no other reason than its long history in the English language but now usually called A Garden of Perpetual Care or Sunset Acres, or some such abomination before the Lord, and most often enclosed by a brick wall that always sends a little shiver down my spine when I invariably wonder what the builders of the wall thought they were walling in or walling out.

I flipped the butt of the fifth cigarette I had smoked since coming out of the hospital and thought: *How utterly goddamn depressing*. Bad enough to die, but to have one's corpse, a corpse as senseless as a stone, given over to the tender mercies of the free enterprise system is an indignity too grotesque to ask even a corpse to bear. (I will spare the sensibilities of the reader the clever work of the embalmer, who, among other things, often has to break his client's jaw to make him smile because of the *risis sardonicus* that rapidly settles on the dead's mouth after death.)

I am grateful every day of my life that my will dictates that I am to be cremated in the nearest furnace available to the place where I die, and my ashes put in a box along with a book of any kind and sent special fourth-class book rate/printed matter enclosed to my son, who has accepted the responsibility of keeping the book and throwing my ashes—without benefit of marker, preacher, flowers, any service, memorial or otherwise—into Big Creek, which separates Bacon County, Georgia, from Applin County. I ate a lot of fish out of Big Creek as a boy and I have always thought that turnabout was fair play.

I knew I had been gone too long and I had to get back up to the hospital room, even though Mama was comatose and was beyond caring whether I was there or not, and my brother was likely getting it on with his God in a voice that suggested he thought his God was deaf or at least very hard of hearing. I didn't know how much more of his praying my nerves could take. I was beginning to feel as I could never remember feeling before. It was as if all of this was happening to somebody else. I felt as if somebody else's mama had died and I was only along to take the pain. I was grieving and hurting, but my mama was fine. She was not on the edge of death because she was never going to die. She was at home making supper. Does that make sense? Of course it doesn't make sense. And I knew it. But it was true, anyway. And it—this feeling, this knowing something was true and not true at the same time—was beginning to unnerve me. And in such a state, I didn't know how long I could keep the peace between my brother and me by sitting on my hands and biting my tongue, neither of which I've ever been much good at. But under the circumstances, I could hardly do otherwise. Too, in a day or two the clan from all over South Georgia would begin heading to Ashburn. Some of them were, no doubt, already on their way. My brother and I had the same hair-trigger temper, and blood could be spilled before this was all over. That would not only dishonor Mama, but also dishonor my brother and me and bring shame upon all the extended family. I did not think I could be provoked enough to get into a bloodletting, but I knew myself well enough to know it was possible. The trick was to keep my hands in my pockets and my mouth shut.

I should have made it clear before now that my brother is not the one with all the faults and failings and that I have all the characteristics of a Boy Scout. The truth is that if we had a scale to weigh genuine nastiness, I would be considerably heavier than he. But he doesn't know that. Because he and I have seen so little of each other over the past three decades, and because he has steadfastly refused to read anything I've written, he has made the potentially dangerous assumption that I am still the fat little crippled boy he once upon a time beat for recreation.

No sane person would maintain it is fair, but the hard truth is, never bedevil, jack up or jack around a writer, because you can't win that war. The hand that holds the pen leaves the record that will last. Take the metaphysical clothes off any human being, especially those clothes he most desperately wants to keep on, and you will find a hairy beast. And the writer's job, it has always seemed to me, is to strip away the clothes that are always an illusion and get to the substance underneath. If the pen I am holding now was in my brother's hand, obviously the story that is developing here would be much different than the one you are reading. But the pen is in my hand, not his.

When I got back up to the room, everything was as it had been, except a formidable machine full of blinking lights and pulsing bar graphs had been placed by Mama's bed to monitor her vital signs. Hoyett was holding her hand. I sat across the bed from him.

"I believe she's squeezing my hand."

I didn't say anything. Maybe he had not heard the doctor say how damaged her brain was hurt.

"She just squeezed it again."

"Good, that's good."

"Miracles do happen."

"I'm told they happen all the time."

"It won't be no heathen talk in this room."

"Sorry," I said.

What in hell was I going to do sitting in this tiny room with this poor devil? I didn't know how I was going to stand these cramped quarters with two comatose people: one comatose from a stroke, one comatose with grief of love and loss. Then he solved it for me. "You pack anything to come up here with?"

"I came with what I have on my back."

"I been thinking and you know what, seem like it made a lot of sense to me? It's two of us and we could, you know, spell one another."

"Spell one another?"

"You could go on back home and rest a day or two, get your clothes and stuff together, and then when you get back, I could go home and look after them dogs of mine. Anne cain't do it by herself."

Anne was his wife and since they had retired, he started a kennel raising thoroughbred American Bull Dogs, enormous animals weighing as much as 170 pounds.

"Like the doctor said, we'll just wear ourselves out sitting here waiting for . . . waiting. If anything happens, neither one of us is very far away. We don't neither one know how long this is going to last."

"You sure this is all right with you?"

"Like I said, I was thinking about it and it made the most sense to me."

"Well. I got two choices. I can go home and get some clothes or buy some here. I'm beginning to stink."

"Go on home. It's not but one of us needed here."

"You mean now. Go right now."

"Might as well. I'm going back up to Ashburn in a little while. Just call me when you start back up here from Gainesville."

"I'll call."

I walked out of the room without looking back and in less than three hours I was in my waterbed with four Valium 10s in my stomach that kept me asleep until ten o'clock the next day. I got up, shaved, showered, packed and picked up the phone.

Hoyett answered in Mama's room.

"I'm heading back."

"You don't have to hurry. Rest up a while." He seemed nervous.

"I feel okay. I'll get up there and let you get back to Rome and take care of your dogs."

"We're taking Mama home." Now he was really nervous and had trouble getting the words out.

I was stunned. "Home? Are you nuts? We can't give her the level of care she needs at home. This is a crazy thing to think, much less do. Nobody knows how long this will go on."

"It won't be long. Maybe four days at most."

"Four days? How could you know that?"

"Genie's here," he said, which hardly answered my question. "She's gone take care of Mother."

I knew that without being told. Eugenia always took care of the terminally ill amongst all our connections and had done so since she was little more than a child.

"How'd Genie know Mama was in the hospital?"

"And the Hospice is gone help, too."

As soon as I heard the word *Hospice*, bells should have gone off. Hell, I knew what Hospice was. I'd given money to the Hospice organization. William Saroyan had died in the care of Hospice. But bells or nothing else went off. I was so confounded I couldn't think of a question to ask. It was like Thorazine Thursday for me. I was half-speed at everything, including thinking.

"I'm leaving now. How long before they take Mama home?"

"Cain't say. Maybe she'll still be in the hospital when you get to Tifton, may not."

"I'll be there as soon as I can," I said and hung up.

I don't remember anything about the trip except that it rained all the way. Walking down the hospital corridor, I saw the doctor, my brother, Eugenia, whom I had not seen since the last family reunion nearly a year ago. I hugged her and thanked her for coming.

"You knew I'd come," she said.

"I guess I did, but I deeply appreciate it, anyway."

A woman I did not know, holding a clipboard and wearing a laminated picture of herself with her name underneath it pinned to her blouse, said: "I'm Flora Jones. I'll be the case worker for your mother."

Still nothing registered. She might as well have told me she was a gorilla from Uganda. Nothing registered. I was tired and confused. My brother had said nothing to me and I don't remember him even looking at me. But that was no surprise. He often did not look at me even when we were talking.

The doctor said: "The EMT is on the way up. I'll remove the oxygen." He turned and went into my mama's room. Looking back on it now, I cannot for the life of me understand why I didn't know what the hell was going on. Knowing how dangerous oxygen was around anybody smoking, maybe I thought he was removing it for the sake of safety. That made no sense, though. But then nothing about death and dying makes any sense. I remember the image of death I had when my four-year-old boy drowned. The image was of a monstrously high black wall of glass which you were obligated to climb, but there was utterly no way to gain purchase with hand or foot. Your blood had passed over the wall and you were left dumbly to stare at the unreasonable slick black wall without explanation or hope or any way to climb over it.

The men driving Mama back to Ashburn arrived with their gurney and the one who was apparently in charge said: "Y'all can go on ahead and we'll be there toreckly."

"Okay," Hoyett said. Then, looking at the Hospice lady: "Too bad we cain't all ride together, but I guess you'll have to follow me. Harry will be all right. He knows the way. Genie does, too."

We were all sitting in the living room when the ambulance came and the attendants got Mama settled into the hospital bed that had been set up in the room she used to share with Mr. Turner, the old man she married while my brother and I were still in the service.

After the ambulance was gone and my brother had gone back to the room and prayed over Mama for about an hour, I went to have a look for myself, knowing that it couldn't possibly matter to Mama because not just my brother and I, but the world and everything in it, had vanished for her.

Eugenia was sitting on the foot of the king-size bed beside the lady from Hospice and Mama, her mouth stretched as wide as it would go, rattled with a strange breathing that she did not have when the oxygen had been there to help her.

"Where's the oxygen?"

"She doesn't get any."

"Doesn't get any?"

"None."

"And the drips? Where are the IV's for her arms?"

"There won't be any. I thought you knew. Didn't the doctor tell you?"

"Nobody told me anything."

"Not even your brother. Surely he . . ."

I turned while she was still talking and walked out of the room, saying over my shoulder: "Especially my brother."

I went back out into the living room and sat down. Hoyett had another *Reader's Digest* open on his lap, his finger moving slowly over the page, his lips almost imperceptibly moving as he read the most vacuous prose of any publication in the country.

I was hurt, confused and livid with anger. The anger was directed at myself. And I was sick with self-loathing for doing nothing to stop what was happening. We had taken the oxygen from the dying lady, which she desperately needed. I did not know how long since she had been given any water, but I did know we intended to never give her water again. And she would be deprived of food as long as she lived. It was no wonder that he had known with such certainty that she would be dead in four days. And this radical end to her life had been decided without a single word to me.

If only my brother had given me a chance to know what he intended to do, to give me time to face and deal with the emotional trauma such a decision would wreak in me, to try to make peace with myself over ending a noble woman's life in such a sorry fashion. Instead I had been presented with the unthinkable fact of my mama dying of dehydration and starvation, her ruined body collapsing upon itself, dying a cell at a time, all the while, day and night, the sound of the strangling baby rattling in her throat from the lack of oxygen.

The Hospice lady came through and said goodbye, assuring us that she would see us again soon. My brother walked her to the door and then came back to the couch and settled himself in with the *Reader's Digest*.

"How often can we expect to be blessed with her presence?"

"How's that?" he said, without looking up from what he was reading.

"Will that lady be coming to visit much?"

"I don't know as they tell you. They just drop in from time to time to see how the patient's coming along. You know, to see that she's being treated all right."

The *patient*. Curious choice of words. But curious or not, I let it pass. I had let so much pass, had been so negligent myself, that I felt absolutely criminal. And I blamed my brother for ignoring me in the last decision of my mother's dying with an intensity that went beyond criminality. Whether the decision was right or wrong, I should have been part of that decision. At that moment I felt like putting the muzzle of a gun in my mouth, or in my brother's mouth or in my mother's mouth. Or a muzzle of a gun in all three. I felt myself part of the most dysfunctional family I could ever have imagined. I had suffered it long enough; why not end it right here?

What stopped me was my mama lying in the next room fighting for the last breaths of her life. If she would have been there and had been able to speak, her love would have forgiven my hatred and my ignominious thoughts and finally my brother, too, saying that he had done what he had done to spare me the horror of perhaps having to do it myself. But Mama knew, as she had reason to, that I would always blame him and never forgive him for what he had done, and then, without warning, let me come home to find her dying not only from the consequences of a stroke but also of lack of oxygen, food, and water.

It should come as a surprise to nobody that I hated myself for the thoughts I had or my inability to forgive myself. And so in that moment I did the only thing I could do. I gave myself over into my dying mama's hands and trusted her to forgive me what I could not forgive myself. It has always been a profound mystery to me that I could find in Mama's world the forgiveness I could not find in my own.

I left my brother on the couch and went to stand at the foot of Mama's bed and for reasons I'll never know—perhaps it was a defense against her dying—I knew that for as long as she lived, whether it was one day or four days or longer—I would be assaulted with memories of Mama, my brother, and me and our lives together.

KEEPING UP WITH HARRY CREWS

A Bibliography of Works, Interviews, and Critical Texts

Damon Sauve

This bibliography is part of an on-going attempt to document all works written by and about Harry Crews, the novelist, essayist, and educator who has written and taught for well over thirty years. A previous bibliography by Michael Hargraves [*Harry Crews: A Bibliography*. Westport, CT: Greenwood P, 1986] recorded the bulk of his early work, but as Crews continues to write and publish, readers and academics have hurried to keep up with the pace. As well, a resurgence of interest in Crews and his work in the late 1980s increased the number of commentaries, both popular and critical. Add to this, a cult-like following attuned to the media's portrayal of Crews as a pugilist-outlaw in the 1990s. Keeping up with Crews requires the stamina and discipline of the boxers, bodybuilders, and martial artists who inhabit his works.

The primary works of Crews are detailed in four sections: Novels, Short Fiction, Nonfiction, and Book Reviews. Two other sections cite Interviews with the author and Critical Texts. A different version of this bibliography appeared in an issue of *The Southern Quarterly* devoted to

Crews ["A Harry Crews Bibliography: Short Work and Critical Response." *Southern Quarterly* 37.1 (Fall 1998): 118–23]. An expanded and regularly updated version can be found online (http://www.levee67.com/crews/).

NOVELS

In 1968, Crews published his first novel *The Gospel Singer*, and over the next eight years, published seven more. After completing his most celebrated work *A Childhood* in 1978, and committing himself to writing nonfiction and several unproduced screenplays, Crews did not publish another major novel until *All We Need of Hell* in 1987. *The Enthusiast*, a limited edition, was published in 1981, but is essentially the first chapter from *All We Need of Hell*, and was reprinted in *Florida Frenzy*.

Except for library collections and used book dealers, finding certain books by Crews can be difficult. Of the fourteen novels Crews has published since *The Gospel Singer*, only half are in print, and of the first eight only four are available in the U.S.

But by the early 1990s, his popularity in France, Italy, and the U.K. enabled publishers there to bring his translated works to European audiences for the first time. In 1993, along with Poseidon in the U.S., the British publisher Gorse released *Classic Crews*, a reader that collected two out-of-print novels, *The Gypsy's Curse* and *Car*, the memoir *A Childhood*, and the essays, "Fathers, Sons, Blood," "The Car," and "Climbing the Tower." In 1995, Gorse also re-released *The Gospel Singer*, coupled with its unpublished sequel, *Where Does One Go When There's No Place Left to Go?* And in 1996, Crews's only dramatic work, *Blood Issue*—commissioned by the Actors Theatre of Louisville—was collected in *By Southern Playwrights*.

His last four novels are available in paperback, and a limited edition of *Where Does One Go When There's No Place Left to Go?* was published in the U.S. in 1998.

The Gospel Singer. NY: William Morrow & Co., 1968.
Naked in Garden Hills. NY: William Morrow & Co., 1969.
This Thing Don't Lead to Heaven. NY: William Morrow & Co., 1970.
Karate Is a Thing of the Spirit. NY: William Morrow & Co., 1971.
Car: A Novel. NY: William Morrow & Co., 1972.
The Hawk Is Dying. NY: Alfred A. Knopf, 1973.
The Gypsy's Curse. NY: Alfred A. Knopf, 1974.
A Feast of Snakes. NY: Atheneum, 1976.
The Enthusiast. Winston-Salem NC: Palaemon P, 1981. [Limited edition of 200 copies.]

All We Need of Hell. NY: Harper & Row, 1987.

The Knockout Artist. NY: Harper & Row, 1988.

Body: A Tragicomedy. NY: Poseidon P, 1990.

Scar Lover. NY: Poseidon P, 1992.

Classic Crews: A Harry Crews Reader. NY: Poseidon P, 1993.

The Mulching of America. NY: Simon & Schuster, 1995.

The Gospel Singer & Where Does One Go When There's No Place Left to Go? London: Gorse Publications, 1995.

Blood Issue. By *Southern Playwrights: Plays from the Actors Theatre of Louisville.* Michael Bigelow Dixon & Michele Volansky, eds. Lexington, KY: University of Kentucky P, 1996. 27–75.

Celebration. NY: Simon & Schuster, 1998.

Where Does One Go When There's No Place Left to Go? Los Angeles, CA: Blood & Guts P, April 1998. [Limited edition of 426 copies.]

SHORT FICTION

During his apprentice years, Crews claims to have written a "room full" of short stories only to have the majority of them rejected. As a result, only a small number, most of them published early in his career, exist in print.

"The Unattached Smile." *The Sewanee Review* 71.2 (April–June 1963): 240–49. [Rpt. in *Craft and Vision: The Best Fiction from* The Sewanee Review. Ed. Andrew Lytle. NY: Delacorte P, 1971. 53–61.]

"It Reminds One of the Opera." *P'an Ku* 1.1 (1964): 20–21. [Crews served as a faculty advisory for this literary magazine while teaching at Broward Community College in Ft. Lauderdale, Florida.]

"A Long Wail." *The Georgia Review* 18.2 (Summer 1964): 217–23. [Rpt. in *Necessary Fictions: Selected Stories from* The Georgia Review. Eds. Stanley W. Lindberg and Stephen Corey. Athens, GA: U Georgia P, 1986. 68–74.]

"The Player Piano." *The Florida Quarterly* 1.2 (Fall 1967): 30–36.

"Becky Lives." *Little Deaths: An Anthology of Erotic Horror.* Ed. Ellen Datlow. NY: Dell, 1995. 35–63.

NONFICTION

Crews has been a regular and prolific contributor of essays, memoirs, and nonfiction to magazines as diverse and popular as *Esquire, Penthouse, Playboy, Playgirl,* and *Sport.* In

July 1976, *Esquire* published the first of fourteen essays for the monthly column "Grits" in which Crews explored themes leading to the book-length memoir *A Childhood: The Biography of a Place* (Harper & Row, 1978). Most of these nonfiction works are collected in four books: *Blood and Grits* (Harper & Row, 1979), *Florida Frenzy* (Gainesville FL: UP Florida, 1982), *2 by Crews* (Northridge CA: Lord John P, 1984), and *Madonna at Ringside* (Northridge, CA: Lord John Press, 1991).

"Teaching and Learning Creative Writing." *Dekalb Literary Arts Journal* 3.2 (1969): 1–16. [Transcripted essay from a lecture delivered to the 1968 Convention of the Georgia Writers' Association.]

"Getting It Together." *The Writer* 84.6 (June 1971): 9–11.

"One Morning in February." *Shenandoah* 25.4 (1974): 90–96. Reprinted in *Shenandoah* 35.2–3 (1984): 105–11. [Early chapter from *A Childhood*.]

"Going Down in Valdeez." *Playboy* 22.2 (February 1975): 108+. [*Blood and Grits*]

"A Walk in the Country." *Playboy* 22.4 (April 1975): 118+. [*Blood and Grits*]

"Charles Bronson Ain't No Pussycat." *Playboy* 22.10 (October 1975): 114+. [*Blood and Grits*]

"The Car." *Esquire* (December 1975): 150–51. [*Blood and Grits, Florida Frenzy, Classic Crews*]

"Harry Crews." *Self-Portrait: Book People Picture Themselves.* Ed. Burt Britton. NY: Random House, 1976. 36. [Crews has drawn a pencil sketch of himself.]

"L. L. Bean Has Your Number, America!" *Esquire* (March 1976): 104+. [*Blood and Grits*]

"Pages from the Life of a Georgia Innocent." *Esquire* (July 1976): 30+.

"The Wonderful World of Winnebagos." *Esquire* (August 1976): 38+. [*Blood and Grits*]

"Building Men the Marine Corps Way." *Esquire* (September 1976): 22+.

"Carny." *Playboy* 23.9 (September 1976): 96+. [*Blood and Grits, Madonna at Ringside*]

"Running Fox." *Esquire* (October 1976): 8+. [*Blood and Grits, Florida Frenzy*]

"Television's Junkyard Dog." *Esquire* (October 1976): 94+. [*Blood and Grits*]

"Reminiscences of a Blind Muleman." *Esquire* (November 1976): 46+.

"A Small Boy on the Floor, Listening." *Esquire* (December 1976): 51+.

"Temple of the Airwaves: A Visit with Garner Ted Armstrong and *The World Tomorrow*." *Esquire* (December 1976): 108+.

"Leaving Pasadena—Resume Safe Speed." *Esquire* (January 1977): 29+. [*Blood and Grits*]

"Tuesday Night with Cody, Jimbo and a Fish of Some Proportion." *Esquire* (February 1977): 26 + . [*Blood and Grits, Florida Frenzy*]

"Cockfighting: An Unfashionable View." *Esquire* (March 1977): 8 + . [*Florida Frenzy*]

"Poaching Gators for Fun and Profit." *Esquire* (April 1977): 54 + . [*Florida Frenzy*]

"The Most Kindest Cut of All: Vasectomy." *Esquire* (May 1977): 60 + . [*Blood and Grits*]

"The Hawk Is Flying." *Esquire*. (June 1977): 32 + . [*Blood and Grits, Florida Frenzy*]

"The Goat Day Olympics." *Esquire* (July 1977): 36 + . [*Florida Frenzy*]

"Comeuppance at the Gatornationals." *Sport* 65 (July 1977): 38 + . [*Florida Frenzy*]

"Climbing the Tower." *Esquire* (August 1977): 38–39. [*Blood and Grits, Classic Crews*]

"The Trucker Militant." *Esquire* (August 1977): 82 + . [*Blood and Grits*]

"Tip on a Live Jockey." *Sport* (January 1978): 38 + . [*Blood and Grits, Florida Frenzy*]

"A Childhood in Georgia." *Penthouse* 10.3 (November 1978): 128 + .

"A Day at the Dogfights." *Esquire* (February 1979): 56 + . [*Florida Frenzy*]

"The Unfeminine Mystique." *Playgirl* 7 (December 1979): 124–25. [*Florida Frenzy*]

"Truckstops, Whores, & Gravy." *Junk Food*. Ed. Charles J. Rubin. NY: Dial P, 1980. 32–35.

"The Buttondown Terror of David Duke." *Playboy* 27.2 (February 1980): 102 + . [*2 by Crews*]

"Why I Live Where I Live." *Esquire* (September 1980): 46–47. [*Florida Frenzy*]

"Jerry Falwell: Reverend of the New Right." *Playgirl* (July 1981). 21 + .

"The Famous Writer's Cooking School." *Playboy* 28.10 (October 1981): 163. [Includes Crews's recipe for "Snake Steak."]

"Man Talk." *Playgirl* 10.2 (July 1982): 44 + .

"Mary Steenburgen: Born with the Gift." *Playgirl* 11.4 (September 1983): 12–13.

"The Violence That Finds Us." *Playboy* 31.4 (September 1983): 98 + . [*2 by Crews*]

"Fathers, Sons, Blood." *Playboy* 32.1 (January 1985): 110 + . [*Madonna at Ringside, Classic Crews*]

"A Stubborn Sense of Place: Forum." *Harper's Magazine* 273.1635 (August 1986): 35–45.

"What Momma Knows." *Southern Magazine* (May 1987): N. pag. [Rpt. and condensed as "Mama Pulled the Load Alone" in *Reader's Digest* 132.789 (January 1988): 55–59.]

"Madonna Goes to the Fights." *San Francisco Chronicle* 31 January 1989: 5B. [*Madonna at Ringside*]

"The Wisdom of the Groin." *Playboy* 36.2 (February 1989): 88 +. [*Madonna at Ringside*]

"Sean Penn Lives to Tell." *Fame* (November 1990): 93 +.

"On Food: From a Telephone Interview August 1986 with Betty Fussell." *Antaeus* 68 (Spring 1992): 125–30.

"Being in Nothingness: The Granite Novelist Reflects on the Tender Zone Where Flesh Meets Fantasy." *Playboy* 40.2 (February 1993): 127 +.

"The Suwannee River: None Prettier." *Forum* (Florida Humanities Council) 27.1 (Spring–Summer 1993): 6–7.

"A Lesson in Desperation and Stupidity." *The Oxford American* (October–November 1996): 47–48.

"Swamp as Metaphor." *The Place Within: Portraits of the American Landscape by Twenty Contemporary Writers.* Ed. Jodi Daynard. NY: Norton, 1997. 27–38.

"Assault of Memory." *Southern Quarterly* 37.1 (Fall 1998): 124–38. [First two chapters of a nonfiction work-in-progress.]

BOOK REVIEWS

The sixteen book reviews that Crews has written are notable for their honesty, humor, and a pedagogical attention to the mechanics of fiction, the craft of writing. Unfortunately, his reviews have yet to be compiled and are available only from their original sources.

"*A Melon for Ecstasy.*" *New York Times Book Review* 8 August 1971: 6. Rev. of *A Melon for Ecstasy*, by John Fortune and John Wells.

"*Going Nowhere:* One Thing You Can Say about Greenberg, He Doesn't Play It Safe." *New York Times Book Review* 29 August 1971: 4. Rev. of *Going Nowhere*, by Alvin Greenberg.

"*Pocock & Pitt:* For Elliot Baker, Roses and One Brick." *New York Times Book Review* 26 September 1971: 2. Rev. of *Pocock & Pitt*, by Elliot Baker.

"*Gray Matters:* In 2400, It Was All Cerebromorphs." *New York Times Book Review* 31 October 1971: 7, 16. Rev. of *Gray Matters*, by William Hjortsberg.

"*An Old-Fashioned Darling:* The Aftermath of Sex." *New York Times Book Review* 21 November 1971: 6. Rev. of *An Old-Fashioned Darling*, by Charles Simmons.

"Between Marriages: A Story of Love, No Love." *Los Angeles Times* 10 June 1973: 23, 27. Rev. of *Starting Over*, by Dan Wakefield.

"A Primal Scream of Despair." *Philadelphia Inquirer* 20 May 1973: 8G. Rev. of *Breakfast of Champions*, by Kurt Vonnegut Jr.

"Football Money: *The Fix*." *New York Times Book Review* 12 November 1978: 66. Rev. of *The Fix*, by Dorian Fliegel.

"Laughing Through Georgia." *Washington Post Book World* 28 September 1980: 3. Rev. of *Crackers*, by Roy Blount Jr.

"Carry On, Doctor." *Washington Post Book World* 16 November 1980: 4. Rev. of *Ray*, by Barry Hannah.

"The Passage to Manhood." *New York Times Book Review* 7 December 1980: 12, 43. Rev. of *The Lords of Discipline*, by Pat Conroy.

"A Tale of Two Texans." *Washington Post Book World* 14 December 1980: 9. Rev. of *Deep in the Heart*, by Wyatt Wyatt.

"Growing Up Black: *Mary*." *New York Times Book Review* 29 March 1981: 12. Rev. of *Mary*, by Mary Mebane.

"On the Lam with Dotty." *New York Times Book Review* 3 July 1988: 5. Rev. of *Vanished*, by Mary McGarry Morris.

"Perfectly Shaped Stones." *Los Angeles Times* 21 October 1990: 3, 8. Rev. of *Big Bad Love*, by Larry Brown.

"A Couple of Predators: The Grifters in This Novel Think They're Pretty Good Guys, But Their Actions Suggest Otherwise." *New York Times Book Review* 20 June 1993: 9. Rev. of *Save Me, Joe Louis*, by Madison Smartt Bell.

INTERVIEWS

Over the last thirty years, Crews's development as a writer has been well-documented by interviews given to newspapers and magazines. Erik Bledsoe unearthed and gathered the best of those interviews in the 1999 anthology *Getting Naked with Harry Crews*.

While the interviews in print offer insights into Crews as a writer, three video documentaries made at the mid-point of his career reveal his charisma, mannerisms, and personality. Wayne Schowalter made the first documentary in 1983, a sobering glimpse of Crews filmed during his nine-year hiatus between novels. Two other documentaries followed in the 1990s, riding a resurgence of Crews's productivity and popularity.

The 1990s also saw the mainstream media take advantage of Crews's well-honed image as a hard-living literary he-man—the South's answer to Hunter S. Thompson and Charles Bukowski. Appearing on *The Dennis Miller Show* in 1992 and *The Late Late Show with Tom Snyder* in 1998, Crews was accorded the respect due to a literary lion but, with a measure of skepticism, courted as a sideshow curiosity.

Bledsoe, Erik, ed. *Getting Naked with Harry Crews: Interviews*. Gainesville, FL: UP of Florida, 1999.

Bonetti, K. *Interview with Harry Crews*. Columbia MO: American Audio Prose Library, 1982. Audio cassette: 60 mins.

Hawkins, Gary, dir. *The Rough South of Harry Crews*. NC: University of North Carolina Center for Public Television, 1992. Videocassette: 54 mins.

Schowalter, Wayne, dir. *Harry Crews: Blood and Words*. Wayne Schowalter Productions, 1983. Videocassette: 52 mins.

Thurman, Tom and Chris Iovenko, dirs. *Harry Crews: Guilty as Charged*. Danville, KY: Fly By Noir Films, 1993. Videocassette: 54 mins.

CRITICAL TEXTS

The academic world was not much engaged by the early works of Crews. His novels were absent of the self-reference or irony in vogue then and deceptively cinematic: all story, character, and device. Reviewing *Craft and Vision* in 1973, Sterling Watson paid a very writerly tribute to Crews's story "The Unattached Smile" by upholding its marriage of "craft, the tool, and vision." It was not until *A Feast of Snakes* and *A Childhood* that academics—including David K. Jeffrey and Gary L. Long, who count among his strongest supporters—recognized the incipient themes of cultural and spiritual malaise in Crews's post-agrarian South. With some foresight, Jeffery edited *A Grit's Triumph: Essays on the Works of Harry Crews* [Port Washington, NY: Associated Faculty P, 1983] which developed these arguments within a critical context. *A Grit's Triumph* remained the major single source of critical inquiry until 1998 when *The Southern Quarterly* published the Harry Crews issue.

Ames, Sanford. "Fast Food/Quick Lunch: Crews, Burroughs, and Pynchon." *Literary Gastronomy*. Ed. David Bevan. Rodopi Perspectives on Modern Literature. Atlanta: Rodopi, 1988. 19–27.

Beatty, Patricia V. "Body Language in Harry Crews's *The Gypsy's Curse*." *Critique: Studies in Contemporary Fiction* 23.2 (Winter 1981–82): 61–66.

———. "Crews's Women." *A Grit's Triumph: Essays on the Works of Harry Crews*. Ed. David K. Jeffrey. Port Washington, NY: Associated Faculty P, 1983. 112–23.

Birden, Lorene M. "A Response to 'Rereading Harry Crews' *A Feast of Snakes*' by Michael Spikes" *Arkansas Review* 4.2 (Fall 1995): 274–76.

Brinkmeyer, Bob. "Wright and Crews: Southern Childhoods." *Southern Exposure* 8.3 (Fall 1980): 120–23.

Brittin, Ruth L. "Harry Crews and the Southern Protestant Church." *A Grit's Triumph: Essays on the Works of Harry Crews*. Ed. David K. Jeffrey. Port Washington, NY: Associated Faculty P, 1983. 79–99.

Buehrer, David. "Crews' Blues: Manic-Depression in *A Feast of Snakes*." *Journal of Evolutionary Psychology* 17.1–2 (March 1996): 37–43.

Carter, Nancy Corson. "1970 Images of the Machine and the Garden: Kosinski, Crews, and Pirsig." *Soundings: A Journal of Interdisciplinary Studies* 61.1 (1978): 105–22.

Connery, Thomas B. "Discovering a Literary Form." *A Sourcebook of American Literary Journalism: Representing Writers in an Emerging Genre*. Ed. Thomas B. Connery. Westport, CT: Greenwood P, 1997. 32.

Covel, Robert C. "The Violent Bear It as Best They Can: Cultural Conflict in the Novels of Harry Crews." *Studies in the Literary Imagination* 27.2 (Fall 1994): 75–86.

DeBord, Larry W. "Crews, Harry." *Encyclopedia of Southern Culture*. Eds. Charles Reagan Wilson and William Ferris. Chapel Hill: U North Carolina P, 1989. 950.

DeBord, Larry W., and Gary L. Long. "Harry Crews's *A Childhood*: A Resource for Teaching Sociology." *Teaching Sociology* 9.4 (July 1982): 452–60.

———. "Harry Crews on the American Dream." *Southern Quarterly* 20.3 (Spring 1982): 35–53.

Dettelbach, Cynthia G. *In the Driver's Seat: The Automobile in American Literature and Popular Culture*. Westport, CT: Greenwood P, 1976. 99–101.

Edwards, Tim. " 'Everthing Is Eating Everthing Else': The Naturalistic Impulse in Harry Crews's *A Feast of Snakes*." *Southern Quarterly* 37.1 (Fall 1998): 42–53.

Guinn, Matthew. "The Grit Émigré in Harry Crews's Fiction." *Southern Quarterly* 38.1 (Fall 1999): 164–72.

Jeffrey, David K. "Crews's Freaks." *A Grit's Triumph: Essays on the Works of Harry Crews*. Ed. David K. Jeffrey. Port Washington, NY: Associated Faculty P, 1983. 67–78.

———. "Murder and Mayhem in Crews' *A Feast of Snakes*." *Critique: Studies in Modern Fiction* 28.1 (1986): 45–54.

Johnson, Donald. "The Athlete's Hand Filling Up: Harry Crews and Sports." *A*

Grit's Triumph: Essays on the Works of Harry Crews. Ed. David K. Jeffrey. Port Washington, NY: Associated Faculty P, 1983. 100–11.

Johnstone, Barbara. "Violence and Civility in Discourse: Uses of Mitigation by Rural Southern White Men." *The SECOL Review (Southeastern Conference on Linguistics)* 16.1 (Spring 1992): 1–19.

———. " 'You Gone Have to Learn to Talk Right': Linguistic Deference and Regional Dialect in Harry Crews's *Body.*" *The Text and Beyond: Essays in Literary Linguistics.* Ed. Cynthia Goldin Bernstein. Tuscaloosa, AL: U Alabama P, 1994. 278–95.

Ketchin, Susan. "The Writer as Shaman." *The Christ-Haunted Landscape: Faith and Doubt in Southern Fiction.* Jackson, MS: U Mississippi P, 1994. 326–29.

Kramer, Victor. "Patterns of Adaptation: Place and Placelessness in Contemporary Southern Fiction." *Studies in the Literary Imagination* 27.2 (Fall 1994): 1–7.

Lake, Elise S. "Having a Hard Time of It: Women in the Novels of Harry Crews." *Southern Quarterly* 37.1 (Fall 1998): 54–65.

Long, Gary L. "Naked Americans: Violence in the Work of Harry Crews." *Southern Quarterly* 32.4 (Summer 1994): 117–30.

———. "Silences, Criticisms, and Laments: Political Implications in the Works of Harry Crews." *Southern Quarterly* 37.1 (Fall 1998): 27–41. [Includes selected bibliography.]

Long, Gary L., and Larry W. DeBord. "Literary Criticism and the Fate of Ideas: The Case of Harry Crews." *The Texas Review* 4.3–4 (Fall–Winter 1983): 69–91. [Includes extensive bibliography.]

———. "Grit Truths: The Journalistic Essays of Harry Crews." *The Texas Review* 9.1–2 (Spring–Summer 1988): 96–109.

Lynskey, Edward C. "Violence in Hometown America: Harry Crews' *A Feast of Snakes.*" *Pembroke Magazine* 19 (1987): 195–200.

———. "Harry Crews: The Unreconstructed Rebel." *Pembroke Magazine* 21 (1989): 172–78.

———. "Early Harry Crews: A True Grit's Religiosity." *Pembroke Magazine* 23 (1991): 143–51.

McGregory, Jerrilyn. "Harry Crews's Home Place: An Excursion into Wiregrass Country and the Carnivalesque." *Southern Quarterly* 37.1 (Fall 1998): 66–73.

Moore, Jack. "The Land and the Ethnics in Crews's Works." *A Grit's Triumph: Essays on the Works of Harry Crews.* Ed. David K. Jeffrey. Port Washington, NY: Associated Faculty P, 1983. 46–66.

Moss, William M. "Postmodern Georgia Scenes: Harry Crews and the Southern

Tradition in Fiction." *A Grit's Triumph: Essays on the Works of Harry Crews*. Ed. David K. Jeffrey. Port Washington, NY: Associated Faculty P, 1983. 33–45.

Nathan, Daniel. "A Boxer's Body: The Cult of Masculinity and Homoeroticism in Harry Crew's [sic] *The Knockout Artist*." *Aethlon: The Journal of Sport Literature* 9.2 (Spring 1992): 29–34.

Noble, Donald R. "Harry Crews Introduces Himself." *A Grit's Triumph: Essays on the Works of Harry Crews*. Ed. David K. Jeffrey. Port Washington, NY: Associated Faculty P, 1983. 7–20.

———. "The Future of Southern Writing." *The History of Southern Literature*. Ed. Louis D. Rubin, Jr. Baton Rouge: Louisiana State UP, 1985. 578–88.

O'Connell, Shaun. "Dream Books." *New Boston Review* 4 (February–March 1979): 6–7.

Papovich, J. Frank. "Place and Imagination in Harry Crews's *A Childhood: The Biography of a Place*." *Southern Literary Journal* 19.1 (Fall 1986): 26–35.

Pearson, Michael. "Rude Beginnings of the Comic Tradition in Georgia Literature." *Journal of American Culture* 11.3 (Fall 1988): 51–54.

Randisi, Jennifer L. "The Scene of the Crime: The Automobile in the Fiction of Harry Crews." *Southern Studies: An Interdisciplinary Journal of the South* 25.3 (Fall 1986): 213–19.

Romine, Scott. "Harry Crews's Away Games: Home and Sport in *A Feast of Snakes* and *Body*." *Southern Quarterly* 37.1 (Fall 1998): 74–87.

Rotenstein, David S. "Ethnography, Journalism and Literature: Ethnographic Text and Southern Author Harry Crews." *Southern Folklore* 54.1 (1997): 40–50.

Ryan, Bryan, ed. "Crews, Harry (Eugene) 1935–." *Major 20th-Century Writers: A Selection of Sketches from* Contemporary Authors. Volume 1: A–D. Detroit: Gale Research Inc., 1991. 739–43.

Schafer, William J. "Partial People: The Novels of Harry Crews." *Mississippi Quarterly: The Journal of Southern Culture* 41.1 (Winter 1987–1988): 69–88.

———. "Crews, Harry (Eugene)." *Contemporary Novelists*. Ed. Lesley Henderson. 5th ed. Chicago: Saint James P, 1991. 220–22.

Seelye, J. "Georgia Boys: The Redclay Satyrs of Erskine Caldwell and Harry Crews." *Virginia Quarterly Review* 56.4 (Autumn 1980): 612–26.

Shelton, Frank W. "A Way of Life and Place." *Southern Literary Journal* 11.2 (1979): 97–102.

———. "Harry Crews: Man's Search for Perfection." *Southern Literary Journal* 12.2 (Spring 1980): 97–113. Reprinted in *A Grit's Triumph* (Jeffrey, 1983. 21–32).

———. "Theme and Technique in Harry Crews's *Car*." *A Grit's Triumph: Essays on the Works of Harry Crews*. Ed. David K. Jeffrey. Port Washington, NY: Associated Faculty P, 1983. 124–31.

———. "The Non-Fiction of Harry Crews: A Review." *Southern Literary Journal* 16.2 (Spring 1984): 132–35.

———. "Harry Crews." *Fifty Southern Writers after 1900*. Eds. Joseph M. Flora and Robert Bain. Westport, CT: Greenwood P, 1987. 111–20.

———. "The Poor-Whites' Perspective: Harry Crews among Georgia Writers." *Journal of American Culture* 11.3 (Fall 1988): 47–50.

———. "Harry Crews after *A Childhood* (Perfection of Mind and Body in His Fiction Novels)." *Southern Literary Journal* 24.2 (Spring 1992): 3–10.

Shepherd, Allen. "Cars in Harry Crews' *Car*." *Notes on Contemporary Literature* 8.1 (1978): 8–9.

———. "Matters of Life and Death: The Novels of Harry Crews." *Critique: Studies in Modern Fiction* 20.1 (September 1978): 53–62.

———. " 'Macho Time': Boxers and Boxing in Harry Crews's *The Knockout Artist*." *Aethlon: The Journal of Sport Literature* 7.1 (Fall 1989): 69–77.

Slay, Jack, Jr. "Delineations in Freakery: Freaks in the Fiction of Harry Crews and Katherine Dunn." *Literature and the Grotesque*. Ed. Michael J. Meyer. Rodopi Perspectives on Modern Literature. Atlanta: Rodopi, 1995. 99–112.

Smith, Dave. "That Appetite for Life So Ravenous." *Shenandoah* 25.4 (Summer 1974): 49–55.

Spikes, Michael P. "Victor over Sin: Harry Crews's Critique of the Phallic Ethic in *A Feast of Snakes*." *University of Mississippi Studies in English* 11–12 (1993–1995): 411–23.

———. "Harry Crews." *American Novelists Since World War II*. Ed. James R. Giles and Wanda H. Giles. 3rd series, vol. 143. *Dictionary of Literary Biography*. Detroit: Gale Research Inc., 1994. 12–23.

———. "Rereading Harry Crews' *A Feast of Snakes*." *The Arkansas Review* 4.1 (Spring 1995): 82–94.

Teague, Matthew. "How Do You Like Your Blue-Eyed Boy Now?" *The Oxford American* (December–January 1995–1996): 69–71.

Vonalt, Larry. "The Other End of Love: Harry Crews's *Car*." *A Grit's Triumph: Essays on the Works of Harry Crews*. Ed. David K. Jeffrey. Port Washington, NY: Associated Faculty P, 1983. 132–39.

Watkins, James H. " 'The Use of *I*, Lovely and Terrifying Word': Autobiographical

Authority and the Representation of 'Redneck' Masculinity in *A Childhood.*" *Southern Quarterly* 37.1 (Fall 1998): 15–26.

Watson, Sterling. "Book Review: Craft and Vision." *Florida Quarterly* 5.2–3 (Spring 1973): 33–39.

Willis, Lonnie L. "Harry Crews' *Car.* A Possible Source." *Notes on Contemporary Literature* 12.5 (November 1982): 9–10.

NOTES

Watkins

I would like to express my gratitude to my colleague, Emily Wright, for her many helpful suggestions as I wrote this essay.

1. For the purposes of this essay, the terms autobiography and memoir will be used more-or-less interchangeably, since both genres interpellate the reader in virtually the same manner by presenting a narrator/author/protagonist who purports to tell the truth of a life.

2. According to Lejeune, because the autobiographer has at his disposal any and all of the formal devices available to the novelist (or historian, for that matter), autobiography can only be distinguished from other genres by means of what he refers to as the "pacte," an informal contract created when the author, narrator, and protagonist are identified as one. To illustrate his point, Lejeune compares the autobiographical novel (in which the protagonist is given a fictional name) to the autobiography: ". . . if the identity [of the author] is not stated positively (as in fiction), the reader will attempt to establish resemblances, in spite of the author; if it is stated positively (as in autobiography), the reader will want to look for differences (errors, deformations, etc.). Confronted with what looks like an autobiographical narrative, the reader often tends to think of himself as a detective, that is to say, to look for breaches of contract . . ." (*On Autobiography* 14). See also Elizabeth Bruss, who argues that we should think of autobiography as an "illocutionary act" rather than as a form. For Bruss, autobiography derives its power from a largely unnoticed but nevertheless influential set of "implicit textual conditions" that govern our responses to the text (*Autobiographical Acts* 4).

3. Although the term "redneck" never appears in *A Childhood*, Crews strongly identifies with the class of people that have come to be associated with that term. In a 1994 interview with Tammy Lytal and Richard R. Russell, Crews is quoted as saying, "Well, you see, what the rest of the country call 'rednecks' I call 'Grits' with a capital G. They're people; they're my people; they're Grits" ("Some of Us Do It Anyway" 540).

4. For discussions of representations of the southern poor white, see John Shelton Reed, *Southern Folk, Plain and Fancy: Native White Social Types* (Athens: University of Georgia Press, 1986), 34–45, especially. Reed distinguishes between the "good old boy" (generally speaking,

a positive designation connoting, among other characteristics, working-class values of self-reliance and hard work), the "redneck" (more commonly associated with virulent racism and a predisposition to violence), and the "hillbilly" (most often connoting ignorance and laziness). Since Crews does not make such distinctions and populates his account with variations on all three types, I will use the terms *redneck, poor white,* and *working-class white* synonymously. See also Sylvia Jenkins Cook, *From Tobacco Road to Route 66: The Southern Poor White in Fiction* (Chapel Hill: University of North Carolina Press, 1977), Grady McWhiney, *Cracker Culture: Celtic Ways in the Old South* (Tuscaloosa: University of Alabama Press, 1988); Patrick Huber, "A Short History of *Redneck*: The Fashioning of a Southern White Male Identity," *Southern Cultures* I.2 (1995): 145–66; Jack Temple Kirby, *The Countercultural South* (Athens: University of Georgia Press, 1995), 57–92; and Duane Carr, *A Question of Class: The Redneck Stereotype in Southern Fiction* (Bowling Green, OH: Bowling Green State University Popular Press, 1996).

5. See Lillian Smith, *Killers of the Dream* (New York: Norton, 1949); Hodding Carter, Jr., *Southern Legacy* (Baton Rouge: LSU Press, 1950) and *Where Main Street Meets the River* (New York: Rinehart, 1952); Frank Smith, *Congressman from Mississippi* (New York: Pantheon, 1954); Ralph McGill, *The South and the Southerner* (Boston: Little Brown, 1959); Sarah Patton Boyle, *The Desegregated Heart: A Virginian's Stand in a Time of Transition* (New York: Morrow, 1962); Willie Morris, *North Toward Home* (Boston: Houghton Mifflin, 1967); and Larry L. King, *Confessions of a White Racist* (New York: Viking, 1968).

6. *A Childhood* is included in its entirety in *Classic Crews: A Harry Crews Reader* (New York: Poseiden, 1993) and is available in an illustrated edition featuring the lovely lithograph etchings of Michael McCurdy (Athens: University of Georgia Press, 1995).

7. For representative reviews, see Robert Sherrill, "A Son of the Hungry South" (*New York Times Book Review,* December 24, 1978) 3, 17; and Shaun O'Connell, "Dream Books" (*New Boston Review* 4:4, Feb.–March, 1979), 6–7. For scholarship focusing on *A Childhood,* see Donald R. Noble, "Harry Crews Introduces Himself," *A Grit's Triumph: Essays on the Works of Harry Crews,* ed. David K. Jeffrey (Port Washington, NY: Associated Faculty Press, 1983) 7–20; and J. Frank Papovich, "Place and Imagination in Harry Crews's *A Childhood,*" *Southern Literary Journal* 19.1 (Fall, 1986): 26–35. Frank W. Shelton discusses *A Childhood* at numerous points in "Harry Crews: Man's Search for Perfection," *Southern Literary Journal* 12 (Spring, 1980): 97–113.

8. Of course, there are numerous reasons for wanting to "tell about the South." While white southerners—conservative defenders and liberal critics alike—have historically identified with the idea of the South much more strongly than have African Americans from the region, the latter group has been equally interested in (re)defining the South in their own terms. Given the canonical status of autobiographies by such southern-born writers as Frederick Douglass, Harriet Jacobs, Booker T. Washington, Richard Wright, and Maya Angelou, it is safe to assume that African American autobiographers have made a more convincing case than have their white counterparts from the South. Historian James Cobb has identified a recent trend in which African American writers are increasingly willing to not only to identify with the South but to celebrate their southernness, as in the cases of autobiographers Clifton Taulbert and Charlayne Hunter-Gault ("Community and Identity" 9–11).

9. Will Campbell's *Brother to a Dragonfly* (New York: Continuum, 1977) and Linda Flowers's *Throwed Away: Failures of Progress in Eastern North Carolina* (Knoxville: University of Tennessee Press, 1990), both of which feature strong—and sober—fathers, serve as the only two exceptions to this trend of which I am aware.

10. See John Shelton Reed, *The Enduring South: Subcultural Persistence in Mass Society* (Toronto: Lexington Books, 1972), Dewey Grantham, *The South in Modern America: A Region at Odds* (New York: HarperPerennial, 1994), 311–31; and Jefferson Humphries, "The Discourse of Southernness: Or How We Can Know There Will Still Be Such a Thing as the South and Southern Literary Culture in the Twenty-First Century," in Humphries and John Lowe, ed., *The Future of Southern Letters* (Oxford, New York: Oxford University Press, 1996), 119–33.

Russell

1. In so doing, he typifies the contemporary southern author whom Fred Hobson has described in his excellent book, *The Southern Writer in the Postmodern World*: "the contemporary southern writer—with the exception of John Barth and, on occasion, writers such as Barry Hannah, Richard Ford, and James Alan McPherson—essentially accepts, rather than invents, his world, is not given to fantasy, does not in his fiction question the whole assumed relationship between narrator and narrative, does not question the nature of fiction itself" (9).

2. Crews repeats this statement in the Bledsoe interview, noting that "I have never been sure of who I am. I was in the university my whole working life; I was in it, but not of it" (105).

3. Later in the Bledsoe interview, Crews goes even further, stating that capitalism is partly responsible for "killing" God: "But wouldn't it be wonderful, and I'm talking about me now, wouldn't it be wonderful for me if I did have something immutable, omnipotent, ubiquitous—all those other English teacher words—and that I could put myself into the keeping of that kind of power and knowledge. And He will . . . or She . . . It will provide. So, no, I believe but there ain't nothing to believe. Said another way. The culture and, God help us, the economic system I live in has killed any semblance of anything that resembles or could resemble a Godhead or first cause or anything like that" (110).

Long

For comments and suggestions, I wish to thank Elise S. Lake and Larry W. DeBord.

1. Crews considers himself an outsider. Literary ambitions separated him from his people; "grit" origins made him an alien among English professor colleagues. See *A Childhood: The Biography of a Place*, 21.

2. Crews describes himself as a believer, neither an atheist nor an agnostic. See "Harry Crews: Interview, His Apartment, December 10, 1978, 12 noon-4:30 p.m.," by David K. Jeffrey and Donald R. Noble, 26–28 (unpublished tape transcript).

3. In his autobiographical book *A Childhood: The Biography of a Place*, Crews describes the desperation, violence, kinship, and love of his childhood. In South Georgia, in the 1930s and 1940s lives were grounded in truths about land and animals, in duty, and in prescribed codes

of behavior. He also recounts the moment when he recognized his alienation from this way of life (170–71).

4. For the importance of the moment in Crews's fiction, see Smith, 55.

5. There are exceptions to the self-destructive pattern. Both *All We Need of Hell* and *Scar Lover* have limp, happy resolutions.

6. Examples in *Childhood* include a hired hand extracting his tooth with pliers, Crews's childhood bout with polio and his fall into a vat of boiling water, tales of altercations and mutilations among people in Bacon County, surgical remedies for sick farm animals, the story about a fetus and a perforated "aner."

7. The pain of eating and passing pieces of an automobile is central in *Car*. Training—discipline and self-denial—is painful in *Body*. Physical workouts are painful in *Hell*, as is physical contact in *Feast*. Pain measures survival in *Heaven* and accomplishment in *Karate*.

8. See *Childhood*, 16–17, 40, and 119.

9. "Building Men the Marine Corps Way" offers a secular analogy. The way Crews handled the beating from his drill sergeant defined his character.

10. See Crews's discussion of Walt Disney movies depicting frontier hardships as character-building in "Pages from the Life of a Georgia Innocent."

11. For a discussion of modern society as inhospitable, and people as tourists, see Long ("Naked Americans"). Crews's attention to shifting, ambiguous standards for achievement in modern America is examined by Long and DeBord ("Grit Truths").

12. On the functions of traditional society see Long ("Naked Americans"). Crews reports his recreation of traditional society in "The Goat Day Olympics."

13. For Crews, standards are important in "The Wonderful World of Winnebagos" and "Tuesday Night with Cody, Jimbo and a Fish of Some Proportion." For his commentary on naked Americans, see "A Day at the Dog Fights."

14. Related is Crews's piece on the lucrative, high-tech, slickly packaged religion of Garner Ted Armstrong, "Temple of the Airwaves."

15. Crews depicts crowds in *Gypsy*, *Karate*, and *Feast*. He describes the crowd in "Dogfights" as individuals disassociated from pasts and futures. His opinions of crowds are apparent in Bellamy, 89–90, and in "Interview with Harry Crews, His Office, University of Florida, December 11, 1978" (Jeffrey and Noble, transcript, 41). Contempt for crowds of tourists is manifest in "Television's Junkyard Dog."

16. Crews's frequently used aphorism "Wish in one hand . . ." is, in its own way, an assertion of the primacy of immediate experience over hopes and dreams. His statement in the interview by Oney is more explicit: ". . . [Y]ou can find out about a thing vicariously . . . from a book, but [not] . . . as well as . . . when you're naked and vulnerable to the experiences of the world" (31).

17. On blood and blood sports, see "Dogfights," "Goat Day," and "Pages." See the recurring phrase "real as blood." For Crews's views on abstractions see "The Violence That Finds Us," "The Wisdom of the Groin," and "The Unfeminine Mystique."

18. Ambivalent about pain, Crews also glorifies pain and uses it as a criterion for the real.

19. For example, George Gattling (*Hawk*) launches himself into the historical regimen

and precise craft of the austringer—hoods, jesses, bells, and live biddies. Leashed to the hawk night and day, training the bird is also a domination of self. Shereel (*Body*) transforms her body through physical discipline. John Kaimon, Gaye Nell, Belt, and members of the karate commune harden their bodies with abuse. Duffy Deeter (*Hell*) concentrates on concentration camp images to control climax during sex. Joe Lon (*Feast*) longs for the physical contact of football practice. In *Gypsy*, Marvin Molar says to himself: "One of the things I've found in my life is that in a tortured muscle there's a kind of peace you can't find anywhere else. Exhaustion drives out the world. . . . [T]he thing about a real workout is that you know you're going to meet pain, and the only question is how you're going to . . . handle it" (131–32).

20. See, for example, "Junkyard Dog" and "Climbing the Tower." Crews's respect for discipline can be found in Summer, 65.

21. Love makes no sense to George Gattling in *Hawk* or to Joe Lon Mackey in *Feast*. In *Heaven*, Pearl Lee Gates believes love can be found at driven-in, Doris Day movies.

22. Crews celebrates his own beatings in "Dogfights," "The Violence," and "Leaving Pasadena—Resume Safe Speed," and his encounters with violence in "A Walk in the Country" and "A Night at a Waterfall." See also Duffy Deeter's celebration of pain in *Hell*, 8. The implications of violence in Crews writings are examined by Long ("Naked Americans").

23. Sympathetic renderings of deformed and unusual people in several of his novels (*Gospel, Naked, Hawk, Heaven, Gypsy*) suggest that Crews considers standards for normality arbitrary. His talk in interviews about the inabilities of the obviously deformed to control their self-presentations, to pass unnoticed like other people, supports this conclusion. (For example, see his interview with Oney, 17, and Betty's statement in *Hawk*: "Normal is for shit," 165.)

24. See Jeffrey and Noble, 11 December, 41.

25. See "Goat Day," "Running Fox," "Cockfighting," and "Dogfights." For Crews the moralist, perhaps the fundamental immorality of modern society is corruption of language and meanings—i.e., the absence of connections between words and intentions, words and action, languages and communities, appearances and essences. In several ways—with phrases such as "Eat-&-Grow-Slim Wafers," and in articles when he writes about contemporary language—Crews suggests a disjunction between symbols and substance. Within modern society, abstractions have displaced and diminished the worth of experience.

In a society organized around illusions, wisdom, craft, and lore—knowledge grounded in experience—are unimportant. People have multiple identities. Appearances and identity claims are not reliable guides for behavior. People and events are no longer what they seem to be. (For example, in *Knockout* characters are misled by the apparent identities of others.)

26. See Jeffrey and Noble, 11 December, 41.

27. Crews is not a propagandist, but his works do contain messages and sophisticated criticisms. *Car* is a tale of alienation. Modern people are diminished by the automobile and a culture of symbolic consumption, dominated by things. But alienation occurs within a vacuum, a problem without historical causes, and without remedies. Not understanding how the thing came to define and control them, Crews's car-characters make only dramatic gestures of

protest against it. With his private rejection of the automobile, Crews does the same. (See "Why I Live Where I Live," 46, and Crews's *Esquire* piece "The Car.")

28. In "Goat Day," Crews describes an individualistic adaptation to modernity. He and friends protest against the present and reverently remember the past with an agrarian theme party. This annual barbecue permits a temporary return to a more "authentic" life, enhances the bonds of friendship, and reminds participants of their estrangement from modernity. As a ritual it changes nothing. In a very real sense, it is not much different than the "escape" into rugged individualism of the woodsman as sold by L. L. Bean, or Gattling's retreat into medieval lore in *Hawk*.

29. In fiction, Crews explores secular beliefs as antidotes to modern life and finds them wanting. Characters are deluded and foolish. Beliefs fail them; their struggles are futile; they tend to come to sad endings. Had Crews's characters been clear-sighted, presumably, they would have "known" better.

For example, magic does not make a midget grow, and pain is not a remedy for age and death in *Heaven*. Wealth and power do not make Dolly's dream of losing her virginity to Fat Man come true in *Naked*. Easy Mack's self-confident mechanical skill does not save him from the crusher in *Car*.

30. Except for discussing his literary "betters"—e.g., Andrew Lytle—Crews seldom talks about social inequality in interviews. He admits to being uncomfortable among professors, and literary types. He seems not to be fond of publishing house representatives.

Crews knows about poverty and powerlessness. He and his people lived without money or control over their fates. Fatalism is a theme in *Childhood*—lack of control is accepted as a fact of life. (See, for example, Crews's discussion of the importance of rituals for creating the illusion of control in *Childhood*, 90.) Perhaps Crews's characters are not sensitive to inequality because he is not. There are silences in Crews's novels on inequality and class barriers as they condition people's life chances. On the other hand, individuals determined to achieve are prominent in his works. Crews persisted in the face of failure; he admits to lusting after an audience. The failures of his characters do not necessarily imply disbelief in individual achievement. Crews is fascinated by belief. Duffy Deeter, Marvin Molar, Al Molarski, the inmates of the retirement home, Herman Mack—all, like Crews—try harder. The silences, the lack of alternatives to individual action, and Crews's outrage about illusions and thwarted individual ambitions are consistent with the criticisms of the true-believer seeking to rectify the faith. "Rugged" individualism is also a component of southern culture.

31. The phrase "Survival is triumph enough" celebrates human endurance. Implicitly it minimizes the value of something larger. Overall, Crews's writings seem to constitute a brief against change.

Edwards

1. In an interview with David K. Jeffrey and Donald R. Noble, Crews has offered the following response to such a "superficial reading": "People have said I write thesis novels or tract novels. That hurts . . . Because I don't think it's fair and I don't think it's true" ("Harry

Crews: An Interview." *A Grit's Triumph: Essays on the Work of Harry Crews*, ed. David K. Jeffrey. New York: Associated Faculty Press, 1983. 140–51. Crews's response appears on 143.)

2. One unpublished dissertation, Martin Kich's "Everyone Goes Around Acting Crazy: A Study of Recent American Hard-Core Naturalists" (*DAI* 50 (1989) 443A (Lehigh University)), recognizes Crews as one of a group of twentieth-century naturalistic novelists. Kich's study, however, focuses primarily on West, Caldwell, Purdy, Kosinski, and Sheen.

3. In some of Crews's most recent work, most notably *Scar Lover* (1992), the novelist has suggested a greater possibility for love and community. But *Scar Lover* somehow seems less satisfying, somehow out of place in Crews's oeuvre, when compared with the darker visions offered by *A Feast of Snakes* and other early novels.

Lake

I would like to thank Gary L. Long for his comments.

McGregory

1. The historic Wiregrass region extends from north of Savannah, sweeps across the rolling meadows into the southwest Georgia coastal plain, fans over into the southeastern corner of Alabama, and dips into the northwestern panhandle of Florida. For insight into the folklife of the Wiregrass region, see McGregory, *Wiregrass Country*. Even the relatively southern enterprise of storytelling possesses a singular meaning within the context of the Wiregrass region. Memorates—personal experience narratives of the supernatural—still form the basis for much of its residents' daily discourse. These forms of narratives are closely related to the grotesqueries Crews is known to manufacture.

2. There is much evidence of befuddled critics striving to situate Crews's literary style. Selecting Nathanael West as a major influence, John Seelye discerns that Crews's fiction embodies a "Hollywoodization of the South" (625), and Edward C. Lynskey likens one novel to "a Sam Peckinpah movie" (195). Christopher Lehmann-Haupt in a book review in *The New York Times*, January 12, 1987, labeled Crews "the founding member of what might be called the shopping-mall-Gothic school of Southern writers" (19).

3. Here, I rely on Bakhtin's *Rabelais and His World*, trans. Helene Iswolsky (Bloomington: Indiana University Press, 1984).

4. Bakhtin writes that the carnivalesque crowd "is the people as a whole, but organized in their own way, the way of the people. It is outside of and contrary to all existing forms of the coercive socioeconomic and political organization, which is suspended for the time of festivity" (255).

5. See Victor Turner, *Dramas, Fields, and Metaphors: Symbolic Action in Human Society* (Ithaca, NY: Cornell University Press, 1974), 23–59, for full definition. Social dramas arise in conflict situations to offer redressive actions in order to resolve social schisms.

6. The term "naked American" is devised by Crews in *Florida Frenzy* (Gainesville: University Presses of Florida, 1982), 57, to describe those who do not adhere strictly to the rules

of a decorous society nor care to be politically correct. Crews writes against the grain of the "official culture," which ignores its own reification of racist ideology.

7. Patricia Beatty writes a very pointed critique of "Crews's Women" in *A Grit's Triumph*. Harry Crews addresses the flack from feminist critics in an interview with Tammy Lytal and Richard R. Russell, in *The Georgia Review*.

Guinn

1. In *A Grit's Triumph: Essays on the Works of Harry Crews*, Donald Johnson describes another recurrent character type in Crews's fiction: the athlete. Johnson stresses that the athlete "epitomizes the duality of mind and body which is at the heart of the human condition" and of Crews's work in general (101). Yet the grit émigré characters augment this general duality with an important cultural one—the stress between the agricultural and the industrial.

2. See for example the *Tobacco Road* motifs in Mirst's mistreatment of the new automobile in *The Gospel Singer* (61, 102).

Romine

1. See especially Moss, whose formulation of Crews's fiction as "Postmodern Georgia Scenes" is an interesting one.

2. Joe Lon, for example, has apparently drowned the salesman for whom his mother left his father (6, 118–20). His father has castrated a black worker for stealing a case of whiskey and killed a white man for undisclosed reasons (40). In this respect, Mystic appears similar to Bacon County as Crews describes it in *A Childhood*: "In Bacon County, the sheriff was the man who tried to keep the peace, but if you had any real trouble, you did not go to him for help to make it right. You made it right yourself or else became known as a man who was defenseless without the sheriff at his back" (8). The setting of *A Feast of Snakes* bears a close relation to Bacon County as Crews describes it in *A Childhood*, as do certain narrative patterns. Joe Lon's failed initiation (see discussion below) is, for example, a systematic inversion of the story Crews tells of his father in *A Childhood*: "Immediately there took place in him a change that has been taking place in men ever since they got out of their caves. As soon as he got himself a wife, he took off that white linen suit and put on a pair of overalls. . . . And he went to work with a vengeance" (24). In a 1992 interview, Crews claimed to "identify with Joe Lon in *Feast of Snakes*—really, really identify with him" ("Some of Us" 542).

3. As Frank W. Shelton observes, the relationship between names and identity is an important one: "Is 'she real' as Shereel, or is she really Dorothy?" (7). Besides the pun suggested by "Shereel," "Dupont" connotes both continental sophistication and plastics (as an allusion to the chemical manufacturer); both connotations stand in stark contrast to the rustic authenticity of "Turnipseed."

4. Russell asserts early in the novel that everything is "fixable" with the exception of bone structure (23). His own career, however, has been limited by "a layer of subcutaneous fat that no amount of sweating, starving, or working could take from between the skin and the muscle. . . . So the skin had defeated him" (174). A third determinant may involve

race, for, according to Russell, small calves are "God's little joke on the nigger" (42). This extension of biological determinants attenuates the domain of control associated with the game; see discussion below.

5. Although Marvella's use of anabolic steroids to build muscle mass might appear to be an example of cheating, Russell's decision to keep Shereel "clean" is clearly ascribed to his belief that "bigness was dead," and not to any belief that steroids are improper (76–77). Nevertheless, the possibility that steroids do affect the outcome of the contest further taints the game's "purity"; see discussion below.

6. In his interviews, Crews speaks extensively on the craft of writing, and often rejects bad craftsmanship on grounds that border on the ethical. In a 1994 interview with Susan Ketchin, for example, Crews claims that "You can fake [dialect] to everybody who doesn't know it, but the guy who knows the dialect, he reads one line of it, he knows you're faking" (Ketchin 343). Similarly, in a 1974 interview with V. Sterling Watson, Crews agreed with Robert Penn Warren that "the idea of going out to deliberately research a novel, in the library or anywhere else, seemed obscene" (65). Interestingly, both Crews and Hemingway (another writer for whom "obscene" was a key word) associate craftsmanship and the cult of experience; life within the "game"—bullfighting or karate, hunting or boxing—enables authentic narration about it.

Spencer

1. See Marx and Engels's *Manifesto of the Communist Party* (77).

2. Tim Edwards demonstrates the naturalism of Crews's writing (43, 44, 52n).

3. For discussions of the regional basis of Crews's portrayals of freaks, see Jeffrey, "Crews's" 67–68 and Slay 101. For other aspects of Crews's work, such as his representation of violence or religion, that place him in the tradition of the southern Gothic, see Covel 75 and Spikes 416. Analyses of Crews as a voice of the language and culture of the poor white south can be found in Johnstone 279; Rotenstein 48; Shelton, "Poor" 47; and Watkins 16.

4. Unfortunately Butler does not name the feminists she has in mind. In "Performative Acts and Gender Constitution: An Essay in Phenomenology and Feminist Theory" Butler does mention Gayatri Spivak and Julia Kristeva as strategic essentialists (280), but here also she is less specific about the absolute essentialist feminists she criticizes.

5. Butler's influence has been especially significant in performance studies, where she has conjoined the perspective of poststructuralist linguistics with the tradition of the study of theatrical performance (McKenzie 218).

6. According to Larry W. DeBord and Gary L. Long, *Karate* depicts a failed attempt to find in the alternative society of the karate commune "escape from industrial society into an uncomplicated past" (41). While this social analysis, like Long's comments elsewhere that Crews's work consistently voices a hankering after a lost agrarian South (32), is very convincing, it should be noted that the karate commune's failure to provide a successful alternative society is expressed in terms of its conceptions of language, spirit, and the body.

7. For an encapsulation of Butler's use of Austin and Derrida, see *Excitable* 43–52.

8. It is important to emphasize the ambivalence of Butler's concept of performativity because, as Jon McKenzie argues, this concept has often been misinterpreted as referring to the transgression rather than the reiteration of social norms (220–25).

9. Peggy Phelan argues that the ontology of performance art is antithetical to that of reproducible art forms, and she is critical of the considerable "pressures brought to bear on performance to succumb to the laws of the reproductive economy" (146). Phelan's opposition between performance and reproduction is relevant to Crews's novel, where Kaimon's concern with sexual reproduction is a pressure that compromises the visibility of the performative basis of normative heterosexuality.

10. A reading of Crews's novel as misogynist has been forwarded by Frank W. Shelton and Patricia V. Beatty, who argue that Gaye Nell Odell is portrayed, respectively, in stereotypical and submissive terms ("Harry" 27–28) and as a debased and modernized mythological Great Mother rather than a real human being ("Crews's" 119, 123). Elise S. Lake notes that while Crews may be guilty of "unconvincingly sentimental romance" (61), the fact that both Kaimon and Gaye Nell Odell give up their karate pursuits indicates that there is no inequality of the sexes in the novel. While Lake is correct to argue that Crews's primary purpose is to show a mutuality and equality in Kaimon and Gaye Nell Odell's renunciation of karate in favor of one another, the fact that it is Kaimon who realizes the flaws of the karate commune and passes what he has learned on to Gaye Nell Odell reflects a misogynist distinction between active males and passive females. Moreover, Crews's portrayal of Gaye Nell Odell in passive terms must be seen as integral to the heterosexual normativity that emerges from this interrogation and not, as Lake contends, as an unrepresentative feature of a feeble narrative conclusion.

11. For Butler's criticisms of the reduction of gender to sex, see *Gender* 6–9.

12. See Long 34–35 for a discussion of Crews's views on his own practice of writing as a bodily ordeal. Kaimon's contradictory feelings towards Faulkner should also be viewed reflexively in terms of Crews's own ambivalent relation, as discussed by William M. Moss, towards his inclusion in a tradition of Southern writing that includes Faulkner (33–35).

13. According to Derrida western philosophy privileges speech over writing because the former is viewed as the expression of the spirit of the subject (*Of Grammatology* 12). Gaye Nell Odell is also guilty of such logocentrism in that her approval of Kaimon's spoken letter to Faulkner is consistent with the karate commune's adherence to the spirit.

14. Crews's representation of language as a displacement of or obstacle to its referent suggests that his fiction conforms to Della Pollock's definition of performative writing (82–83).

15. There is a growing amount of Crews criticism that refers to theorists and theoretical concepts, such as René Girard (Covel 85; Romine 76–77), Mikhail Bakhtin and the carnivalesque (McGregory 72), postmodernism (Moss 42), Foucault (Schafer 72, 80–81), Derrida (Spikes 411–12), and psychoanalysis (Watkins 17).

WORKS CITED

Allain, Marie-Francoise. *The Other Man: Conversations with Graham Greene.* London: The Bodley Head, 1983.

Bakhtin, Mikhail. *Rabelais and His World.* Trans. Helene Iswolsky. Bloomington: Indiana UP, 1984.

Beatty, Patricia V. "Body Language in Harry Crews's *The Gypsy's Curse.*" *Critique: Studies in Contemporary Fiction* 23.2 (1981–82): 61–66.

———. "Crews's Women." Jeffrey, *A Grit's.* 112–23.

Bellamy, Joe David. "Harry Crews: An Interview." *Fiction International,* 6/7 (1976): 83–93.

Blackburn, Sara. "A Gallery of Hurt Animals and People." *New York Times Book Review* 25 March 1973: 47.

Bledsoe, Erik. "An Interview with Harry Crews." *Southern Quarterly* 37.1 (1998): 97–117.

———. "Introduction." *Southern Quarterly* 37.1 (1998): 5–7.

Bonetti, Kay. "An Interview with Harry Crews." *Missouri Review* 6 (1983): 145–64.

Brittin, Ruth L. "Harry Crews and the Southern Protestant Church." Jeffrey, *A Grit's.* 79–99.

Bruss, Elizabeth. *Autobiographical Acts: The Changing Situation of a Literary Genre.* Baltimore: Johns Hopkins UP, 1976.

Burke, Peter. *Popular Culture in Early Modern Europe.* New York: Harper, 1978.

Burt, Al. "Sears Inspired Novelist in Harry Crews." Ed. Barbara Nykoruk. Vol. 1, *Authors in the News.* Detroit: Gale, 1976. 117–19.

Butler, Judith. *Bodies That Matter: On the Discursive Limits of "Sex."* New York and London: Routledge, 1993.

———. *Excitable Speech: A Politics of the Performative.* New York and London: Routledge, 1997.

———. *Gender Trouble: Feminism and the Subversion of Identity.* New York and London: Routledge, 1990.

———. "Performative Acts and Gender Constitution: An Essay in Phenomenology and Feminist Theory." *Performing Feminisms: Feminist Critical Theory and Theatre.* Ed. Sue-Ellen Case. Baltimore: Johns Hopkins UP, 1990. 270–82.

Cargill, Oscar. *Intellectual America: Ideas on the March.* New York: Macmillan, 1941.

Civello, Paul. *American Literary Naturalism and Its Twentieth-Century Transformations: Frank Norris, Ernest Hemingway, Don DeLillo.* Athens: U of Georgia P, 1994.

Cobb, James C. "Community and Identity: Redefining Southern Culture." *Georgia Review* 50:1 (Spring 1995) 9–24.

Covel, Robert C. "The Violent Bear It as Best They Can: Cultural Conflict in the Novels of Harry Crews." *Studies in the Literary Imagination* 27.2 (1994): 75–86.

Crews, Harry. *All We Need of Hell.* New York: Harper & Row, 1987.

———. *Blood and Grits.* New York: Harper & Row, 1979.

———. *Body.* New York: Poseidon, 1990.

———. "Building Men the Marine Corps Way." *Esquire* 86 (Sept. 1976): 22 + .

———. *Car.* New York: William Morrow, 1972.

———. "The Car." *Esquire* 84 (Dec. 1975): 150–51.

———. "Carny." *Playboy* 23 (Sept. 1976): 96 + .

———. *A Childhood: The Biography of a Place.* New York: Harper & Row, 1978.

———. "Climbing the Tower." *Blood and Grits.* New York: Harper & Row, 1976. 208–13.

———. "Cockfighting: An Unfashionable View." *Esquire* 87 (Mar. 1977): 8 + .

———. "A Day at the Dogfights." *Esquire* 91 (Feb. 79): 56 + .

———. *A Feast of Snakes.* New York: Atheneum, 1976.

———. *Florida Frenzy.* Gainesville: UP of Florida, 1982.

———. "The Goat Day Olympics." *Esquire* 88 (July 1977): 36 + .

———. "Going Down in Valdeez." *Playboy* 22 (Feb. 1975): 108 + .

———. *The Gospel Singer.* New York: William Morrow, 1968.

———. *The Gypsy's Curse.* New York: Alfred A. Knopf, 1974.

———. *The Hawk Is Dying.* New York: Alfred A. Knopf, 1973.

———. "The Hawk Is Flying." *Esquire* 87 (June 1977): 24 + .

———. "Introduction." *A Childhood: The Biography of a Place. Classic Crews.* New York: Poseidon, 1993. 9–17.

———. *Karate Is a Thing of the Spirit.* New York: William Morrow, 1971.

———. *The Knockout Artist.* New York: Harper & Row, 1988.

———. "L. L. Bean Has Your Number, America!" *Blood and Grits.* 24–30.

———. "A Lesson in Desperation and Stupidity." *Oxford American* (Oct.–Nov. 1996): 47–48.

———. "Leaving Pasadena—Resume Safe Speed." *Esquire* 87 (Jan. 1977): 29 + .

———. *The Mulching of America.* New York: Simon & Schuster, 1995.

———. "The Mythic Mule." *Southern Magazine* 1 (Oct. 1986): 21 + .

———. *Naked in Garden Hills.* New York: William Morrow, 1969.

———. "A Night at a Waterfall." *Blood and Grits.* 31–44.

———. "Pages from the Life of a Georgia Innocent." *Esquire* 86 (July 1976): 30 + .

———. "Poaching Gators for Fun and Profit." *Esquire* 87 (Apr. 1977): 54 + .

———. "Reminiscences of a Blind Muleman." *Esquire* 86 (Nov. 1976): 46 + .

———. "Running Fox." *Esquire* 86 (Oct. 1976): 8 + .

———. *Scar Lover.* New York: Poseidon, 1992.

———. "Television's Junkyard Dog." *Esquire* 86 (Oct. 1976): 94 + .

———. "Temple of the Airwaves." *Esquire* 86 (Dec. 1976): 108 + .

———. *This Thing Don't Lead to Heaven*. New York: William Morrow, 1970.

———. "The Trucker Militant." *Esquire* 88 (Aug. 1977): 82 + .

———. "Tuesday Night with Cody, Jimbo and a Fish of Some Proportion." *Esquire* 87 (Feb. 1977): 26 + .

———. "The Unfeminine Mystique." *Playgirl* (Dec. 1979): 124–25.

———. "The Violence That Finds Us." *Playboy* 31 (Apr. 1984): 98 + .

———. "A Walk in the Country." *Blood and Grits*. 1–23.

———. "Why I Live Where I Live." *Esquire* 94 (Sept. 1980): 46–47.

———. "The Wisdom of the Groin." *Playboy* 36 (Feb. 1989): 88 + .

———. "The Wonderful World of Winnebagos." *Esquire* 86 (Aug. 1976): 38 + .

Crowder, A. B. "Harry Crews." Ed. C. C. Barfoot, Hans Bertens, Theo D'haen, and Erik Kooper. Vol. 78, *Writing in the Southern Tradition: Interviews with Five Contemporary Authors*. Costerus New Series, Atlanta, GA: 1990. 80–115.

de Lauretis, Teresa. *Technologies of Gender: Essays on Theory, Film, and Fiction*. Bloomington and Indianapolis: U of Indiana P, 1987.

DeBord, Larry W., and Gary L. Long. "Harry Crews on the American Dream." *Southern Quarterly* 20.3 (1982): 35–53.

———. "Harry Crews's *A Childhood*: A Resource for Teaching Sociology." *Teaching Sociology* 9 (July 1982): 452–60.

Derrida, Jacques. "Signature Event Context." *Limited Inc*. Evanston, IL: Northwestern UP, 1988. 1–23.

———. *Of Grammatology*. Trans. Gayatri Chakravorty Spivak. Baltimore and London: Johns Hopkins UP, 1976.

Edwards, Tim. " 'Everthing Is Eating Everthing Else': The Naturalistic Impulse in Harry Crews's *A Feast of Snakes*." *Southern Quarterly* 37.1 (1998): 42–53.

Foata, Anne. "Interview with Harry Crews, May 1972." *Recherches Anglaises et Americaines* 5 (1972): 207–25.

Forte, Jeanie. "Focus on the Body: Pain, Praxis, and Pleasure in Feminist Performance." *Critical Theory and Performance*. Ed. Janelle G. Reinelt and Joseph R. Roach. Ann Arbor: U of Michigan P, 1992. 248–62.

Friedman, Susan Stanford. "Women's Autobiographical Selves: Theory and Practice." *The Private Self: Theory and Practice of Women's Autobiographical Writings*. Ed. Shari Benstock. Chapel Hill: U of North Carolina P, 1988.

Gelphant, Blanche H. "What More Can Carrie Want? Naturalistic Ways of Consuming Women." *The Cambridge Companion to American Realism and Naturalism: Howells to London*. Ed. Donald Pizer. Cambridge: Cambridge UP, 1995. 178- 210.

Graves, Tom. "Harry Crews: An Interview." *Southern Exposure* 7 (Summer 1979): 151–52.

Green, Michelle. "Life-scarred and Weary of Battle, a Literary Guerilla Calls Truce." *People Weekly* 8 June 1987: 75 + .

Greene, Graham. *The Power and the Glory*. New York: Penguin, 1991.

————. *A Sort of Life*. New York: Simon and Schuster, 1971.

Hemphill, Paul. *The Good Old Boys*. New York: Simon and Schuster, 1974.

Hobson, Fred. *The Southern Writer in the Postmodern World*. Athens, GA: U of Georgia P, 1991.

————. *Tell About the South: The Southern Rage to Explain*. Baton Rouge: Louisiana State UP, 1983.

Howard, June. *Form and History in American Literary Naturalism*. Chapel Hill: U of North Carolina P, 1985.

Huber, Patrick. "A Short History of *Redneck*: The Fashioning of a Southern White Masculinity." *Southern Cultures* 1.2 (1995): 145–66.

Jeffrey, David K. "Crews's Freaks." Jeffrey, *A Grit's*. 67–78.

————. "Murder and Mayhem in Crews's *A Feast of Snakes*." *Critique: Studies in Contemporary Fiction* 28.1 (1986): 45–53.

————, ed. *A Grit's Triumph: Essays on the Works of Harry Crews*. Port Washington, NY: Associated Faculty P, 1983.

Jeffrey, David K., and Donald R. Noble. "Harry Crews: An Interview." Jeffrey, *A Grit's*. 140–51.

————. "Harry Crews: Interview, His Apartment, December 10, 1978, 12 noon–4:30 pm" and "Interview with Harry Crews, His Office, University of Florida, December 11, 1978." Tape Transcripts.

Johnson, Donald. "The Athlete's Hand Filling Up: Harry Crews and Sports." Jeffrey, *A Grit's*. 100–11.

Johnstone, Barbara. " 'You Gone Have to Learn to Talk Right': Linguistic Deference and Regional Dialect in Harry Crews's *Body*." *The Text and Beyond: Essays in Literary Linguistics*. Ed. Cynthia Goldin Bernstein. Tuscaloosa and London: U of Alabama P, 1994.

Kazin, Alfred. *God and the American Writer*. New York: Alfred A. Knopf, 1997.

Lake, Elise S. "Having a Hard Time of It: Women in the Novels of Harry Crews." *Southern Quarterly* 37.1 (1998): 54–65.

Lejeune, Philippe. *On Autobiography*. Ed. and Foreword John Paul Eakin. Trans. Katherine Leary. Minneapolis: U of Minnesota P, 1989.

Long, Gary L. "Naked Americans: Violence in the Work of Harry Crews." *Southern Quarterly* 32.4 (1994): 117–30.

————. "Silences, Criticisms, and Laments: Political Implications in the Work of Harry Crews." *Southern Quarterly* 37.1 (1998): 27–41.

Long, Gary L., and Larry W. DeBord. "Grit Truths: The Journalistic Essays of Harry Crews." *Texas Review* 9 (Spring/Summer 1988): 96–109.

————. "Literary Criticism and the Fate of Ideas: The Case of Harry Crews." *Texas Review* 4 (Fall/Winter 1983): 69–91.

Lynskey, Edward C. "Violence in Hometown America: Harry Crews's *A Feast of Snakes*." *Pembroke Magazine* 19 (1987): 195–200.

Lytal, Tammy, and Richard R. Russell. "Some of Us Do It Anyway: An Interview with Harry Crews." *Georgia Review* 48 (1994): 537–53.

Marx, Karl, and Friedrich Engels. "Manifesto of the Communist Party." *The Revolutions of 1848: Political Writings Volume I.* Ed. David Fernbach. New York: Vintage, 1974. 62–98.

Mason, Mary G. "The Other Voice: Autobiographies of Women Writers." *Autobiography: Essays Theoretical and Critical.* Ed. James Olney. Princeton, NJ: Princeton UP, 1980.

McGregory, Jerrilyn. "Harry Crews's Home Place: An Excursion into Wiregrass Country and the Carnivalesque." *Southern Quarterly* 37.1 (1998): 66–73.

———. *Wiregrass Country.* Jackson: UP of Mississippi, 1997.

McKenzie, Jon. "Genre Trouble: (The) Butler Did It." Phelan and Lane 217–35.

Meriwether, James B., and Michael Millgate. *Lion in the Garden: Interviews with William Faulkner.* Lincoln: U of Nebraska P, 1968.

Miller, R. H. *Understanding Graham Greene.* Columbia: U of South Carolina P, 1990.

Moss, William M. "Postmodern Georgia Scenes: Harry Crews and the Southern Tradition in Fiction." Jeffrey, *A Grit's.* 33–45

Noble, Donald R. "Harry Crews Introduces Himself." Jeffrey, *A Grit's.* 7–20.

Nuwer, Hank. "Harry Crews Plays with Pain." *Dynamic Years* (Sept./Oct. 1984): 44+.

O' Prey, Paul. *A Reader's Guide to Graham Greene.* Worcester, England: Thames and Hudson, 1988.

Oney, Steve. "Harry Crews Is a Stomp-Down Hard-Core Moralist." *Atlanta Journal and Constitution Magazine* (15 May 1977): 7, 30+.

———. "The Making of the Writer." *New York Times Book Review* (24 Dec. 1978): 3+.

Parker, Andrew, and Eve Kosofsky Sedgwick. "Introduction: Performativity and Performance." Parker and Sedgwick, *Performativity and Performance* 1–18.

———, eds. *Performativity and Performance.* New York and London: Routledge, 1995.

Penley, Constance. "Crackers and Whackers: The White Trashing of Porn." *White Trash: Race and Class in America.* Ed. Matt Wray and Annalee Newitz. New York and London: Routledge, 1997. 89–112.

Phelan, Peggy. *Unmarked: The Politics of Performance.* London and New York: Routledge, 1993.

Phelan, Peggy, and Jill Lane, eds. *The Ends of Performance.* New York and London: New York UP, 1998.

Pizer, Donald. *The Theory and Practice of American Literary Naturalism: Selected Essays and Reviews.* Carbondale and Edwardsville: Southern Illinois UP, 1993.

———. *Twentieth-Century American Literary Naturalism: An Interpretation.* Carbondale and Edwardsville: Southern Illinois UP, 1982.

Pollock, Della. "Performing Writing." Phelan and Lane. 73–103.

Romine, Scott. "Harry Crews's Away Games: Home and Sport in *A Feast of Snakes* and *Body.*" *Southern Quarterly* 37.1 (1998): 74–87.

Rotenstein, David S. "Ethnography, Journalism and Literature: Ethnographic Text and Southern Author Harry Crews." *Southern Folklore* 54.1 (1997): 40–50.

Schafer, William J. "Partial People: The Novels of Harry Crews." *Mississippi Quarterly* 41 (Summer 1987–88): 69–88.

Schmich, Mary T. "Still in the Game: On the Straight and Narrow with Writer Harry Crews." *Atlanta Weekly* (27 Jan. 1985): 7+.

Seelye, John. "Georgia Boys: The Redclay Satyrs of Erskine Caldwell and Harry Crews." *Virginia Quarterly Review* 56 (Autumn 1980): 612–26.

Shelton, Frank W. "Harry Crews after *A Childhood*." *Southern Literary Journal* 24.2 (1992): 3–10.

———. "Harry Crews: Man's Search for Perfection." Jeffrey, *A Grit's*. 21–32.

———. "The Nonfiction of Harry Crews: A Review." *Southern Literary Journal* 16 (Spring 1984): 132–35.

———. "The Poor Whites' Perspective: Harry Crews among Georgia Writers." *Journal of American Culture* 11.3 (1988): 47–50.

———. "A Way of Life and Place." *Southern Literary Journal* 11 (Spring 1979): 97–102.

Shepherd, Allen. "Harry Crews." *American Novelists Since World War II*. Ed. James E. Kibler, Jr. Vol. 6, *Dictionary of Literary Biography*. Detroit: Bruccoli Clark, 1980. 65–69.

———. "Matters of Life and Death: The Novels of Harry Crews." *Critique: Studies in Modern Fiction* 20.1 (1978): 53–62.

Slay, Jack, Jr. "Delineations in Freakery: Freaks in the Fiction of Harry Crews and Katherine Dunn." *Literature and the Grotesque*. Ed. Michael Meyer. Amsterdam: Rodopi, 1995. 99–112.

Smith, Dave. "That Appetite for Life So Ravenous." *Shenandoah* 25 (Summer 1974): 49–55.

Spikes, Michael. "Rereading Harry Crews's *A Feast of Snakes*." *Arkansas Review: A Journal of Criticism* 4.1 (1995): 82–94.

———. "Victory over Sin: Harry Crews's Critique of the Phallic Ethic in *A Feast of Snakes*." *University of Mississippi Studies in English* 11–12 (1993–95): 411–23.

Stallybrass, Peter and Allon White. *The Politics and Poetics of Transgression*. Ithaca, NY: Cornell UP, 1986.

Stratford, Philip, ed. "Editor's Introduction." *The Portable Graham Greene*. New York: Penguin, 1994. ix–xv.

Sullivan, Walter. "Fiction in a Dry Season: Some Signs of Hope." *Sewanne Review* 77.1 (1969): 154–64.

Summer, Bob. "Harry Crews." *Publisher's Weekly* (15 Apr. 1988): 64–65.

Tannenbaum, Frank. *Darker Phases of the South*. New York: Negro UP, 1924.

Tate, Allen. *Collected Essays*. Denver: Alan Swallow, 1959.

Teague, Matthew. "How Do You Like Your Blue-Eyed Boy Now?" *Oxford American* (Dec. 1995/Jan. 1996): 69–71.

Thomson, Rosemarie Garland. "Introduction: From Wonder to Error—A Genealogy of Freak Discourse in Modernity." *Freakery: Cultural Spectacles of the Extraordinary Body*. Ed. Rosemarie Garland Thomson. New York and London: New York UP, 1996. 1–19.

Walcutt, Charles Child. *American Literary Naturalism, A Divided Stream*. Westport, Connecticut: Greenwood, 1956.

Walsh, William. "An Interview with Harry Crews." *Pembroke Magazine* 22 (1990): 121–29.

Watkins, James H. " 'The Use of *I*, Lovely and Terrifying Word': Autobiographical Authority and the Representation of 'Redneck' Masculinity in *A Childhood*." *Southern Quarterly* 37.1 (1998): 15–26.

Watson, V. Sterling. "Arguments over an Open Wound: An Interview with Harry Crews." *Prairie Schooner* 48.1 (1974): 60–74.

Watts, Cedric. *A Preface to Greene.* New York: Addison Wesley Longman Inc., 1997.

Weaver, Angela Kaye. "Sexual Salvation: Men, Women, and Identity in Three Novels by Harry Crews." Thesis. U of Georgia, Athens, 1995.

White, Allon. *Carnival, Hysteria, and Writing.* New York: Oxford UP, 1993.

Notes on Contributors

Erik Bledsoe is an instructor of English and American studies at the University of Tennessee, Knoxville. He is the editor of *Getting Naked with Harry Crews: Interviews* and has published in *Southern Quarterly, Faulkner Journal, Mississippi Quarterly,* and *Southern Cultures* among other journals.

Larry Brown lives in Mississippi with his family. His most recent novel, *Fay,* was published in the spring of 2000 and is a sequel to *Joe.*

Harry Crews still lives in Florida and he still writes. And on occasion, he still howls at the moon.

Tim Edwards, assistant professor of English at the University of the Ozarks, has authored several forthcoming articles on southern modernist Evelyn Scott. He is presently revising his dissertation—an examination of Scott's major prose works—for a book manuscript.

Matthew Guinn is the author of *After Southern Modernism: Fiction of the Contemporary South* (UP of Mississippi, 2000).

Elise S. Lake is an associate professor of sociology at the University of Mississippi, where she teaches family sociology, criminology, and deviance. She has published articles on family violence, criminal victimization, and ethics in teaching.

Gary L. Long is a professor of sociology at the University of Mississippi. He is interested in literature, war, professional ethics, and issues in teaching.

Jerrilyn McGregory is an associate professor of folklore in the department of English at Florida State University. She is the author of *Wiregrass Country* and is currently working on a book-length study of African American sacred music traditions within this region of the South.

Tim McLaurin is still teaching at North Carolina State University and still doing snake shows. His most recent book is *The River Less Run*, a memoir that updates *Keeper of the Moon.*

Scott Romine is an assistant professor of English at the University of North Carolina at

Greensboro, where he teaches American and southern literature. His essays have appeared in such journals as *Mississippi Quarterly, Style, Southern Quarterly, Southern Literary Journal, South Atlantic Review*, and *Critical Survey*. His first book, *The Narrative Forms of Southern Community*, was published by Louisiana State University Press.

Richard Rankin Russell is a Ph.D. candidate in English at the University of North Carolina at Chapel Hill, writing a dissertation on Northern Irish. His essay on poetic responses by Thomas Kinsella and Seamus Heaney to Bloody Sunday is forthcoming in *Troubled Voices: Contemporary Northern Irish Writers*, and an article on W. B. Yeats, Eavan Boland, and postcolonialism is forthcoming in a volume of essays on Yeats and postcolonialism. He is currently on a dissertation research fellowship at the Institute for Irish Studies in Belfast, Northern Ireland.

Damon Sauve holds master's degrees from both the University of Florida and the University of North Carolina at Chapel Hill. He is the publisher and fiction editor of *Oyster Boy Review*, a print and online journal of fiction and poetry, as well as web editor for *Brightleaf: A Southern Review of Books*. Between 1988 and 1990, he attended four semesters of Harry Crews's undergraduate creative writing class.

Nicholas Spencer was educated at St. John's College, Oxford and Emory University. He is an assistant professor in the department of English at the University of Nebraska-Lincoln, and his publications include essays in *Contemporary Literature* and *Angelaki*.

James H. Watkins is assistant professor of English at Berry College in Rome, Georgia, where he teaches, among other subjects, southern literature and autobiography studies. He is the editor of *Southern Selves: A Collection of Autobiographical Writing* and his work has appeared in the *Southern Quarterly, South Atlantic Review*, and *Georgia Historical Quarterly*. He is currently completing a study of autobiography and southern white masculinity.

INDEX

Vietnam War, 67, 103
Violence, 23, 25–26, 121–26, 172
Vonnegut, Kurt, 66

Walcutt, Charles Child, 66; *American Literary Naturalism, A Divided Stream*, 65
Walsh, William, 76
Warren, Robert Penn, 219n 6
Was, Don, 160
Washington, Booker T., 212n 8
Watkins, Jim, xii
Watson, Sterling V., 30, 171, 204, 219n 6; *The Calling*, 171
Watts, Cedric, 32
Waycross, Ga., 112, 126
Weaver, Angela, 81
West, Nathanael, *The Day of the Locust*, 64, 119

White, Allon, 102, 104; *The Politics and Poetics of Transgression*, 97
Whitman, Charles, 76, 77
Willalee Bookatee, 170–71
William Morrow and Company, Inc., 148–49, 151
Williams, Tennessee, 167–68; *The Glass Menagerie*, 168
Wiregrass Country, 97, 101, 104; defined, 95–96, 217n 1
Wittig, Monique, 139
Wolfe, Thomas, 166; *Look Homeward Angel*, 166
Women, depiction of by Crews, 72–75, 79–93, 220n 10
World Publishing Company, 148
Wright, Richard, 212n 8; *Native Son*, 75
Writers Guild West, 161

Young, Stephen Flinn, xi